CHOOSE A CHRISTIAN COLLEGE

A Guide to Academically Challenging Colleges Committed to a Christ-Centered Campus Life

Third Edition

Peterson's Guides
Princeton, New Jersey

Published in association with
the Christian College Coalition

Library of Congress Cataloging-in-Publication Data

Choose a Christian College: a guide to academically challenging colleges committed to a Christ-centered campus life / Christian College Coalition.

      p. cm.
    Includes index.
    ISBN 1-56079-217-5
    1. Christian colleges—United States—Directories. I. Christian College Coalition (U.S.)
L901.C57 1992
378.73—dc20

                            92-22622

Composition and design by Peterson's Guides

Cover design by Laurie Lohne

Printed in the United States of America

10 9 8 7 6 5 4 3

Printed on recycled paper.

Contents

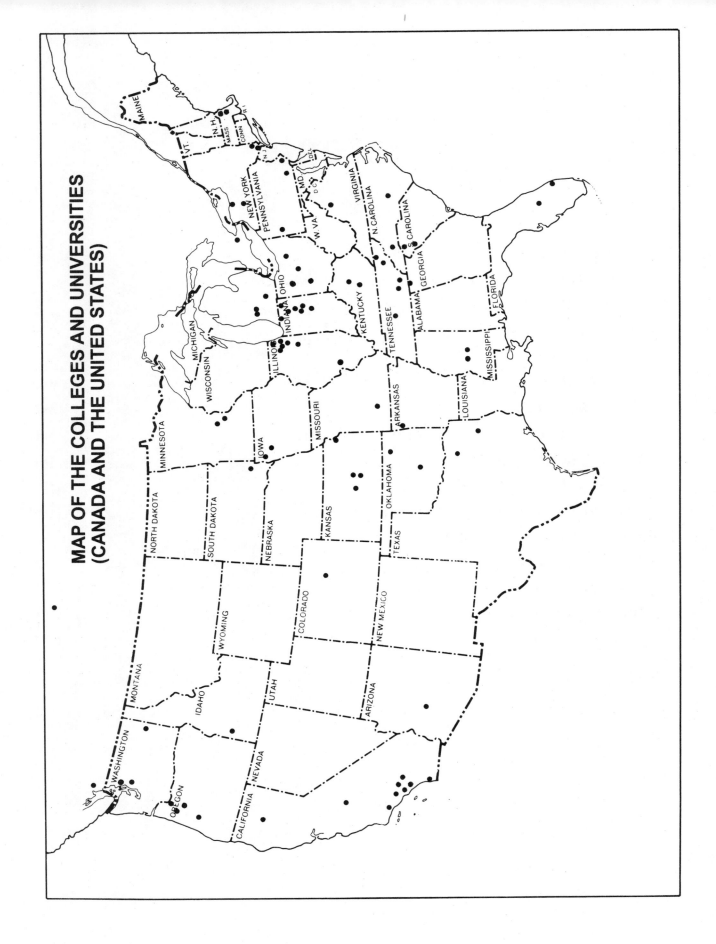

MAP OF THE COLLEGES AND UNIVERSITIES
(CANADA AND THE UNITED STATES)

Christian College Coalition Colleges and Universities

How to
Use This Book

It is likely you are reading this book because you are a student (or the parent of one) who is thinking seriously about going to college and wondering how to select a school that will best allow you to get everything you want out of your college years. If you believe that a college with an active Christian orientation might provide what you are seeking, this book can help you by providing information on eighty-four colleges and universities that combine academically challenging programs in the liberal arts and sciences with a Christ-centered campus life.

The Introduction: Why Choose a Christian College?

The introductory essay can help you to determine whether a Christian college is the best choice for you. It provides a rich overview of what you can expect from a Christian liberal arts school compared to other colleges and universities.

The College Profiles

The heart of the book is detailed profiles of the eighty-four member schools of the Christian College Coalition, containing data supplied by each of them.

Each one provides information on things like enrollment, academic offerings, costs, athletics programs, admission procedures, and financial aid. Familiarizing yourself with the format of the profiles will help you review them and compare schools easily.

A special note from the president of each school appears at the end of each profile. These notes include information about the school's mission, special programs and curricula emphases, and campus life.

Programs Sponsored by the Christian College Coalition

The Coalition makes available five independent study programs. These programs provide for off-campus study in Washington, D.C., Michigan, California, Costa Rica, and England. Consider such opportunities when choosing a college since they can not only round out your studies but also provide a rich opportunity for personal growth.

The Indexes

We've provided indexes at the back of the book to assist you in picking out the profiles you wish to review based on four criteria: academic majors, intercollegiate athletics, study-abroad opportunities,

---

About the Christian College Coalition

The Christian College Coalition is an association of Christ-centered colleges and universities of the liberal arts and sciences. It is committed to cultivating communities of educational excellence in which the Lordship of Jesus Christ is central. Coalition institutions meet eight criteria for membership: an institutional commitment to the centrality of Jesus Christ to all campus life, integration of biblical faith with academics and student life, hiring practices that require a personal Christian commitment from each full-time faculty member and administrator, accreditation and primary orientation as a four-year liberal arts college, fundraising activities consistent with the standards set by the Evangelical Council for Financial Accountability, a commitment to participating in Coalition programs, cooperation with and support of other Coalition colleges, and responsible financial operation. For more information, please contact the Christian College Coalition at 329 Eighth Street NE, Washington, D.C. 20002.

Profile Highlights Lists facts about each school such as its total enrollment, tuition and fees, entrance difficulty, and denominational affiliation.

General Information Gives an overall sense of the school by detailing the degrees awarded, the faculty, and library and computer resources.

Financial Aid Shows how many students applied for aid and were judged to have need as well as the amount of the average aid package.

Athletics Details the intercollegiate and intramural sports available and their member affiliation.

Freshman Admissions Includes required tests and the application deadline.

WHEATON COLLEGE
Wheaton, Illinois

Total Enrollment: 2,520
UG Enrollment: 2,214 (52% W)
Application Deadline: 2/15
Tuition & Fees: $10,280
Room & Board: $3970
Entrance: very difficult
SAT ≥ 500: 77% V, 91% M
ACT ≥ 21: 95%
Denominational Affiliation: interdenominational

GENERAL INFORMATION Independent comprehensive coed institution. Founded 1860. Awards B, M. Primary accreditation: regional. Suburban setting, with easy access to Chicago; 80-acre campus. Total enrollment 2,520. Faculty: 254 (146 full-time, 108 part-time); 63% of full-time faculty have terminal degrees; graduate assistants teach no undergraduate courses. Library holdings: 356,289 bound volumes, 127,119 titles on microform, 2,164 periodical subscriptions, 11,809 records/tapes/CDs. Computer terminals/PCs available for student use: 40, located in computer center, computer labs.

UNDERGRADUATE PROFILE Fall 1991: 2,214 undergraduates (545 freshmen) from 50 states and territories and 10 foreign countries; 2% part-time; 22% state residents; 12% transfers; 55% financial aid recipients; 52% women; 1% African Americans, 1% Hispanics; 5% Asian Americans; 1% international students, 2% of undergraduates 25 years of age or older.

1991 FRESHMAN DATA: 1,311 students applied for fall 1991 admission; 71% were accepted; 59% of those accepted enrolled. 40 freshmen were National Merit Scholarship Finalists; all received a National Merit Scholarship. 50% of freshmen were in top 10% of secondary school class, 85% were in top 25%, 98% were in top half.

ENROLLMENT PATTERNS 92% of fall 1990 freshmen returned for fall 1991 term. 81% of 1987 freshmen graduated within 5 years.

FRESHMAN ADMISSIONS Preference given to Christians. Options: early action, deferred entrance. Required: essay, high school transcript, 2 recommendations, interview, SAT or ACT, TOEFL (for foreign students). Recommended: 3 years of high school math and science, 2 years of high school foreign language, Achievement Tests, English Composition Test. Test scores used for admission. Application deadlines: 2/15, 12/1 for early action.

Notification dates: 4/10, 2/10 for early action. College's own assessment of entrance difficulty level: very difficult.

TRANSFER ADMISSIONS Required: essay, high school transcript, 2 recommendations, interview, college transcript. Recommended: 3 years of high school math and science, 2 years of high school foreign language. Application deadline: 3/1. Notification date: 4/15. College's own assessment of entrance difficulty level: moderately difficult.

EXPENSES (1992–93) Comprehensive fee of $14,250 includes full-time tuition ($10,280) and college room and board ($3970). College room only: $2300. Part-time tuition: $430 per hour.

FINANCIAL AID College-administered aid for all 1991–92 undergraduates: 1,191 need-based scholarships (average $3360); 155 non-need scholarships (average $747); low-interest long-term loans from college funds (average $1001), from external sources (average $2347); SEOG; College Work-Study; part-time jobs. Supporting data: FAF required; IRS required for some. Priority application deadline: 3/15.

CAMPUS LIFE/STUDENT SERVICES Mandatory chapel; drama/theater group; student-run newspaper and radio station. Institution provides health clinic, personal/psychological counseling.

STUDY ABROAD SITES England, France, Germany, Israel, Spain, the Netherlands, Asia.

ATHLETICS Member NCAA (Division III). Intercollegiate sports: basketball M, W; cross-country running M, W; football M; golf M; soccer M, W; softball W; swimming and diving M, W; tennis M, W; track and field M, W; volleyball W; wrestling M. Intramural sports: badminton, baseball, basketball, football, racquetball, soccer, softball, tennis, ultimate frisbee, volleyball, weight lifting.

MAJORS Archaeology; art education; art/fine arts; art history; biblical languages; biblical studies; biology/biological sciences; broadcasting; business economics; chemistry; classics; communication; computer science; (pre)dentistry sequence; economics; elementary education; environmental sciences; French; geology; German; history; interdisciplinary studies; journalism; (pre)law sequence; literature; mathematics; (pre)medicine sequence; modern languages; music; music business; music education; music history; philosophy; physical education; physics; piano/organ; political science/government; psychology; religious education; religious studies; science education; secondary education; sociology; Spanish; speech/rhetoric/public address/debate; stringed instruments; studio art; theater arts/drama; voice; wind and percussion instruments. Most popular majors of class of 1991: business economics, literature, psychology.

SPECIAL NOTE FROM THE COLLEGE Convinced that "all truth is God's truth," Wheaton College actively pursues the integration of biblical Christianity with rigorous academic study in the liberal arts, with the goal of serving Christ in this world. Wheaton has a national reputation built upon a distinguished teaching and dedicated faculty known for its outstanding teaching and scholarship and a student body that is committed to academic achievement, leadership, and Christian service. Extensive athletic and other student activities add to the friendly and supportive community on campus.

CONTACT Mr. Dan Crabtree, Director of Admissions, Wheaton College, 501 East College Avenue, Wheaton, IL 60187, 708-752-5005 or toll-free 800-222-2419 (out-of-state).

---

and graduate programs. In addition, to make it easy to pick out the schools that are in a particular geographical area, we've provided a geographical listing and map which appear at the front of the book immediately following the contents page.

Codes Used in the Profiles

Profile Highlights:
UG—undergraduate
N/R—not reported
N/Avail—not available
V—verbal SAT scores
M—math SAT scores

General Information:
Degrees Awarded:
A—associate degree
B—bachelor's degree
M—master's degree
D—doctoral and professional degrees

Freshman Admissions:
PSAT—Preliminary Scholastic Aptitude Test
SAT—Scholastic Aptitude Test
ACT—American College Testing Program's ACT Assessment
TOEFL—Test of English as a Foreign Language
WPCT—Washington Pre-College Test

Financial Aid:
SEOG—Supplemental Educational Opportunity Grants, a federally funded needs-based award program administered by colleges
AFSA/SAR—the federal government's Application for Federal Student Aid/Student Aid Report
FAF—Financial Aid Form of the College Scholarship Service
FFS—Family Financial Statement of the American College Testing Program
IRS—federal income tax form 1040

Athletics:
NCAA—National Collegiate Athletic Association
NAIA—National Association of Intercollegiate Athletics
NJCAA—National Junior College Athletic Association
NLCAA—National Little College Athletic Association

Individual Sports:
M—offered for men
F—offered for women
(s)—scholarships available
(c)—club sport

Why Choose a Christian College?

A college education is a big investment. But trying to make sense of the hundreds of recruitment brochures and promotional videos confronting today's high school students can be a confusing and frustrating experience. It's no surprise, then, that families are eager for advice.

For families looking for a special school, such as a Christian college or university, the search can be even more confusing. Bible colleges and Christian colleges can sound a lot alike. If students are unfamiliar with the important differences among them, they can be misled in their choice. Other students, though deeply committed to Christianity, may not be certain that a Christ-centered college education is really so important or that the differences between a Christian college and a secular school are so great.

This guide is a resource for all those who are already considering a Christian college and those who are not yet convinced that such a choice matters. We at the Christian College Coalition are absolutely convinced that a Christ-centered college education is the right choice for tens of thousands of young people. *Choose a Christian College* provides a brief overview of eighty-four very special colleges and universities—places of learning where the spiritual and the academic go hand in hand.

By inviting students and parents to consider a Christian college or university, this guide can be the first step toward a wise and informed choice.

The Christian College Difference

There are approximately 3,300 colleges and universities in the United States, but only 600 or 700 maintain some tie to a specific church denomination or religious tradition. Of this subgroup, about 125 are what we refer to as "Christ-centered." Eighty-four of these colleges and universities are members of the Christian College Coalition, an association of re-

gionally accredited four-year colleges and universities.

On the surface, most small colleges look a lot alike. They all promise a strong academic program, varied cocurricular offerings, a pleasant campus, and a friendly faculty. What sets Christ-centered colleges apart is the educational environment: the way in which faith, learning, and life come together and work together.

The Christian faith is at the very heart of what a Christ-centered college or university is all about. These institutions seek to provide a Christian view of education, bringing to every major important questions of origins, meaning, and purpose. At Christian schools, combining faith and learning is ongoing. The Christian college environment helps students integrate faith and learning and prepares

people who have experienced the Christian-college difference. As God's ambassadors to a sinful and hurting world, graduates of Christian colleges are working for good in America and abroad. Theirs is a voice for peace, justice, and the abundant life that comes from knowing Christ.

Alike But Different

The eighty-four members of the Christian College Coalition differ in size, location, traditions, denominational ties, range of academic offerings, and lifestyle expectations. Christian colleges are located within a reasonable distance of almost any point in North America. About half are in major cities or urban areas, while the remainder call a small town home. Most Christian colleges are residential campuses, although older students who commute to campuses are increasing.

The academic programs offered by Christian colleges also provide prospective students with considerable choice. Within the Coalition, a number of colleges continue to offer a traditional liberal arts curriculum, while others have expanded their course offerings to include professional programs of study. Several of the colleges emphasize technological programs of study, while others focus more on service areas such as nursing and social work. Many of the colleges allow students to shape their own interdisciplinary majors.

them to live out their faith in all areas of life.

Faculty members play a key role in making Christian colleges and universities truly Christ-centered. Although very committed to their academic disciplines, faculty members at Christian colleges are believers first. Classroom instruction is first-rate. Professors are not afraid to pose tough questions and challenge young scholars to think deeply about their faith. These professors are willing to reveal their own imperfections as humans and their uncertainties as Christians, thereby freeing students to ask the "stupid" questions or to take the courageous "leap of faith." For many students, faculty members become much more than teachers—they are role models, mentors, and lifelong friends.

In today's troubled times, the need is great for

Different But Alike

No matter what their uniqueness, all Christian colleges take seriously the need to prepare students for lives of service to God, His world, and His church. Across the membership of the Coalition, faculty and administrators share the following beliefs:

- That we live in a world that was created by God.
- That God is love.
- That Jesus Christ is the Son of God and the "author and finisher of our faith."
- That the key to abundant life is a relationship with Jesus Christ.

Different But Alike
All Christian colleges take seriously the need to prepare men and women for lives of service to God, the world, and the Church

- That a high-quality education must deal with matters of the heart as well as of the mind.
- That a college education should provide a solid foundation for living an active, meaningful, and contributing life in God's world and that a curriculum that is firmly grounded in the liberal arts is the surest basis for such a foundation.
- That faculty members should serve as academic and spiritual mentors to their students.
- That cocurricular and resident-life activities are an important part of an educational experience.
- That in addition to a degree, sharpened intellectual skills, and current information, students should graduate with an enhanced sense of wholeness and the courage to ask the right questions.

- That no college experience, if it is to be whole and valuable, can ignore the problems of society or the major issues of the modern world.

Life on a Christian College Campus . . .

As is the case at all small, residential colleges, campus life is an important part of the Christian college experience. However, the Christian emphasis of the colleges is clearly evident. Whether serving in student government or singing in the college choir, students are encouraged to use their talents and skills for the glory of God. Additionally, the Christian college campus is a place where students can "Just Say Yes" to a life-style that is free from alcohol and drug abuse.

Life on a Christian College Campus
An atmosphere of compassion and caring, of
teamwork and trust characterizes campus
life at Christian colleges

. . . and Beyond

Christian colleges are known for their commitment to service, which finds fulfillment in the outreach activities of the young people they enroll. Students at Christian colleges participate in volunteer efforts and Christian service projects in the United States and abroad. They tutor the young and read to the old. They march for hunger and speak out on social issues. They visit teenagers in jail and work with the terminally ill. They participate in political causes and lead Young Life groups. In short, these students witness to God's love with their time and with their actions, as well as their words.

Cultural diversity is a fact of life on Christian campuses as students from other countries come to study in the United States. Additionally, many Christian colleges provide students with international study experiences around the world.

The Christian College Coalition sponsors several off-campus programs that are available to students from member institutions: the American Studies Program in Washington, D.C.; the Latin American Studies Program in San José, Costa Rica; the Los Angeles Film Studies Center; and the Oxford Summer School Program in England. Other unique study opportunities are available through the Au Sable Institute of Environmental Studies in Michigan and the Oregon Extension Fall Semester. (Other foreign-study opportunities available through Christian College Coalition member institutions are provided in the Study Abroad Index on page 127.)

When looking back at their undergraduate years, alumni of Christian colleges and universities speak of the lifelong friendships that continue to grow out of a shared commitment to Christ. Campus life is designed to encourage healthy friendships. Christian college campuses are not split into competitive Greek houses or divided by ethnic or religious categories. "Community" is more than just an idea, it is a reality on these campuses. And when students do encounter the day-to-day tensions present with any group of people living together, such problems are tempered by an atmosphere of compassion and caring, of teamwork and trust.

Life After College

That graduates of Christian colleges have little trouble finding a first job or gaining admittance to graduate or professional schools is no accident. The colleges work hard at providing students with a broad array of resources and at helping alumni succeed in life after college.

Notable alumni who have graduated from a Christian college include evangelist Billy Graham; founder and president of Focus on the Family James

Narrowing the Choice
The college years are the most exciting of a
young person's life. They are also the
stepping stones to things to come

Dobson; award-winning recording artist Sandi Patti; Olympic track-and-field star Airat Bakare; U.S. congressmen Dennis Hastert, Paul Henry, and Bob McEwen; NFL running back Christian Okoye; U.S. senator Dan Coats; chairman of the board of the ServiceMaster Company Kenneth Wessner; and sociologist, speaker, and author Tony Campolo. Other alumni are also making their mark on society as they serve in North America and abroad. Their collective faithfulness in dealing with life's minor as well as major issues stands as a testimony to the lifelong impact of a Christian college education.

most likely to encourage their full development. The college years are the most exciting in a young person's life. They are also the stepping stones to things to come—a career, new friends, and a lifetime walk with God.

By inviting students and parents to consider a Christian school, we hope this guide will be the first step toward many wise and informed college choices.

Dr. Myron Augsburger
President
Christian College Coalition

Meeting the Cost of a Christian College Education

A Christian college education is a major investment. However, many thousands of families have found a Christian college education well worth the price, even if it is a bit more than what is charged by public colleges and universities. Parents and alumni alike agree that it is impossible to place a dollar value on the lifelong benefits of a Christ-centered undergraduate experience.

Most Christian colleges and universities provide generous aid packages to financially and/or academically qualified students. Indeed, at many Christian colleges about two thirds of all students receive some form of institutional aid. Financial aid officers are eager to work with families in structuring financial aid packages that fit individual situations. Students enrolled full-time at a Christian college may also be eligible for federal and state grants, scholarships, loans, and work-study opportunities.

Narrowing the Choice

With over 3,000 colleges and universities to choose from, narrowing the field to one school can be tough. Most students attend only one college during their undergraduate career.

It is important that students conduct the search carefully and prayerfully, seeking the college that is

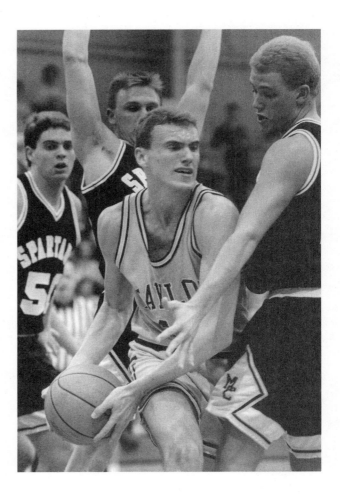

ANDERSON UNIVERSITY

Anderson, Indiana

Total Enrollment: 2,162

UG Enrollment: 2,050 (58% W)

Application Deadline: 9/1

Tuition & Fees: $8780

Room & Board: $3120

Entrance: moderately difficult

SAT ≥ 500: 24% V, 44% M

ACT ≥ 21: 56%

Denominational Affiliation: Church of God

GENERAL INFORMATION Independent comprehensive coed institution. Founded 1917. Awards A (college transfer and terminal), B, M. Primary accreditation: regional. Suburban setting, with easy access to Indianapolis; 100-acre campus. Total enrollment: 2,162. Faculty: 119 (61 full-time, 58 part-time); 50% of full-time faculty have terminal degrees; graduate assistants teach no undergraduate courses. Library holdings: 155,000 bound volumes, 12,152 titles on microform, 1,100 periodical subscriptions, 11,640 records/tapes/CDs. Computer terminals/PCs available for student use: 125, located in computer center, instructional materials center.

UNDERGRADUATE PROFILE Fall 1991: 2,050 undergraduates (547 freshmen) from 44 states and territories and 16 foreign countries; 13% part-time; 60% state residents; 3% transfers; 90% financial aid recipients; 58% women; 5% African Americans; 1% Native Americans; 0% Hispanics; 0% Asian Americans; 1% international students; 22% of undergraduates 25 years of age or older..

1991 FRESHMAN DATA 1,362 students applied for fall 1991 admission; 79% were accepted; 51% of those accepted enrolled. 23% of freshmen were in top 10% of secondary school class, 45% were in top 25%, 74% were in top half.

ENROLLMENT PATTERNS 82% of fall 1990 freshmen returned for fall 1991 term. 38% of 1986 freshmen graduated within 5 years.

FRESHMAN ADMISSIONS Options: early entrance, early decision, deferred entrance. Required: high school transcript, 2 recommendations, SAT or ACT, TOEFL (for foreign students). Recommended: 3 years of high school math and science, 1 year of high school foreign language. Test scores used for counseling/placement. Application deadlines: 9/1, 12/1 for early decision. Notification dates: continuous until 9/6, continuous until 1/15 for early decision. College's own assessment of entrance difficulty level: moderately difficult.

TRANSFER ADMISSIONS Required: high school transcript, 2 recommendations, college transcript, minimum 2.0 grade point average. Application deadline: 9/1. College's own assessment of entrance difficulty level: moderately difficult.

EXPENSES (1992–93) Comprehensive fee of $11,900 includes full-time tuition ($8780) and college room and board ($3120). College room only: $1680. Part-time tuition: $366 per semester hour.

FINANCIAL AID College-administered aid for all 1991–92 undergraduates: 400 need-based scholarships (average $1180); 600 non-need scholarships (average $1520); low-interest long-term loans from external sources (average $2700); SEOG; College Work-Study; 300 part-time jobs. Supporting data: institutional form required; FFS, FAF, AFSA/SAR acceptable. Priority application deadline: 3/1.

CAMPUS LIFE/STUDENT SERVICES Mandatory chapel; drama/theater group; student-run newspaper and radio station. Institution provides health clinic, personal/psychological counseling. Social organizations: 11 social clubs.

ATHLETICS Member NAIA. Intercollegiate sports: baseball M; basketball M, W; cross-country running M, W; football M; golf M; soccer M; softball W; tennis M, W; track and field M, W; volleyball W. Intramural sports: basketball, football, golf, soccer, softball, tennis, track and field, volleyball.

MAJORS Accounting; American studies; art education; art/fine arts; athletic training; biblical studies; biology/biological sciences; broadcasting; business administration/commerce/management; business education; chemistry; child care/child and family studies; communication; computer science; criminal justice; (pre)dentistry sequence; early childhood education; ecology/environmental studies; economics; education; elementary education; (pre)engineering sequence; English; environmental sciences; French; German; graphic arts; health education; history; journalism; (pre)law sequence; marketing/retailing/merchandising; marriage and family counseling; mathematics; medical technology; (pre)medicine sequence; museum studies; music; music business; music education; nursing; pastoral studies; philosophy; physical education; physics; piano/organ; political science/government; psychology; public affairs and policy studies; public relations; recreation and leisure services; religious studies; sacred music; secondary education; secretarial studies/office management; social work; sociology; Spanish; speech/rhetoric/public address/debate; sports medicine; theater arts/drama; (pre)veterinary medicine sequence; voice. Most popular majors of class of 1991: elementary education, business administration/commerce/management, marketing/retailing/merchandising.

SPECIAL NOTE FROM THE COLLEGE Anderson University is a community of Christian higher education where high-quality learning and Christian service come alive. Believing that scholarship and scholars should serve a purpose, Anderson University is a mission-minded school that offers students a strong liberal arts foundation on which to build career credentials. Business, computer science, education, music, religious studies, social work, and sociology are among the most popular of the 60 majors and programs offered. The Tri-S program (study, serve, and share) is probably most representative of the spirit of the University. Through this program, more than 500 students volunteer each year for 50 different cross-cultural work projects throughout the world. Bill and Gloria Gaither and Sandi Patti are a few of the nearly 25,000 loyal alumni who make up the University's international alumni association and whose strength is not only in their numbers but also in their belief.

CONTACT Director of Admissions, Anderson University, 1100 East Fifth Street, Anderson, IN 46012, 317-641-4080 or toll-free 800-428-6414.

ASBURY COLLEGE

Wilmore, Kentucky

Total Enrollment: 1,086 (all UG)

Women: 55%

Application Deadline: rolling

Tuition & Fees: $7863

Room & Board: $2614

Entrance: moderately difficult

SAT ≥ 500: 32% V, 41% M

ACT ≥ 21: 61%

Denominational Affiliation: nondenominational

GENERAL INFORMATION Independent 4-year coed college. Founded 1890. Awards B. Primary accreditation: regional. Small-town setting; 400-acre campus. Total enrollment: 1,086. Faculty: 102 (33 full-time, 69 part-time). Library holdings: 135,178 bound volumes, 564 titles on microform, 974 periodical subscriptions, 6,733 records/tapes/CDs. Computer terminals/PCs available for student use: 40, located in computer center.

UNDERGRADUATE PROFILE Fall 1991: 1,086 undergraduates (315 freshmen) from 45 states and territories and 18 foreign countries; 5% part-time; 26% state residents; 8% transfers; 92% financial aid recipients; 55% women; 1% African Americans; 1% Hispanics; 1% Asian Americans; 3% international students; 11% of undergraduates 25 years of age or older.

1991 FRESHMAN DATA 648 students applied for fall 1991 admission; 72% were accepted; 68% of those accepted enrolled. 4 freshmen were National Merit Scholarship Finalists. 26% of freshmen were in top 10% of secondary school class, 46% were in top 25%, 82% were in top half.

ENROLLMENT PATTERNS 82% of fall 1990 freshmen returned for fall 1991 term. 78% of 1986 freshmen graduated within 5 years; 45% of students completing a degree program went on for further study.

FRESHMAN ADMISSIONS Options: early entrance, deferred entrance. Required: high school transcript, 3 recommendations, SAT or ACT, TOEFL (for foreign students). Recommended: 3 years of high school math and science, some high school foreign language. Required for some: essay, interview. Test scores used for admission. Application deadline: rolling. College's own assessment of entrance difficulty level: moderately difficult.

TRANSFER ADMISSIONS Required: high school transcript, 2 recommendations, college transcript, minimum 2.0 grade point average. Recommended: standardized test scores, 3 years of high school math and science, some high school foreign language. Required for some: essay, interview. Application deadline: rolling. College's own assessment of entrance difficulty level: moderately difficult.

EXPENSES (1992–93) Comprehensive fee of $10,477 includes full-time tuition ($7740), mandatory fees ($123), and college room and board ($2614). Part-time tuition and fees per semester hour: $314.

FINANCIAL AID College-administered aid for all 1991–92 undergraduates: 507 need-based scholarships (average $1575); 310 non-need scholarships (average $1350); low-interest long-term loans from college funds (average $925), from external sources (average $2950); SEOG; College Work-Study; 390 part-time jobs. Supporting data: FAF, institutional form required; IRS, state form required for some; FFS, AFSA/SAR acceptable. Priority application deadline: 3/15.

CAMPUS LIFE/STUDENT SERVICES Dress code; mandatory chapel; drama/theater group; student-run newspaper and radio station. Institution provides health clinic, personal/psychological counseling.

STUDY ABROAD SITES France, Latin America, England.

ATHLETICS Member NCAA (Division III), NAIA. Intercollegiate sports: baseball M; basketball M, W; cross-country M, W; soccer M; softball W; swimming M, W; tennis M, W; volleyball W. Intramural sports: basketball, football, soccer, softball, table tennis (Ping Pong), tennis, volleyball.

MAJORS Accounting; applied mathematics; art education; art/fine arts; biblical languages; biblical studies; biology/biological sciences; broadcasting; business administration/commerce/management; chemistry; computer science; education; elementary education; English; French; history; human services; journalism; literature; mathematics; medical technology; (pre)medicine sequence; ministries; music; music education; philosophy; physical education; psychology; recreation and leisure services; science education; social work; sociology; Spanish; speech/rhetoric/public address/debate. Most popular majors of class of 1991: education, business administration/commerce/management, psychology.

SPECIAL NOTE FROM THE COLLEGE At Asbury College students join in a century-long tradition of personal, spiritual, and professional excellence. Selected as one of the nation's "top fifty liberal arts schools" by the *National Review College Guide,* Asbury offers programs ranging from accounting and broadcast communication to education and psychology. A leadership program complements outstanding academics, which enables students to realize their full potential. Students come from 45 states and 18 countries and live on a campus featuring stately white columns and Central Kentucky's rolling landscape. Lexington's educational, commercial, and cultural resources are within a 20-minute commute of Wilmore's relaxed tree-lined streets.

CONTACT Mr. Stan F. Wiggam, Dean of Admissions, Asbury College, 1 Macklem Drive, Wilmore, KY 40390, 606-858-3511 Ext. 142.

AZUSA PACIFIC UNIVERSITY

Azusa, California

Total Enrollment: 2,955

UG Enrollment: 1,754 (60% W)

Application Deadline: rolling

Tuition & Fees: $9992

Room & Board: $3700

Entrance: moderately difficult

SAT ≥ 500: 21% V, 38% M

ACT ≥ 21: 42%

Denominational Affiliation: Interdenominational

GENERAL INFORMATION Independent comprehensive coed institution. Founded 1899. Awards B, M. Primary accreditation: regional. Small-town setting, with easy access to Los Angeles; 73-acre campus. Total enrollment: 2,955. Faculty: 177 (90 full-time, 87 part-time); graduate assistants teach a few undergraduate courses. Library holdings: 97,000 bound volumes, 415,000 titles on microform, 950 periodical subscriptions, 5,000 records/tapes/CDs. Computer terminals/PCs available for student use: 82, located in computer center.

UNDERGRADUATE PROFILE Fall 1991: 1,754 undergraduates. (359 freshmen) from 35 states and territories and 27 foreign countries; 7% part-time; 70% state residents; 81% financial aid recipients; 60% women; 4% African Americans; 1% Native Americans; 6% Hispanics; 4% Asian Americans; 4% international students; 16% of undergraduates 25 years of age or older.

1991 FRESHMAN DATA 720 students applied for fall 1991 admission; 81% were accepted; 62% of those accepted enrolled. 25% of freshmen were in top 10% of secondary school class, 52% were in top 25%, 75% were in top half.

ENROLLMENT PATTERNS 84% of fall 1990 freshmen returned for fall 1991 term.

FRESHMAN ADMISSIONS Option: deferred entrance. Required: essay, high school transcript, 2 recommendations, SAT or ACT, English Composition Test (with essay), TOEFL (for foreign students). Required for some: interview. Test scores used for admission. Application deadline: rolling. Notification date: continuous. College's own assessment of entrance difficulty level: moderately difficult.

TRANSFER ADMISSIONS Required: essay, 2 recommendations, college transcript, minimum 2.0 grade point average. Required for some: standardized test scores, high school transcript, interview. Application deadline: rolling. Notification date: continuous. College's own assessment of entrance difficulty level: moderately difficult.

EXPENSES (1992–93) Comprehensive fee of $13,692 includes full-time tuition ($9992) and college room and board ($3700 minimum). College room only: $1650 (minimum). Part-time tuition: $405 per unit.

FINANCIAL AID College-administered aid for all 1991–92 undergraduates: need-based scholarships; 105 non-need scholarships (average $2358); low-interest long-term loans from external sources (average $2500); SEOG; College Work-Study; part-time jobs. Supporting data: FAF, IRS, institutional form, AFSA/SAR required; state form acceptable. Priority application deadline: 3/1.

CAMPUS LIFE/STUDENT SERVICES Mandatory chapel; drama/theater group; student-run newspaper. Institution provides health clinic, personal/psychological counseling.

STUDY ABROAD SITES Ecuador, Japan, Taiwan, Costa Rica.

ATHLETICS Member NAIA. Intercollegiate sports: baseball M(s); basketball M(s), W(s); cross-country running M(s), W(s); football M(s); soccer M(s), W; softball W; tennis M(s); track and field M(s), W(s); volleyball W(c,s). Intramural sports: badminton, basketball, bowling, football, golf, racquetball, skiing (cross-country), skiing (downhill), soccer, tennis, track and field, volleyball, wrestling.

MAJORS Accounting; applied art; art/fine arts; biblical languages; biblical studies; biochemistry; biology/biological sciences; business administration; chemistry; communication; computer science; (pre)dentistry sequence; education; elementary education; English; history; international studies; (pre)law sequence; liberal arts/general studies; management information systems; marketing; mathematics; (pre)medicine sequence; ministries; music; music education; nursing; pastoral studies; philosophy; physical education; physics; political science/government; psychology; religious studies; secondary education; social science; social work; sociology; theology; (pre)veterinary medicine sequence. Most popular majors of class of 1991: business administration, liberal arts/general studies, music, psychology.

SPECIAL NOTE FROM THE COLLEGE Asuza Pacific has a widely acclaimed and innovative student leadership training program. This dynamic program takes APU students outside the comfort of everyday life to prepare them for leadership positions at the University and beyond. Every year student government leaders and resident assistants travel to the Sierra Nevada region for a 9-day wilderness Walk-About, including group exercises in risk-taking, interpersonal communication, and problem solving. Azusa Pacific's Bridges Program exposes student leaders to the needs of the homeless, AIDS victims, and those living in need on the streets of inner-city San Francisco. Wherever their training takes place, students learn that service to others is the cornerstone to effective leadership.

CONTACT Ms. Karen Sauvé, Dean of Enrollment Management, Azusa Pacific University, 901 East Alosta Avenue, P.O. Box 7000, Azusa, CA 91702, 818-812-3016.

BARTLESVILLE WESLEYAN COLLEGE

Bartlesville, Oklahoma

Total Enrollment: 446 (all UG)

Women: 57%

Application Deadline: rolling

Tuition & Fees: $5950

Room & Board: $2900

Entrance: minimally difficult

SAT ≥ 500: N/R

ACT ≥ 21: 46%

Denominational Affiliation: Wesleyan Church

GENERAL INFORMATION Independent 4-year coed college. Founded 1909. Awards A (college transfer), B. Primary accreditation: regional. Small-town setting, with easy access to Tulsa; 27-acre campus. Total enrollment: 446. Faculty: 67 (42 full-time, 25 part-time); 51% of full-time faculty have terminal degrees. Library holdings: 132,148 bound volumes, 35,997 titles on microform, 300 periodical subscriptions, 1,076 records/tapes/CDs. Computer terminals/PCs available for student use: 20, located in computer center.

UNDERGRADUATE PROFILE Fall 1991: 446 undergraduates (88 freshmen) from 24 states and territories and 6 foreign countries; 31% part-time; 54% state residents; 18% transfers; 92% financial aid recipients; 57% women; 2% African Americans; 3% Native Americans; 2% Hispanics; 1% Asian Americans; 2% international students; 34% of undergraduates 25 years of age or older.

1991 FRESHMAN DATA 120 students applied for fall 1991 admission; 82% were accepted; 90% of those accepted enrolled. 15% of freshmen were in top 10% of secondary school class, 32% were in top 25%, 72% were in top half.

ENROLLMENT PATTERNS 82% of fall 1990 freshmen returned for fall 1991 term.

FRESHMAN ADMISSIONS Options: early entrance, deferred entrance. Required: high school transcript, SAT or ACT.

Required for some: TOEFL (for international students). Test scores used for counseling/placement. Application deadline: rolling. College's own assessment of entrance difficulty level: minimally difficult.

TRANSFER ADMISSIONS Required: high school transcript, college transcript, minimum 2.0 grade point average. Application deadline: rolling. College's own assessment of entrance difficulty level: minimally difficult.

EXPENSES (1992–93) Comprehensive fee of $8850 includes full-time tuition ($5950) and college room and board ($2900 minimum). Part-time tuition: $195 per semester hour.

FINANCIAL AID College-administered aid for all 1991–92 undergraduates: 25 need-based scholarships (average $1330); 250 non-need scholarships (average $843); low-interest long-term loans from external sources (average $2625); SEOG; College Work-Study; 30 part-time jobs. Supporting data: FFS, IRS, state form, institutional form, AFSA/SAR required; FAF acceptable. Priority application deadline: 5/1.

CAMPUS LIFE/STUDENT SERVICES Dress code; mandatory chapel; student-run newspaper. Institution provides health clinic, personal/psychological counseling.

ATHLETICS Member NAIA. Intercollegiate sports: basketball M(s), W(s); cross-country running M(s), W(s); golf M; soccer M(s), W(s); tennis M; volleyball W. Intramural sports: basketball, football, golf, racquetball, softball, swimming and diving, tennis, volleyball.

MAJORS Accounting; applied computer information systems; behavioral science; biology; business administration; business education; chemistry; communications; cross-cultural ministry; elementary education; English; English education; general science; general studies; history; history/political science; management of human resources; mathematics; math education; ministerial studies; office administration; physical education; physical education/recreation; science education; social studies education; social studies/history; youth ministry.

SPECIAL NOTE FROM THE COLLEGE Bartlesville Wesleyan College is a distinctive Christian college. The campus community strongly believes in providing a Christ-centered educational experience that will produce lifelong results. It is located in the south-central part of the United States, 45 miles north of Suburban Tulsa. Bartlesville is a cosmopolitan city of 40,000 and is the world headquarters of Phillips Petroleum Company. Local cultural opportunities include a choral society, a civic ballet, a theater guild, a symphony orchestra, and an annual International OK Mozart festival. The focal point of the 27-acre campus is an elegant 60-year-old, 32-room, Spanish-style mansion overlooking a beautiful lake.

CONTACT Mr. Robert Hubbard, Enrollment Services Administrator, Bartlesville Wesleyan College, 2201 Silver Lake Road, Bartlesville, OK 74006, 918-333-6151 Ext. 377.

BELHAVEN COLLEGE

Jackson, Mississippi

Total Enrollment: 967 (all UG)

Women: 56%

Application Deadline: rolling

Tuition & Fees: $6470

Room & Board: $2420

Entrance: moderately difficult

SAT ≥ 500: N/R

ACT ≥ 21: 53%

Denominational Affiliation: Presbyterian

GENERAL INFORMATION Independent 4-year coed college. Founded 1883. Awards B. Primary accreditation: regional. Urban setting; 42-acre campus. Total enrollment: 967. Faculty: 71 (32 full-time, 39 part-time); 75% of full-time faculty have terminal degrees; graduate assistants teach no undergraduate courses. Library holdings: 79,990 bound volumes, 174 titles on microform, 334 periodical subscriptions, 6,660 records/tapes/CDs. Computer terminals/PCs available for student use: 39, located in computer center, business building.

UNDERGRADUATE Profile Fall 1991: 967 undergraduates (99 freshmen) from 20 states and territories and 25 foreign countries; 31% part-time; 88% state residents; 14% transfers; 95% financial aid recipients; 56% women; 13% African Americans; 0% Native Americans; 1% Hispanics; 1% Asian Americans; 4% international students; 36% of undergraduates 25 years of age or older.

1991 FRESHMAN DATA 201 students applied for fall 1991 admission; 84% were accepted; 93% of those accepted enrolled. 21% of freshmen were in top 10% of secondary school class, 41% were in top 25%, 66% were in top half.

FRESHMAN ADMISSIONS Options: early entrance, deferred entrance. Required: high school transcript, SAT or ACT, TOEFL (for foreign students). Test scores used for admission. Application deadline: rolling. College's own assessment of entrance difficulty level: moderately difficult.

TRANSFER ADMISSIONS Required: 2 recommendations, college transcript, minimum 2.0 grade point average. Recommended: standardized test scores, high school transcript. Application deadline: rolling. College's own assessment of entrance difficulty level: moderately difficult.

EXPENSES (1992–93) Comprehensive fee of $8890 includes full-time tuition ($6340), mandatory fees ($130), and college room and board ($2420). Part-time tuition per semester ranges from $210 to $2840 for day students; part-time tuition for evening students: $150 per semester hour.

FINANCIAL AID College-administered aid for all 1991–92 undergraduates: need-based and honors scholarships; 600 non-need scholarships (average $1950); low-interest long-term loans from college funds (average $1000), from external sources (average $2760); SEOG; College Work-Study. Supporting data: IRS, institutional form, AFSA/SAR required; FFS, FAF acceptable. Priority application deadline: 7/31.

CAMPUS LIFE/STUDENT SERVICES Weekly chapel; drama/theater group; student-run newspaper. Health clinic, Reformed University Fellowship (RUF), Student Mission Fellowship (SMF), career center.

ATHLETICS Member NAIA. Intercollegiate sports: baseball M(s); basketball M(s), W(s); cross-country M(s), W(s); golf M(s); soccer M(s); tennis M(s), W(s). Intramural sports: basketball, football, soccer, softball, swimming and diving, tennis, softball.

MAJORS Accounting; art/fine arts; biblical studies; biology/biological sciences; business administration/commerce/management; chemistry; computer science; (pre)dentistry sequence; elementary education; engineering sciences; English; history; humanities; (pre)law sequence; mathematics; (pre)medicine sequence; ministries; music; nursing; philosophy; piano/organ; psychology; sacred music; science; stringed instruments; (pre)veterinary medicine sequence; voice. Most popular majors of class of 1991: business administration/commerce/management, elementary education, psychology.

SPECIAL NOTE FROM THE COLLEGE Founded in 1883, Belhaven College is located in a historic neighborhood of Jackson, Mississippi, the thriving center of cultural, educational, and political life in a state known for its Southern hospitality. Belhaven is a coeducational, liberal arts Christian college serving students throughout the Southeast and beyond. Dedicated to the integration of academic excellence with a biblically based world view, Belhaven encourages young men and women to develop strong lifelong moral values. The emphasis on personal development was recognized nationally in 1992 when Belhaven was 1 of 111 schools selected from over 800 nominees and named to the John Templeton Foundation Honor Roll for Character Building Colleges. Belhaven's 42-acre campus, graced by traditional Southern architecture, provides a sense of Christian community with its small classes, dedicated faculty, and friendships that last a lifetime.

CONTACT Mrs. Mary I. Word, Director of Admissions, Belhaven College, 1500 Peachtree Street, Jackson, MS 39202-1789, 601-968-5940.

BETHEL COLLEGE

Mishawaka, Indiana

Total Enrollment: 782

UG Enrollment: 769 (60% W)

Application Deadline: rolling

Tuition & Fees: $8150

Room & Board: $2900

Entrance: moderately difficult

SAT ≥ 500: 17% V, 44% M

ACT ≥ 21: 37%

Denominational Affiliation: Missionary Church

GENERAL INFORMATION Independent comprehensive coed institution. Founded 1947. Awards A (college transfer and terminal), B, M. Primary accreditation: regional. Suburban setting; 60-acre campus. Total enrollment: 782. Faculty: 84 (45 full-time, 39 part-time); 40% of full-time faculty have terminal degrees; graduate assistants teach no undergraduate courses. Library holdings: 68,393 bound volumes, 3,655 titles on microform, 435 periodical subscriptions, 1,208 records/tapes/CDs. Computer terminals/PCs available for student use: 18, located in computer center.

UNDERGRADUATE PROFILE Fall 1991: 769 undergraduates (277 freshmen) from 16 states and territories and 5 foreign countries; 25% part-time; 79% state residents; 17% transfers; 80% financial aid recipients; 60% women; 7% African Americans; 0% Native Americans; 1% Hispanics; 0% Asian Americans; 1% international students; 28% of undergraduates 25 years of age or older.

1991 FRESHMAN DATA 449 students applied for fall 1991 admission; 70% were accepted; 88% of those accepted enrolled. 15% of freshmen were in top 10% of secondary school class, 36% were in top 25%, 69% were in top half.

ENROLLMENT PATTERNS 70% of fall 1990 freshmen returned for fall 1991 term.

FRESHMAN ADMISSIONS Options: early entrance, deferred entrance. Required: high school transcript, 1 recommendation, SAT or ACT, TOEFL (for foreign students). Recommended: 2 years of high school foreign language, interview. Test scores used for counseling/placement. Application deadline: rolling. College's own assessment of entrance difficulty level: moderately difficult.

TRANSFER ADMISSIONS Required: high school transcript, 1 recommendation, college transcript, minimum 2.0 grade point average. Recommended: standardized test scores, 2 years of high school foreign language, interview. Application deadline: rolling. College's own assessment of entrance difficulty level: moderately difficult.

EXPENSES (1991–92) Comprehensive fee of $10,850 includes full-time tuition ($7950), mandatory fees ($200), and college room and board ($2900). Part-time tuition per semester hour ranges from $189 to $295. Part-time fees per semester: $25.

FINANCIAL AID College-administered aid for all 1991–92 undergraduates: need-based scholarships; 778 non-need scholarships (average $2696); low-interest long-term loans from college funds (average $1315), from external sources (average $2652); SEOG; College Work-Study; 60 part-time jobs. Supporting data: FAF, institutional form required; IRS required for some; FFS, AFSA/SAR acceptable. Priority application deadline: 3/1.

CAMPUS LIFE/STUDENT SERVICES Dress code; mandatory chapel; drama/theater group; student-run newspaper and radio station. Institution provides personal/psychological counseling.

ATHLETICS Member NAIA. Intercollegiate sports: baseball M(s); basketball M(s), W(s); cross-country running M(s), W(s); golf M(s), W(s); soccer M(s); softball W(s); tennis M(s), W(s); volleyball W(s). Intramural sports: basketball, football, soccer, softball, table tennis (Ping Pong), tennis, track and field, volleyball, weight lifting.

MAJORS Accounting; art/fine arts; biblical languages; biblical studies; biology/biological sciences; business administration/commerce/management; business education; chemistry; commercial art; communication; computer science; (pre)dentistry sequence; early childhood education; economics; education; elementary education; English; French; gerontology; health education; history; human resources; journalism; liberal arts/general studies; mathematics; (pre)medicine sequence; ministries; music; music education; nursing; pastoral studies; philosophy; physical education; piano/organ; psychology; recreation and leisure services; religious studies; sacred music; science; science education; secondary education; secretarial studies/office management; social science; sociology; Spanish; theater arts/drama; voice. Most popular majors of class of 1991: elementary education, business administration/commerce/management, psychology.

SPECIAL NOTE FROM THE COLLEGE Bethel College is located in northern Indiana on a beautiful 60-acre wooded campus. Bethel is a college of the Missionary Church, an evangelical denomination with roots in Methodist and Mennonite traditions. Since its founding in 1947, the hallmark of the College has been an emphasis on excellent teaching and warm student-faculty relationships. Bethel cares about its students. Bethel College has a challenging and participatory environment: students work hard in the classroom, on the athletic field, in performance, and in ministry opportunities. Bethel is a college with a deep Christian commitment. There is an open and joyful emphasis on the Christian life. Chapel meets 3 times a week and is the center of the campus culture. "With Christ at the helm" is more than a motto—it is the purpose and intent of living and studying together.

CONTACT Mr. Steve Matteson, Director of Admissions, Bethel College, 1001 West McKinley Avenue, Mishawaka, IN 46545, toll-free 800-422-4101.

BETHEL COLLEGE

North Newton, Kansas

Total enrollment: 576 (all UG)

Women: 57%

Application Deadline: 8/15

Tuition & Fees: $7980

Room & Board: $3000

Entrance: moderately difficult

SAT ≥ 500: N/R

ACT ≥ 21: 69%

Denominational Affiliation: General Conference Mennonite Church

GENERAL INFORMATION Independent 4-year coed college. Founded 1887. Awards B. Primary accreditation: regional. Small-town setting; 45-acre campus. Total enrollment: 576. Faculty: 59 (38 full-time, 21 part-time); 80% of full-time faculty have terminal degrees; graduate assistants teach no undergraduate courses. Library holdings: 125,000 bound volumes, 100 titles on microform, 725 periodical subscriptions, 1,500 records/tapes/CDs. Computer terminals/PCs available for student use: 25, located in computer center.

UNDERGRADUATE PROFILE Fall 1991: 576 undergraduates (118 freshmen) from 30 states and territories and 12 foreign countries; 15% part-time; 68% state residents; 11% transfers; 97% financial aid recipients; 57% women; 5% African Americans; 1% Native Americans; 1% Hispanics; 1% Asian Americans; 3% international students; 22% of undergraduates 25 years of age or older.

1991 FRESHMAN DATA 369 students applied for fall 1991 admission; 95% were accepted; 34% of those accepted enrolled. 19% of freshmen were in top 10% of secondary school class, 46% were in top 25%, 71% were in top half. 1 freshman was a National Merit Finalist and received a National Merit Scholarship.

ENROLLMENT PATTERNS 64% of fall 1990 freshmen returned for fall 1991 term.

FRESHMAN ADMISSIONS Options: early entrance, deferred entrance. Required: high school transcript, 2 recommendations, interview, SAT or ACT, TOEFL (for foreign students). Recommended: 3 years of high school math and science, some high school foreign language. Test scores used for admission. Application deadline: 8/15. Notification date: continuous.

College's own assessment of entrance difficulty level: moderately difficult.

TRANSFER Admissions Required: high school transcript, 1 recommendation, interview, college transcript, minimum 2.0 grade point average. Recommended: 3 years of high school math and science, some high school foreign language. Required for some: standardized test scores. Application deadline: 8/15. Notification date: continuous. College's own assessment of entrance difficulty level: moderately difficult.

EXPENSES (1992–93) Comprehensive fee of $10,980 includes full-time tuition ($7780), mandatory fees ($200), and college room and board ($3000). Part-time tuition per credit hour ranges from $130 to $260.

FINANCIAL AID College-administered aid for all 1991–92 undergraduates: 369 need-based scholarships (average $715); 400 non-need scholarships (average $1753); low-interest long-term loans from external sources (average $2600); SEOG; College Work-Study; 130 part-time jobs. Supporting data: IRS required for some; FFS, FAF, institutional form, AFSA/SAR acceptable. Priority application deadline: 3/1.

CAMPUS LIFE/STUDENT SERVICES Debate/forensics; drama/theater group; student-run newspaper and radio station. Institution provides personal/psychological counseling.

STUDY ABROAD SITES Germany, England, Spain, China, France, Japan.

ATHLETICS Member NAIA. Intercollegiate sports: basketball M(s), W(s); football M(s); soccer M(s); tennis M(s), W(s); track and field M(s), W(s); volleyball W(s). Intramural sports: badminton, basketball, football, golf, table tennis (Ping Pong), tennis, volleyball, weight lifting.

MAJORS Accounting; art/fine arts; biblical studies; biology/biological sciences; business administration; chemistry; communication; computer science; (pre)dentistry sequence; early childhood education; economics; education; elementary education; English; environmental sciences; German; graphic design; health and physical education; history; home economics education; human services; interdisciplinary studies; international studies; (pre)law sequence; liberal arts/general studies; mathematics; (pre)medicine sequence; music; natural sciences; nursing; peace studies; philosophy; physics; political science/government; psychology; religious studies; secondary education; social science; social work; sociology; special education; theater arts/drama.

SPECIAL NOTE FROM THE COLLEGE Bethel College in Kansas offers academic excellence firmly rooted in a Christian heritage. Founded in 1887 by Mennonite immigrants, Bethel affirms a commitment to social justice, service to others, and conflict resolution. While support of these ideals by Bethel remains a cornerstone at the college, a prospective student does not need to be Mennonite to attend Bethel. In fact, approximately 50% of the Bethel student population have a religious orientation other than Mennonite. Within this context of spiritual belief, Bethel College offers a distinguished array of undergraduate liberal arts programming. Students at Bethel choose from among a variety of academic majors to study on the 45-acre, wooded campus. Bethel is noted for high academic standards and achievements. Bethel College is "the educated choice" for a Christian college.

CONTACT Mr. J. Michael Lamb, Director of Admissions, Bethel College, 300 East 27th Street, North Newton, KS 67117, 316-283-2500 Ext. 230 or toll-free 800-522-1887.

BETHEL COLLEGE

St. Paul, Minnesota

Total Enrollment: 2,001

UG Enrollment: 1,783 (59% W)

Application Deadline: rolling

Tuition & Fees: $10,540

Room & Board: $3790

Entrance: moderately difficult

SAT ≥ 500: 30% V, 57% M

ACT ≥ 21: 62%

Denominational Affiliation: Baptist General Conference

GENERAL INFORMATION Independent comprehensive coed institution. Founded 1871. Awards A (college transfer), B, M. Primary accreditation: regional. Suburban setting; 231-acre campus. Total enrollment: 2,001. Faculty: 181 (110 full-time, 71 part-time); 68% of full-time faculty have terminal degrees; graduate assistants teach no undergraduate courses. Library holdings: 129,000 bound volumes, 640 periodical subscriptions, 3,700 records/tapes/CDs. Computer terminals/PCs available for student use: 74, located in computer center, dormitories.

UNDERGRADUATE PROFILE Fall 1991: 1,783 undergraduates (393 freshmen); 6% part-time; 65% state residents; 9% transfers; 91% financial aid recipients; 59% women; 1% African Americans; 1% Native Americans; 1% Hispanics; 2% Asian Americans; 1% international students.

1991 FRESHMAN DATA 882 students applied for fall 1991 admission; 78% were accepted; 57% of those accepted enrolled. 29% of freshmen were in top 10% of secondary school class, 87% were in top half.

FRESHMAN ADMISSIONS Required: high school transcript with rank, 3 recommendations, SAT or ACT, TOEFL (for foreign students), PSAT. Recommended: interview. Test scores used for admission. Application deadline: rolling. College's own assessment of entrance difficulty level: moderately difficult.

TRANSFER ADMISSIONS Required: 3 recommendations, college transcript, minimum 2.0 grade point average. Recommended: interview. Required for some: high school transcript, standardized test score. Application deadline: rolling.

College's own assessment of entrance difficulty level: moderately difficult.

EXPENSES (1992–93 estimated) Comprehensive fee of $14,330 includes full-time tuition ($10,540) and college room and board ($3790). College room only: $2090. Part-time tuition: $397 per credit hour.

FINANCIAL AID College-administered aid for all 1991–92 undergraduates: 1,227 need-based scholarships (average $2000); non-need scholarships (average $800); short-term loans (average $330); low-interest long-term loans from external sources (average $2750); SEOG; College Work-Study; 500 part-time jobs. Supporting data: FFS, IRS, institutional form required; state form required for some; FAF acceptable. Priority application deadline: 4/15.

CAMPUS LIFE/STUDENT SERVICES Drama/theater group; student-run newspaper and radio station. Institution provides health clinic, personal/psychological counseling.

STUDY ABROAD SITES England, Israel, Sweden, Germany

ATHLETICS Member NCAA (Division III). Intercollegiate sports: baseball M; basketball M, W; cross-country running M, W; football M; golf M; ice hockey M; soccer M, W; softball W; tennis M, W; track and field M, W; volleyball W. Intramural sports: basketball, football, golf, racquetball, table tennis (Ping Pong), tennis, track and field, volleyball, weight lifting.

MAJORS Accounting; adult and continuing education; anthropology; art education; art/fine arts; art history; biblical studies; biology/biological sciences; business administration/commerce/management; chemistry; child care/child and family studies; child psychology/child development; communication; computer science; creative writing; (pre)dentistry sequence; early childhood education; economics; education; elementary education; (pre)engineering sequence; English; finance/banking; health education; history; international studies; (pre)law sequence; liberal arts/general studies; literature; management information systems; mathematics; (pre)medicine sequence; ministries; molecular biology; music; music education; natural sciences; nursing; philosophy; physical education; physics; political science/government; psychology; sacred music; science education; secondary education; social science; social work; sociology; Spanish; speech/rhetoric/public address/debate; studio art; theater arts/drama; theology; (pre)veterinary medicine sequence; youth ministry. Most popular majors of class of 1991: business administration/commerce/management, education, nursing.

SPECIAL NOTE FROM THE COLLEGE From the first day of classes at Bethel, students find an atmosphere of active questioning, both intellectual and spiritual. Bethel believes that this questioning results in clearer understanding and a deepening faith. Students at Bethel find not only an educational experience but also spiritual maturity. Life and learning are celebrated at Bethel.

CONTACT Mr. John C. Lassen, Director of Admissions, Bethel College, 3900 Bethel Drive, St. Paul, MN 55112, 612-638-6242 or toll-free 800-255-8706.

BIOLA UNIVERSITY

La Mirada, California

Total Enrollment: 2,600

UG Enrollment: 1,830 (59% W)

Application Deadline: 6/1

Tuition & Fees: $10,756

Room & Board: $4546

Entrance: moderately difficult

Denominational Affiliation: nondenominational

GENERAL INFORMATION Independent coed university. Founded 1908. Awards B, M, D. Primary accreditation: regional. Small-town setting, with easy access to Los Angeles; 100-acre campus. Total enrollment: 2,600. Faculty: 216 (132 full-time, 84 part-time); 55% of full-time faculty have terminal degrees; graduate assistants teach a few undergraduate courses. Library holdings: 207,983 bound volumes, 328,604 titles on microform, 1,174 periodical subscriptions, 7,500 records/tapes/CDs. Computer terminals/PCs available for student use: 60, located in computer center, dormitories, computer labs.

UNDERGRADUATE PROFILE Fall 1991: 1,830 undergraduates (639 freshmen); 7% part-time; 70% state residents; 10% transfers; 85% financial aid recipients; 59% women; 3% African Americans; 1% Native Americans; 5% Hispanics; 12% Asian Americans; 7% international students.

1991 FRESHMAN DATA 1,382 students applied for fall 1991 admission; 76% were accepted; 61% of those accepted enrolled.

ENROLLMENT PATTERNS 81% of fall 1990 freshmen returned for fall 1991 term. 77% of 1986 freshmen graduated within 5 years.

FRESHMAN ADMISSIONS Options: early entrance, deferred entrance. Required: high school transcript, 2 recommendations, interview, SAT or ACT, TOEFL (for foreign students). Recommended: 3 years of high school math and science, some high school foreign language. Test scores used for admission. Application deadline: 6/1. College's own assessment of entrance difficulty level: moderately difficult.

TRANSFER ADMISSIONS Required: high school transcript, 2 recommendations, interview, college transcript, minimum 2.0 grade point average. Recommended: 3 years of high school math and science, some high school foreign language, minimum 3.0 grade point average. Required for some: standardized test scores.

Application deadline: 6/1. College's own assessment of entrance difficulty level: moderately difficult.

EXPENSES (1992–93) Comprehensive fee of $15,302 includes full-time tuition ($10,756) and college room and board ($4546). Part-time tuition: $448 per unit.

FINANCIAL AID College-administered aid for all 1991–92 undergraduates: 488 need-based scholarships (average $2800); 1,049 non-need scholarships (average $2945); low-interest long-term loans from college funds (average $1660); from external sources (average $2906); SEOG; College Work-Study; 500 part-time jobs. Supporting data: FAF, state form required for some. Priority application deadline: 3/2.

CAMPUS LIFE Dress code; mandatory chapel; drama/theater group; student-run newspaper and radio station. Institution provides legal services, health clinic, personal/psychological counseling.

STUDY ABROAD SITES Germany, Israel, Costa Rica, England.

ATHLETICS Member NAIA. Intercollegiate sports: baseball M(s); basketball M(s), W(s); cross-country running M(s), W(s); soccer M, W; softball W; tennis M(s), W(s); track and field M(s), W(s); volleyball W(s). Intramural sports: badminton, basketball, cross-country running, football, racquetball, skiing (cross-country), skiing (downhill), soccer, softball, table tennis (Ping Pong), tennis, track and field, volleyball, water polo.

MAJORS Accounting; adult and continuing education; anthropology; art education; art/fine arts; art therapy; biblical studies; biochemistry; biology/biological sciences; broadcasting; business administration/commerce/management; business economics; business education; business machine technologies; chemistry; communication; computer information systems; computer programming; computer science; economics; education; elementary education; English; European studies; film studies; Greek; history; humanities; international studies; journalism; liberal arts/general studies; literature; marketing/retailing/merchandising; mathematics; (pre)medicine sequence; ministries; modern languages; music; music education; nursing; painting/drawing; pastoral studies; philosophy; physical education; physical sciences; physics; piano/organ; psychology; public relations; radio and television studies; religious education; religious studies; social science; sociology; Spanish; speech pathology and audiology; speech therapy; theater arts/drama; theology; voice. Most popular majors of class of 1991: business administration/commerce/management, communication, psychology.

SPECIAL NOTE FROM THE COLLEGE Biola University's suburban campus is just a short drive from the beach, the mountains, Disneyland, Hollywood, cultural events in Los Angeles, and many other Southern California attractions. Of the 84 members of the Christian College Coalition, which requires faculty members to be Christian, only 14 of them require that their students be Christian. Of those, Biola is 1 of 2 ranked by the Carnegie Commission as a Level II degree-granting institution, and it is the only one given *U.S. News & World Report*'s highest ranking, that of a National University. Selected to the John Templeton Foundation Honor Roll for Character Building Colleges for 1992, Biola offers a solid biblical foundation, with 30 required units of Bible. Students may choose from among 123 programs and enjoy close contact with a highly qualified and caring staff.

CONTACT Mr. Greg Vaughan, Director Enrollment Management, Biola University, 13800 Biola Avenue, La Mirada, CA 90639, 310-903-4752.

BLUFFTON COLLEGE

Bluffton, Ohio

Total Enrollment: 698 (all UG)

Women: 55%

Application Deadline: 8/15

Tuition & Fees: $8685

Room & Board: $3513

Entrance: moderately difficult

SAT ≥ 500: 26% V, 48% M

ACT ≥ 21: 65%

Denominational Affiliation: General Conference Mennonite Church

GENERAL INFORMATION Independent 4-year coed college. Founded 1899. Awards B. Primary accreditation: regional. Small-town setting, with easy access to Toledo; 65-acre campus. Total enrollment: 698. Faculty: 71 (46 full-time, 25 part-time); 63% of full-time faculty have terminal degrees; graduate assistants teach no undergraduate courses. Library holdings: 130,000 bound volumes, 50,000 titles on microform, 800 periodical subscriptions. Computer terminals/PCs available for student use: 39, distributed around campus.

UNDERGRADUATE PROFILE Fall 1991: 698 undergraduates (186 freshmen) from 14 states and territories and 18 foreign countries; 10% part-time; 88% state residents; 6% transfers; 95% financial aid recipients; 55% women; 2% African Americans; 0% Native Americans; 1% Hispanics; 1% Asian Americans; 5% international students; 1% of undergraduates 25 years of age or older.

1991 FRESHMAN DATA 562 students applied for fall 1991 admission; 80% were accepted; 42% of those accepted enrolled. 17% of freshmen were in top 10% of secondary school class, 52% were in top 25%, 82% were in top half.

ENROLLMENT PATTERNS 71% of fall 1990 freshmen returned for fall 1991 term. 46% of 1986 freshmen graduated within 5 years; 6% of students completing a bachelor's program went on for further study.

FRESHMAN ADMISSIONS Options: early entrance, deferred entrance. Required: high school transcript, 2 recommendations, SAT or ACT, TOEFL (for foreign students). Recommended: 3 years of high school math and science, 3 years of high school foreign language, interview. Test scores used for admission. Application deadline: 8/15. College's own assessment of entrance difficulty level: moderately difficult.

TRANSFER ADMISSIONS Required: high school transcript, 2 recommendations, college transcript, minimum 2.0 grade point average. Recommended: 3 years of high school math and science, some high school foreign language, interview. Required for some: standardized test scores. Application deadline: rolling. College's own assessment of entrance difficulty level: moderately difficult.

EXPENSES (1992–93) Comprehensive fee of $12,198 includes full-time tuition ($8685) and college room and board ($3513). College room only: $1422. Part-time tuition: $193 per quarter hour.

FINANCIAL AID College-administered aid for all 1991–92 undergraduates: need-based scholarships; non-need scholarships; low-interest long-term loans from external sources (average $1000); SEOG; College Work-Study; part-time jobs. Supporting data: FAF required; IRS required for some; FFS, AFSA/SAR acceptable. Priority application deadline: 6/1.

CAMPUS LIFE/STUDENT SERVICES Drama/theater group; student-run newspaper. Institution provides health clinic, personal/psychological counseling.

STUDY ABROAD SITES Commonwealth of Independent States (USSR), Mexico, Poland, Central America.

ATHLETICS Member NCAA. Intercollegiate sports: baseball M; basketball M, W; cross-country M, W; football M; golf M; soccer M, W; softball W; tennis M, W; track and field M, W; volleyball W. Intramural sports: badminton, basketball, bowling, football, golf, racquetball, soccer, table tennis (Ping Pong), tennis, volleyball, weight lifting.

MAJORS Accounting; art education; art/fine arts; biology/biological sciences; business administration/commerce/management; business education; chemistry; child care/child and family studies; communication; computer science; criminal justice; dietetics; early childhood education; economics; education; elementary education; English; fashion merchandising; health education; history; home economics; home economics education; humanities; (pre)law sequence; liberal arts/general studies; mathematics; (pre)medicine sequence; ministries; music; music education; nutrition; peace studies; philosophy; physical education; physical fitness/human movement; physics; political science/government; psychology; recreation and leisure services; religious studies; secondary education; social science; social work; sociology; Spanish; special education; speech/rhetoric/public address/debate; sports management; textiles and clothing; wellness. Most popular majors of class of 1991: business administration/commerce/management, education, recreation and leisure services.

SPECIAL NOTE FROM THE COLLEGE Unique to Bluffton College is a seriously Mennonite peace church orientation with genuine openness to students of all racial, ethnic, and denominational backgrounds, including approximately 40 international students. Within this widely diverse and deeply caring Christian community, faculty, staff, and students seek to apply the insights of both the academic disciplines and the Bible to the problems of offender ministries, racial discrimination, oppression and poverty, and violence and war. Academic integrity, broad social concern, a caring community, spiritual nurturing, and a beautiful natural environment are all distinguishing characteristics of Bluffton.

CONTACT Mr. Michael Hieronimus, Director of Admissions, Bluffton College, 280 West College Avenue, Bluffton, OH 45817-1196, 419-358-3257 or toll-free 800-488-3257.

CALIFORNIA BAPTIST COLLEGE

Riverside, California

Total Enrollment: 750

UG Enrollment: 705 (52% W)

Application Deadline: rolling

Tuition & Fees: $6742

Room & Board: $3704

Entrance: minimally difficult

Denominational Affiliation: Southern Baptist

GENERAL INFORMATION Independent comprehensive coed institution. Founded 1950. Awards B, M. Primary accreditation: regional. Suburban setting, with easy access to Los Angeles; 75-acre campus. Total enrollment: 750. Faculty: 82 (44 full-time, 38 part-time); 70% of full-time faculty have terminal degrees; graduate assistants teach no undergraduate courses. Library holdings: 70,000 bound volumes, 8,200 titles on microform, 400 periodical subscriptions, 2,500 records/tapes/CDs. Computer terminals/PCs available for student use: 60, located in computer center, library, business administration department.

UNDERGRADUATE PROFILE Fall 1991: 705 undergraduates (150 freshmen) from 30 states and territories and 21 foreign countries; 16% part-time; 69% state residents; 38% transfers; 88% financial aid recipients; 52% women; 7% African Americans; 1% Native Americans; 5% Hispanics; 2% Asian Americans; 7% international students.

1991 FRESHMAN DATA 463 students applied for fall 1991 admission; 78% were accepted; 42% of those accepted enrolled. 37% of freshmen were in top 25% of secondary school class, 72% were in top half.

FRESHMAN ADMISSIONS Options: deferred entrance. Required: high school transcript, 2 recommendations, SAT or ACT, TOEFL (for foreign students). Recommended: 3 years of high school math and science, some high school foreign language, Achievement Tests, English Composition Test. Test scores used for admission and counseling/placement. Application deadline: rolling. College's own assessment of entrance difficulty level: minimally difficult.

TRANSFER ADMISSIONS Required: 2 recommendations, college transcript, minimum 2.0 grade point average. Required for some: standardized test scores, high school transcript. Application deadline: rolling.

EXPENSES (1992–93) Comprehensive fee of $10,446 includes full-time tuition ($6370), mandatory fees ($372), and college room and board ($3704). Part-time tuition ranges from $245 to $3027.

FINANCIAL AID College-administered aid for all 1991–92 undergraduates: 540 need-based scholarships; 300 non-need scholarships (average $2405); low-interest long-term loans from external sources (average $2625); SEOG; College Work-Study; 76 part-time jobs. Supporting data: FAF, IRS, institutional form, AFSA/SAR required; state form required for some. Priority application deadline: 4/15.

CAMPUS LIFE/STUDENT SERVICES Mandatory chapel; drama/theater group; student-run newspaper. Institution provides health clinic, personal/psychological counseling.

STUDY ABROAD SITE China.

ATHLETICS Member NAIA. Intercollegiate sports: baseball M(s); basketball M(s), W(s); soccer M(s); softball W(s); tennis M(s), W(s); volleyball W(s). Intramural sports: baseball, basketball, football, golf, softball, volleyball.

MAJORS Art/fine arts; behavioral sciences; biology/biological sciences; business administration/commerce/management; communication; education; elementary education; English; history; liberal arts/general studies; music; physical education; physical sciences; political science/government; psychology; public administration; recreation and leisure services; religious studies; secondary education; social science; sociology; Spanish; theater arts/drama. Most popular majors of class of 1991: business administration/commerce/management, psychology, education.

SPECIAL NOTE FROM THE COLLEGE California Baptist College is located in southern California's Inland Empire, which is one of the most rapidly growing areas in the nation. Cal Baptist emphasizes a life of assisting others, whether in a service-oriented career such as counseling and teaching or in business, which is based on biblical principles. The College is diverse in its ethnicity, denominational affiliation, and the age of its student body, providing students with a global outlook in all areas of campus life. Cal Baptist, with offerings of 17 undergraduate majors and a master's degree in marriage, family, and child counseling, provides students with a diverse and challenging academic program and the opportunity for active participation in experiential learning and development. At California Baptist College, knowledge is enhanced through personal experience.

CONTACT Mr. Kent Dacus, Director of Admissions, California Baptist College, 8432 Magnolia Avenue, Riverside, CA 92504, 714-689-5771 or toll-free 800-782-3382.

CALVIN COLLEGE

Grand Rapids, Michigan

Total Enrollment: 4,025

UG Enrollment: 3,841 (55% W)

Application Deadline: rolling

Tuition & Fees: $8630

Room & Board: $3520

Entrance: moderately difficult

SAT ≥ 500: 53% V, 73% M

ACT ≥ 21: 83%

Denominational Affiliation: Christian Reformed Church

GENERAL INFORMATION Independent comprehensive coed institution. Founded 1876. Awards B, M. Primary accreditation: regional. Suburban setting; 370-acre campus. Total enrollment: 4,025. Faculty: 281 (242 full-time, 39 part-time); 83% of full-time faculty have terminal degrees; graduate assistants teach no undergraduate courses. Library holdings: 550,798 bound volumes, 476,090 titles on microform, 2,830 periodical subscriptions, 16,840 records/tapes/CDs. Computer terminals/PCs available for student use: 220, located in computer center, student center, library, dormitories.

UNDERGRADUATE PROFILE Fall 1991: 3,841 undergraduates (862 freshmen) from 47 states and territories and 36 foreign countries; 5% part-time; 55% state residents; 4% transfers; 88% financial aid recipients; 55% women; 1% African Americans; 1% Native Americans; 1% Hispanics; 2% Asian Americans; 8% international students; 5% of undergraduates 25 years of age or older.

1991 FRESHMAN DATA 1,440 students applied for fall 1991 admission; 95% were accepted; 63% of those accepted enrolled. 17 freshmen were National Merit Scholarship Finalists; 14 received a National Merit Scholarship. 31% of freshmen were in top 10% of secondary school class, 56% were in top 25%, 85% were in top half.

ENROLLMENT PATTERNS 81% of fall 1990 freshmen returned for fall 1991 term. 60% of 1986 freshmen graduated within 5 years; 22% of students completing a degree program went on for further study.

FRESHMAN ADMISSIONS Options: early entrance, deferred entrance. Required: high school transcript, 1 recommendation, ACT, TOEFL (for foreign students). Recommended: 3 years of high school math and science, 2 years of high school foreign language. Test scores used for admission and counseling/placement. Application deadline: rolling. College's own assessment of entrance difficulty level: moderately difficult.

TRANSFER ADMISSIONS Required: standardized test scores, high school transcript, 1 recommendation, college transcript, minimum 2.0 grade point average. Recommended: 3 years of high school math and science. Application deadline: rolling. College's own assessment of entrance difficulty level: moderately difficult.

EXPENSES (1992–93) Comprehensive fee of $12,150 includes full-time tuition ($8630) and college room and board ($3520). Part-time tuition: $1120 per course. Tuition prepayment plan available.

FINANCIAL AID College-administered aid for all 1991–92 undergraduates: 2,600 need-based scholarships (average $1730); 3,900 non-need scholarships (average $660); short-term loans (average $100); low-interest long-term loans from college funds (average $2220), from external sources (average $2580); SEOG; College Work-Study; 700 part-time jobs. Supporting data: FAF required; IRS required for some; FFS acceptable. Priority application deadline: 2/15.

CAMPUS LIFE/STUDENT SERVICES Drama/theater group; student-run newspaper and radio station. Institution provides health clinic, personal/psychological counseling.

STUDY ABROAD SITES Spain, England, Wales, Germany, the Netherlands, China, Mexico, Costa Rica, France, Austria.

ATHLETICS Member NCAA (Division III). Intercollegiate sports: baseball M; basketball M, W; cross-country running M, W; golf M, W; ice hockey M; soccer M, W; softball W; swimming and diving M, W; tennis M, W; track and field M, W; volleyball W. Intramural sports: badminton, basketball, football, golf, ice hockey, racquetball, soccer, softball, table tennis, tennis, volleyball, waterpolo, weight lifting.

MAJORS Accounting; art education; art/fine arts; art history; biblical studies; biochemistry; biology/biological sciences; business administration/commerce/management; business economics; chemistry; civil engineering; classics; communication; computer science; criminal justice; (pre)dentistry sequence; economics; education; electrical engineering; elementary education; engineering (general); English; European studies; French; geography; geology; German; Germanic languages and literature; Greek; history; humanities; interdisciplinary studies; Latin; (pre)law sequence; liberal arts/general studies; literature; mathematics; mechanical engineering; medical technology; (pre)medicine sequence; music; music education; nursing; philosophy; physical education; physical sciences; physics; political science/government; psychology; recreation and leisure services; religious education; religious studies; sacred music; science; science education; secondary education; social science; social work; sociology; Spanish; special education; speech/rhetoric/public address/debate; telecommunications; theology; voice. Most popular majors of class of 1991: education, business administration/commerce/management, engineering (general).

SPECIAL NOTE FROM THE COLLEGE Calvin College is one of the largest, oldest, and most respected of the Coalition schools. Calvin's modern 370-acre campus provides the setting for over 4,000 students and 250 faculty members to explore a broad range of majors and programs. While awarding over half of its degrees in accredited professional programs such as education, engineering, nursing, and business, Calvin remains committed to a liberal arts approach to learning. Eager to become a partner with students in their Christian maturation, the College encourages students to make faithful and responsible decisions about how they will use their time and talents—without imposing an excessive list of rules and regulations.

CONTACT Mr. Thomas E. McWhertor, Director of Admissions, Calvin College, 3201 Burton Street, SE, Grand Rapids, MI 49546, 616-957-6106 or toll-free 800-748-0122.

CAMPBELLSVILLE COLLEGE

Campbellsville, Kentucky

Total Enrollment: 1,010

Women: 51%

Application Deadline: rolling

Tuition & Fees: $5400

Room & Board: $2890

Entrance: moderately difficult

SAT ≥ 500: 40% V, 20% M

ACT ≥ 21: 39%

Denominational Affiliation: Baptist

GENERAL INFORMATION Independent 4-year coed college. Founded 1906. Awards A (college transfer and terminal), B. Primary accreditation: regional. Small-town setting; 35-acre campus. Total enrollment: 1,010. Faculty: 60 (47 full-time, 13 part-time); 51% of full-time faculty have terminal degrees; graduate assistants teach no undergraduate courses. Library holdings: 105,000 bound volumes, 500 titles on microform, 465 periodical subscriptions, 4,000 records/tapes/CDs. Computer terminals/PCs available for student use: 30, located in computer center, library, classrooms.

UNDERGRADUATE PROFILE Fall 1991: 1,010 undergraduates (297 freshmen) from 17 states and territories and 8 foreign countries; 18% part-time; 91% state residents; 8% transfers; 89% financial aid recipients; 51% women; 8% African Americans; 1% Native Americans; 1% Hispanics; 1% Asian Americans; 1% international students; 27% of undergraduates 25 years of age or older.

1991 FRESHMAN DATA 452 students applied for fall 1991 admission; 76% were accepted; 87% of those accepted enrolled. 22% of freshmen were in top 10% of secondary school class, 49% were in top 25%, 74% were in top half.

FRESHMAN ADMISSIONS Options: early entrance, deferred entrance. Required: high school transcript, SAT or ACT, TOEFL (for foreign students). Recommended: essay, 3 years of high school math and science, recommendations, interview. Test scores used for admission. Application deadline: rolling. Notification date: continuous. College's own assessment of entrance difficulty level: moderately difficult.

TRANSFER ADMISSIONS Required: college transcript, minimum 2.0 grade point average. Recommended: essay, 3 years of high school math and science, recommendations, interview. Required for some: standardized test scores, high school transcript. Application deadline: rolling. Notification date: continuous. College's own assessment of entrance difficulty level: moderately difficult.

EXPENSES (1992–93) Comprehensive fee of $8290 includes full-time tuition ($5400) and college room and board ($2890). Part-time tuition: $225 per credit.

FINANCIAL AID College-administered aid for all 1991–92 undergraduates: 40 need-based scholarships (average $500); 300 non-need scholarships (average $1300); short-term loans (average $800); low-interest long-term loans from college funds (average $1000), from external sources (average $2500); SEOG; College Work-Study; 20 part-time jobs. Supporting data: FAF, institutional form required; IRS required for some; AFSA/SAR acceptable. Priority application deadline: 4/15.

CAMPUS LIFE/STUDENT SERVICES Dress code; mandatory chapel; drama/theater group; student-run newspaper and television station; marching band.

STUDY ABROAD SITES England, France, Israel.

ATHLETICS Member NAIA. Intercollegiate sports: baseball M(s); basketball M(s), W(s); cross-country running M(s), W(s); football M; golf M(s); soccer M(s); swimming and diving M(s), W(s); tennis M(s), W(s). Intramural sports: basketball, football, soccer, table tennis (Ping Pong), tennis, volleyball, weight lifting.

MAJORS Accounting; art education; biology/biological sciences; business administration/commerce/management; chemistry; Christian studies; church music; communications; computer information systems; (pre)dentistry sequence; elementary education; economics; English; health education; history; (pre)law sequence; mathematics; medical technology; (pre)medicine sequence; music; music education; organizational administration; physical education; piano/organ; political science/government; psychology; recreation and leisure services; religious education; sacred music; science education; secondary education; office management; sociology; (pre)veterinary medicine sequence; voice. Most popular majors of class of 1991: elementary education, business administration, music, religious education.

SPECIAL NOTE FROM THE COLLEGE Campbellsville College is a 4-year liberal arts, science, and business institution that is affiliated with the Kentucky Baptist Convention. Campbellsville is situated in central Kentucky, minutes from the beautiful Green River Reservoir and Lake. Students benefit from individual attention from the 125 caring, dedicated faculty and staff members. Academic work at Campbellsville is not confined only to the classroom. This past year, study groups traveled to Europe, New York, and the western states. Students are active in many phases of mission work. As Dr. Kenneth W. Winters, president of Campbellsville College, has said, "Campbellsville College is a place where significant areas of life are being explored. For whatever you want to be, Campbellsville College is the place to start."

CONTACT Mr. R. Trent Argo, Director of Admissions, Campbellsville College, 200 West College Street, Campbellsville, KY 42718-2799, 502-789-5220 or toll-free 800-264-6014.

CAMPBELL UNIVERSITY

Buies Creek, North Carolina

Total Enrollment: 5,777

UG Enrollment: 4,777 (53% W)

Application Deadline: rolling

Tuition & Fees: $7150

Room & Board: $2590

Entrance: moderately difficult

SAT ≥ 500: 22% V, 42% M

ACT ≥ 21: 26%

Denominational Affiliation: Baptist

GENERAL INFORMATION Independent coed university. Founded 1887. Awards A (college transfer), B, M, D. Primary accreditation: regional. Rural setting, with easy access to Raleigh; 850-acre campus. Total enrollment: 5,777. Faculty: 261 (139 full-time, 122 part-time); 76% of full-time faculty have terminal degrees; graduate assistants teach no undergraduate courses. Library holdings: 256,000 bound volumes, 300,000 titles on microform, 1,006 periodical subscriptions, 4,200 records/tapes/CDs. Computer terminals/PCs available for student use: 36, located in computer center.

UNDERGRADUATE PROFILE Fall 1991: 4,777 undergraduates (731 freshmen) from 50 states and territories and 41 foreign countries; 13% part-time; 55% state residents; 12% transfers; 88% financial aid recipients; 53% women; 8% African Americans; 1% Native Americans; 3% Hispanics; 9% Asian Americans; 8% international students; 17% of undergraduates 25 years of age or older.

1991 FRESHMAN DATA 1,319 students applied for fall 1991 admission; 70% were accepted; 79% of those accepted enrolled. 14% of freshmen were in top 10% of secondary school class, 27% were in top 25%, 64% were in top half.

ENROLLMENT PATTERNS 85% of fall 1990 freshmen returned for fall 1991 term.

FRESHMAN ADMISSIONS Options: early entrance, deferred entrance. Required: high school transcript, 3 years of high school math and science, SAT or ACT, TOEFL (for foreign students). Recommended: some high school foreign language, recommendations, interview. Test scores used for admission and counseling/placement. Application deadline: rolling. Notification date: continuous. College's own assessment of entrance difficulty level: moderately difficult.

TRANSFER ADMISSIONS Required: high school transcript, college transcript, minimum 2.0 grade point average, good standing at previous institution. Recommended: standardized test scores, 3 years of high school math, recommendations, interview. Required for some: minimum 2.0 grade point average. Application deadline: rolling. Notification date: continuous.

EXPENSES (1991–92) Comprehensive fee of $9740 includes full-time tuition ($7150) and college room and board ($2590). College room only: $1120. Part-time tuition: $110 per semester hour.

FINANCIAL AID College-administered aid for all 1991–92 undergraduates: 3,134 need-based scholarships (average $4946); 240 non-need scholarships (average $2300); low-interest long-term loans from external sources (average $3000); SEOG; College Work-Study; 324 part-time jobs. Supporting data: FFS, institutional form, AFSA/SAR required; IRS, state form required for some; FAF acceptable. Priority application deadline: 3/15.

CAMPUS LIFE/STUDENT SERVICES Mandatory assembly; drama/theater group; student-run newspaper and radio station. Institution provides health clinic, personal/psychological counseling.

STUDY ABROAD SITES Wales, Mexico, France.

ATHLETICS Member NCAA (Division I). Intercollegiate sports: baseball M(s); basketball M(s), W(s); cross-country running M(s), W(s); golf M(s), W(s); soccer M(s), W(s); softball W(s); tennis M(s), W(s); track and field M(s), W(s); volleyball W(s); wrestling M(s). Intramural sports: basketball, football, golf, soccer, softball, swimming and diving, table tennis, tennis, track and field, volleyball, wrestling.

MAJORS Accounting; advertising; applied mathematics; art/fine arts; biblical studies; biology/biological sciences; biomedical technologies; broadcasting; business administration/commerce/management; business economics; chemistry; child care/child and family studies; commercial art; communication; computer information systems; computer science; data processing; (pre)dentistry sequence; early childhood education; earth science; economics; education; educational administration; elementary education; (pre)engineering sequence; English; fashion design and technology; fashion merchandising; finance/banking; food services management; French; health education; health science; history; home economics; home economics education; interior design; international business; journalism; (pre)law sequence; liberal arts/general studies; mathematics; medical technology; (pre)medicine sequence; military science; music; music education; natural sciences; pastoral studies; physical education; physical fitness/human movement; physical therapy; physician's assistant studies; piano/organ; political science/government; psychology; public administration; public relations; radio and television studies; religious education; sacred music; science education; secondary education; social science; social work; Spanish; sports administration; studio art; theater arts/drama; theology; (pre)veterinary medicine sequence; voice.

SPECIAL NOTE FROM THE COLLEGE Campbell University is a private liberal arts institution in southeastern North Carolina, born of a vision 100 years ago—a vision that lives on today. Campbell's curriculum meets individual needs and interests and offers the range of majors that today's students expect from a high-quality institution, including preprofessional and professional studies. A comprehensive financial aid program helps families meet educational costs. The University has adapted to changing times and needs without losing sight of its heritage and mission to provide educational opportunities in a Christian environment.

CONTACT Mr. Herbert Kerner, Dean of Admissions, Campbell University, Box 546, Buies Creek, NC 27506, 919-893-4111 Ext. 2275 or toll-free 800-334-4111 (out-of-state).

CEDARVILLE COLLEGE

Cedarville, Ohio

Total Enrollment: 2,046 (all UG)

Women: 57%

Application Deadline: rolling

Tuition & Fees: $6402

Room & Board: $3579

Entrance: moderately difficult

SAT ≥ 500: 45% V, 59% M

ACT ≥ 21: 72%

Denominational Affiliation: Baptist

GENERAL INFORMATION Independent 4-year coed college. Founded 1887. Awards A (terminal), B. Primary accreditation: regional. Rural setting, with easy access to Columbus and Dayton; 105-acre campus. Total enrollment: 2,046. Faculty: 126 (91 full-time, 35 part-time); 58% of full-time faculty have terminal degrees; graduate assistants teach no undergraduate courses. Library holdings: 114,795 bound volumes, 1,898 titles on microform, 971 periodical subscriptions, 15,737 records/tapes/CDs. Computer terminals/PCs available for student use: 100, located in computer center, library, dormitories, business administration building, science center.

UNDERGRADUATE PROFILE Fall 1991: 2,046 undergraduates (605 freshmen) from 45 states and territories and 14 foreign countries; 3% part-time; 38% state residents; 7% transfers; 84% financial aid recipients; 57% women; 1% African Americans; 1% Native Americans; 1% Hispanics; 1% Asian Americans; 1% international students; 4% of undergraduates 25 years of age or older.

1991 FRESHMAN DATA 950 students applied for fall 1991 admission; 91% were accepted; 70% of those accepted enrolled. 5 freshmen were National Merit Scholarship Finalists. 24% of freshmen were in top 10% of secondary school class, 52% were in top 25%, 77% were in top half.

ENROLLMENT PATTERNS 75% of fall 1990 freshmen returned for fall 1991 term. 54% of 1986 freshmen graduated within 5 years.

FRESHMAN ADMISSIONS Options: early entrance, deferred entrance. Required: essay, high school transcript, SAT or ACT, TOEFL (for foreign students), 2 recommendations. Recommended: 3 years of high school math and science, 2 years of high school foreign language. Required for some: interview. Test scores used for counseling/placement. Application deadline: rolling. College's own assessment of entrance difficulty level: moderately difficult.

TRANSFER ADMISSIONS Required: essay, high school transcript, 2 recommendations, college transcript, minimum 2.0 grade point average. Recommended: 2 years of high school foreign language. Required for some: standardized test scores, interview. Application deadline: rolling. College's own assessment of entrance difficulty level: moderately difficult.

EXPENSES (1992–93) Comprehensive fee of $9981 includes full-time tuition ($5712), mandatory fees ($690), and college room and board ($3579). College room only: $1704. Part-time tuition: $119 per quarter hour.

FINANCIAL AID College-administered aid for all 1991–92 undergraduates: need-based scholarships; non-need scholarships; short-term loans (average $1000); low-interest long-term loans from college funds (average $1200), from external sources (average $2000); SEOG; College Work-Study; 214 part-time jobs. Supporting data: FAF, institutional form, AFSA/SAR required; IRS, state form required for some; FFS acceptable. Priority application deadline: 3/1.

CAMPUS LIFE/STUDENT SERVICES Dress code; mandatory chapel; drama/theater group; student-run newspaper and radio station. Institution provides health clinic, personal/psychological counseling.

STUDY ABROAD SITE Spain.

ATHLETICS Member NAIA. Intercollegiate sports: baseball M(s); basketball M(s), W(s); cross-country running M(s), W(s); golf M(s); soccer M(s); softball W(s); tennis M(s), W(s); track and field M(s), W(s); volleyball W(s). Intramural sports: basketball, bowling, football, golf, racquetball, skiing (downhill), soccer, table tennis (Ping Pong), tennis, volleyball.

MAJORS Accounting; American studies; behavioral sciences; biblical studies; biology/biological sciences; broadcasting; business administration/commerce/management; business economics; business education; chemistry; communication; computer information systems; criminal justice; (pre)dentistry sequence; early childhood education; economics; education; electrical engineering; elementary education; (pre)engineering sequence; English; environmental biology; finance/banking; health education; history; international business; international economics; international studies; (pre)law sequence; marketing/retailing/merchandising; mathematics; mechanical engineering; medical technology; (pre)medicine sequence; music; music education; music history; nursing; pastoral studies; physical education; physical fitness/human movement; political science/government; psychology; public administration; radio and television studies; religious education; sacred music; science; science education; secondary education; secretarial studies/office management; social science; social work; sociology; Spanish; special education; speech/rhetoric/public address/debate; sports administration; technical writing; theater arts/drama; theology; (pre)veterinary medicine sequence; voice.

SPECIAL NOTE FROM THE COLLEGE Cedarville College's mission is "to offer an education consistent with biblical truth." Commitment and achievement characterize this education. All students and faculty members can testify to personal faith in Christ. A Bible minor complements every major. Relevant daily chapels encourage spiritual growth. Over 100 local and worldwide ministries provide avenues for outreach. Cedarville teams consistently finish among top universities in national academic competitions. National, regional, and local employers and graduate schools recruit students who pursue any of 75 academic programs. IBM supports the College's new campuswide computer network as a national showcase account. Reasonable costs and financial aid make Cedarville affordable.

CONTACT Mr. Roscoe F. Smith, Associate Director of Admissions, Cedarville College, P.O. Box 601, Cedarville, OH 45314, 513-766-7700 or toll-free 800-777-2211.

CENTRAL WESLEYAN COLLEGE

Central, South Carolina

Total Enrollment: 1,091

UG Enrollment: 1,004

Women: 53%

Application Deadline: 8/10

Tuition & Fees: $7500

Room & Board: $3080

Entrance: minimally difficult

SAT ≥ 500: 14% V, 24% M

ACT ≥ 21: 0%

Denominational Affiliation: Wesleyan Church

GENERAL INFORMATION Independent 4-year coed college. Founded in 1906. Two programs: traditional day format on main campus (traditional age students) and Leadership Education for Adult Professionals (LEAP) format in several locations throughout South Carolina (restricted to working adults at least 23 years old). Traditional program awards B. LEAP program awards A, B, M. Primary accreditation: regional. Small-town setting; 140-acre campus. Total enrollment: 1,091. Faculty: 132 (37 full-time, 95 part-time); 61% of full-time faculty have terminal degrees. Library holdings: 72,453 bound volumes, 345 titles on microform, 389 periodical subscriptions, 2,537 records/tapes/CDs. Computer terminals/PCs available for student use: 40, located in computer center, library.

UNDERGRADUATE PROFILE Fall 1991 total enrollment for traditional and LEAP programs: 1,004 undergraduates (76 freshmen) from 17 states and territories and 5 foreign countries; 3% part-time; 80% state residents; 50% transfers; 90% financial aid recipients; 53% women; 12% African Americans; 0% Native Americans; 0% Hispanics; 1% Asian Americans; 1% international students; 75% of undergraduates 25 years of age or older.

1991 FRESHMAN DATA Traditional program: 134 students applied for fall 1991 admission; 88% were accepted; 64% of those accepted enrolled. 7% of freshmen were in top 10% of secondary school class, 28% were in top 25%, 58% were in top half.

ENROLLMENT PATTERNS Traditional program: 70% of fall 1990 freshmen returned for fall 1991 term. 37% of 1986 freshmen graduated within 5 years.

FRESHMAN ADMISSIONS (For traditional program) Options: early entrance, deferred entrance. Required: high school transcript, recommendations, SAT or ACT, TOEFL (for foreign students). Required for some: interview. Test scores used for admission. Application deadline: 8/10. Notification date: continuous. College's own assessment of entrance difficulty level: minimally difficult.

TRANSFER ADMISSIONS (For traditional program) Required: college transcript, recommendations. Recommended: minimum 2.0 grade point average. Required for some: standardized test scores, high school transcript, interview. Application deadline: 8/10. College's own assessment of entrance difficulty level: minimally difficult.

EXPENSES Traditional program: (1992–93) comprehensive fee of $10,580 includes full-time tuition ($7300), mandatory fees ($200), and college room and board ($3080). College room only: $1000. Part-time tuition: $250 per hour. Tuition prepayment plan available.

FINANCIAL AID (For traditional program) College-administered aid for all 1991–92 undergraduates: need-based scholarships; 345 non-need scholarships (average $2400); low-interest long-term loans from external sources (average $2482); SEOG; College Work-Study; 25 part-time jobs. Supporting data: institutional form required; IRS, state form, AFSA/SAR required for some; FFS, FAF acceptable. Priority application deadline: 4/15.

CAMPUS LIFE/STUDENT SERVICES Traditional program: dress code; mandatory chapel; curfew; drama/theater productions; Fellowship of Christian Athletes (FCA); Baptist Student Union (BSU). Institution provides health clinic, personal/psychological counseling.

STUDY ABROAD SITE England.

ATHLETICS Member NAIA. Intercollegiate sports: baseball M; basketball M(s), W(s); golf M(s); soccer M(s); volleyball W(s). Intramural sports: basketball, soccer, table tennis (Ping Pong), tennis, volleyball.

MAJORS Traditional program: accounting; biology; business administration; chemistry; elementary education; English; history; mathematics; medical technology; music; nursing; physical education; psychology; recreation; religion; social studies; special education. LEAP program: general business; business administration; management of human resources; elementary/early childhood education; special education; management of organizations; Christian ministries. Most popular majors of class of 1991: business administration/commerce/management, education, psychology.

SPECIAL NOTE FROM THE COLLEGE Central Wesleyan College is committed to providing a high-quality education from a very Christian perspective. The issues of faith are explored in each course of study and practiced in daily life. The faculty's personal dedication and skills enable it to serve students from a wide variety of backgrounds—ranging from those who might be underprepared to National Merit Finalists—by providing the right amount of support and the right amount of challenge. A cooperative program with nearby Clemson University allows Central Wesleyan's students to experience the atmosphere and fellowship of a Christian campus and the academic diversity of a large university. Graduates have distinguished themselves in their careers while maintaining active involvement in service to their communities and churches. An education at Central Wesleyan provides what's needed for a career and for a satisfying and balanced life.

CONTACT Mr. Tim Wilkerson, Dean of Enrollment Management, Central Wesleyan College, 1 Wesleyan Drive, Central, SC 29630-1020, 803-639-2453 Ext. 327.

COLORADO CHRISTIAN UNIVERSITY

Lakewood, Colorado

Total Enrollment: 1,000

UG Enrollment: 670 (52% W)

Application Deadline: rolling

Tuition & Fees: $5785

Room & Board: $3040

Entrance: moderately difficult

Denominational Affiliation: interdenominational

GENERAL INFORMATION Independent comprehensive coed institution. Founded 1914. Awards A (college transfer), B, M. Primary accreditation: regional and AABC. Urban setting, with easy access to Denver; 25-acre campus. Total enrollment: 1,000. Faculty: 81 (41 full-time, 40 part-time); graduate assistants teach no undergraduate courses. Library holdings: 40,000 bound volumes, 25 titles on microform, 300 periodical subscriptions, 1,530 records/tapes/CDs. Computer terminals/PCs available for student use: 32, located in computer center.

UNDERGRADUATE PROFILE Fall 1991: 670 undergraduates (305 freshmen) from 38 states and territories and 10 foreign countries; 10% part-time; 68% state residents; 42% transfers; 85% financial aid recipients; 52% women; 4% African Americans; 3% Hispanics; 1% Asian Americans; 1% international students; 35% of undergraduates 25 years of age or older.

1991 FRESHMAN DATA 745 students applied for fall 1991 admission; 80% were accepted; 51% of those accepted enrolled.

FRESHMAN ADMISSIONS Options: early entrance, deferred entrance. Required: essay, high school transcript, SAT or ACT, TOEFL (for foreign students). Recommended: 3 years of high school math and science, some high school foreign language, 2 recommendations, all interview. Some test scores used for admission. Application deadline: rolling. College's own assessment of entrance difficulty level: moderately difficult.

TRANSFER ADMISSIONS Required: college transcript, minimum 2.0 grade point average. Required for some: high school transcript, 2 recommendations, some. Application deadline: rolling. College's own assessment of entrance difficulty level: moderately difficult.

EXPENSES (1992–93) Comprehensive fee of $8825 includes full-time tuition ($5280), mandatory fees ($505), and college room and board ($3040).Part-time tuition: $220 per semester hour.

FINANCIAL AID College-administered aid for all 1991–92 undergraduates: need-based scholarships; non-need scholarships; short-term loans; low-interest long-term loans from external sources (average $2000); SEOG; College Work-Study. Supporting data: FFS, IRS, institutional form, AFSA/SAR required; state form required for some; FAF acceptable. Priority application deadline: 4/1.

CAMPUS LIFE/STUDENT SERVICES Mandatory chapel; drama/theater group; student-run newspaper. Institution provides personal/psychological counseling.

ATHLETICS Member NCAA (Division II). Intercollegiate sports: basketball M(s), W(s); golf M; soccer M(s), W(s); tennis M(s), W(s); volleyball W(s).

MAJORS Accounting; adult and continuing education; biblical studies; biology/biological sciences; business administration/commerce/management; communication; computer information systems; elementary education; English; history; humanities; liberal arts/general studies; mathematics; ministries; music; music education; pastoral studies; psychology; sacred music; secondary education; theater arts/drama; theology; voice. Most popular majors of class of 1991: ministries, psychology, business administration/commerce/management.

SPECIAL NOTE FROM THE COLLEGE Colorado Christian University emphasizes the integration of biblical principles into every aspect of the student's life. Educating the whole person is the focus; preparing each student for a successful life of leadership and service is the goal. In an ideal setting of dynamic urban Denver, the Colorado Christian student benefits from various internship opportunities as well as cultural stimulation to help prepare for the realities of the everyday world. The campus offers natural open space and a caring community to encourage creative educational growth. The University's location in Colorado allows every student a wealth of recreational opportunities, including skiing, hiking, camping, and biking. Students are invited to come and experience an education at Colorado Christian University—an education designed for life.

CONTACT Ms. Carrie Mowery, Admissions Office Manager, Colorado Christian University, 180 South Garrison Street, Lakewood, CO 80226, 303-238-5386 Ext. 125.

COVENANT COLLEGE

Lookout Mountain, Georgia

Total Enrollment: 727

UG Enrollment: 707 (52% W)

Application Deadline: rolling

Tuition & Fees: $8400

Room & Board: $3480

Entrance: moderately difficult

ACT ≥ 21: 82%

Denominational Affiliation: Presbyterian Church in America

GENERAL INFORMATION Independent comprehensive coed institution. Founded 1955. Awards A (college transfer and terminal), B, M. Primary accreditation: regional. Small-town setting, with easy access to Atlanta and Nashville; 300-acre campus. Total enrollment: 727. Faculty: 63 (37 full-time, 26 part-time); 76% of full-time faculty have terminal degrees; graduate assistants teach no undergraduate courses. Library holdings: 69,000 bound volumes, 22,500 titles on microform, 480 periodical subscriptions, 7,500 records/tapes/CDs. Computer terminals/PCs available for student use: 54, located in computer center, library.

UNDERGRADUATE PROFILE Fall 1991: 707 undergraduates (149 freshmen) from 39 states and territories and 17 foreign countries; 5% part-time; 21% state residents; 5% transfers; 86% financial aid recipients; 52% women; 3% African Americans; 1% Native Americans; 1% Hispanics; 1% Asian Americans; 5% international students; 25% of undergraduates 25 years of age or older.

1991 FRESHMAN DATA 366 students applied for fall 1991 admission; 77% were accepted; 53% of those accepted enrolled. 27% of freshmen were in top 10% of secondary school class, 51% were in top 25%, 81% were in top half.

ENROLLMENT PATTERNS 79% of fall 1990 freshmen returned for fall 1991 term. 45% of 1986 freshmen graduated within 5 years.

FRESHMAN ADMISSIONS Options: early entrance, deferred entrance. Required: essay, high school transcript, 3 years of high school math, interview, 2 recommendations, SAT or ACT, TOEFL (for foreign students). Recommended: 2 years of high school foreign language, English Composition Test. Test scores used for admission. Application deadline: rolling. College's own assessment of entrance difficulty level: moderately difficult.

TRANSFER ADMISSIONS Required: essay, high school transcript, 3 years of high school math, interview, 2 recommendations, college transcript, minimum 2.0 grade point average. Recommended: standardized test scores, 2 years of high school foreign language. Application deadline: rolling. College's own assessment of entrance difficulty level: moderately difficult.

EXPENSES (1992–93 estimated) Comprehensive fee of $12,060 includes full-time tuition ($8400), mandatory fees ($180), and college room and board ($3480). College room only: $1640.

FINANCIAL AID College-administered aid for all 1991–92 undergraduates: 472 need-based scholarships (average $3600); 18 non-need scholarships (average $2714); low-interest long-term loans from college sources (average $3371), from external sources (average $1900); SEOG; College Work-Study; 35 part-time jobs. Supporting data: FAF, IRS required; AFSA/SAR required for some; FFS acceptable. Priority application deadline: 3/31.

CAMPUS LIFE/STUDENT SERVICES Mandatory chapel; drama/theater group; student-run newspaper. Institution provides health clinic, personal/psychological counseling.

ATHLETICS Member NAIA. Intercollegiate sports: basketball M(s), W(s); cross-country running M, W; soccer M(s); volleyball W. Intramural sports: basketball, football, soccer, tennis, volleyball.

MAJORS Biblical studies; biology/biological sciences; business administration/commerce/management; chemistry; computer science; elementary education; (pre)engineering sequence; English; health science; history; interdisciplinary studies; (pre)law sequence; (pre)medicine sequence; music; music education; natural sciences; nursing; piano/organ; psychology; sociology; stringed instruments; voice; wind and percussion instruments. Most popular majors of class of 1991: business administration/commerce/management, interdisciplinary studies, English.

SPECIAL NOTE FROM THE COLLEGE "In all things . . . Christ preeminent" is more than a motto at Covenant College. It is a way of teaching, a way of learning, and a way of living. Covenant College provides a broad liberal arts education emphasizing a personal commitment to Christ. The College offers both associate and baccalaureate degrees in liberal arts disciplines and selected preprofessional programs. The primary goal is to provide an environment of academic excellence that encourages students to develop an active Christian mind. More than two thirds of the faculty members have earned doctorates. More than 500 students come to Covenant from 39 states and 19 foreign countries. Christian commitment and academic excellence are knit together in a warm spirit of friendship that makes Covenant unique.

CONTACT Dr. Richard Allen, Director of Admissions, Covenant College, Lookout Mountain, GA 30750, 706-820-1560 Ext. 145.

DALLAS BAPTIST UNIVERSITY

Dallas, Texas

Total Enrollment: 2,635

UG Enrollment: 2,240 (52% W)

Application Deadline: rolling

Tuition & Fees: $6550

Room & Board: $3130

Entrance: moderately difficult

SAT ≥ 500: 11% V, 34% M

ACT ≥ 21: 39%

Denominational Affiliation: Southern Baptist

GENERAL INFORMATION Independent comprehensive coed institution. Founded 1965. Awards B, M. Primary accreditation: regional. Suburban setting; 200-acre campus. Total enrollment: 2,635. Faculty: 177 (62 full-time, 115 part-time); 48% of full-time faculty have terminal degrees; graduate assistants teach no undergraduate courses. Library holdings: 162,092 bound volumes, 303,839 titles on microform, 612 periodical subscriptions, 2,298 records/tapes/CDs. Computer terminals/PCs available for student use: 56, located in computer center, library.

UNDERGRADUATE PROFILE Fall 1991: 2,240 undergraduates (129 freshmen) from 33 states and territories and 43 foreign countries; 65% part-time; 89% state residents; 41% transfers; 62% financial aid recipients; 52% women; 19% African Americans; 1% Native Americans; 6% Hispanics; 2% Asian Americans; 9% international students; 69% of undergraduates 25 years of age or older.

1991 FRESHMAN DATA 245 students applied for fall 1991 admission; 87% were accepted; 57% of those accepted enrolled. 19% of freshmen were in top 10% of secondary school class, 42% were in top 25%, 71% were in top half.

ENROLLMENT PATTERNS 59% of fall 1990 freshmen returned for fall 1991 term.

FRESHMAN ADMISSIONS Options: early entrance, deferred entrance. Required: high school transcript, SAT or ACT, TOEFL (for foreign students). Recommended: 3 years of high school math and science, some high school foreign language, campus interview, rank in upper 50% of high school class. Required for some: recommendations. Test scores used for admission.

Application deadline: rolling. Notification date: continuous. College's own assessment of entrance difficulty level: moderately difficult.

TRANSFER ADMISSIONS Required: college transcript, minimum 2.0 grade point average. Required for some: standardized test scores, high school transcript, recommendations, interview. Application deadline: rolling. Notification date: continuous. College's own assessment of entrance difficulty level: minimally difficult.

EXPENSES (1991–92) Comprehensive fee of $9680 includes full-time tuition ($6000), mandatory fees ($550), and college room and board ($3130). College room only: $1130. Part-time tuition: $200 per credit hour.

FINANCIAL AID College-administered aid for all 1991–92 undergraduates: 99 need-based scholarships (average $1497); 765 non-need scholarships (average $2183); low-interest long-term loans from college funds (average $2500), from external sources (average $3426); SEOG; College Work-Study. Supporting data: FAF, IRS, institutional form, AFSA/SAR required. Priority application deadline: 6/1.

CAMPUS LIFE/STUDENT SERVICES Dress code; mandatory chapel; drama/theater group. Institution provides health clinic, personal/psychological counseling. Social organizations: local fraternities, local sororities, social clubs.

STUDY ABROAD SITE England.

ATHLETICS Member NAIA. Intercollegiate sports: baseball M(s); volleyball W(s); soccer M(s). Intramural sports: badminton, basketball, bowling, football, golf, table tennis (Ping Pong), tennis, track and field, volleyball, weight lifting.

MAJORS Accounting; accounting/information science; art (fine arts); aviation management; biblical studies; biology; business administration; church music; computer science; computer systems management; criminal justice; counseling; (pre)dentistry; economics; education; elementary education; English; finance; general studies; history; interdisciplinary academic studies; (pre)law; marketing; mathematics; management; (pre)medicine; multidisciplinary studies; music (piano/organ); music (vocal); (pre)occupational therapy; (pre)optometry; pastoral ministries; (pre)pharmacy; physical education; (pre)physical therapy; (pre)podiatry; political science; psychology; public administration; religious education; secondary education; social services; sociology.

SPECIAL NOTE FROM THE COLLEGE DBU's strategic location in southwest Dallas is easily accessible to all the amenities of one of the nation's most exciting metropolitan areas. From its multicultural opportunities to its high-tech industry, the Dallas-Fort Worth metroplex is an excellent place to live and learn. DBU's scenic campus, known as University Hill, overlooks beautiful Mountain Creek Lake. This peaceful haven provides a setting designed to encourage students to develop intellectually, emotionally, physically, and spiritually. The primary goal of the University is to graduate students expertly trained by Christian faculty and who are deeply committed to God's service.

CONTACT Mr. John Plotts, Admissions Office, Dallas Baptist University, 3000 Mountain Creek Parkway, Dallas, TX 75211, 214-333-5360.

DORDT COLLEGE

Sioux Center, Iowa

Total Enrollment: 1,046 (all UG)

Women: 50%

Application Deadline: 9/1

Tuition & Fees: $8600

Room & Board: $2570

Entrance: moderately difficult

ACT ≥ 21: 70%

Denominational Affiliation: Christian Reformed

GENERAL INFORMATION Independent 4-year coed college. Founded 1955. Awards A (terminal), B. Primary accreditation: regional. Small town setting; 45-acre campus. Total enrollment: 1,046. Faculty: 90 (72 full-time, 18 part-time); 57% of full-time faculty have terminal degrees; graduate assistants teach no undergraduate courses. Library holdings: 120,157 bound volumes, 14,819 titles on microform, 489 periodical subscriptions, 3,616 records/tapes/CDs. Computer terminals/PCs available for student use: 100, located in computer center, student center, library.

UNDERGRADUATE PROFILE Fall 1991: 1,046 undergraduates (292 freshmen) from 36 states and territories and 8 foreign countries; 4% part-time; 40% state residents; 3% transfers; 95% financial aid recipients; 50% women; 0% African Americans; 0% Native Americans; 0% Hispanics; 1% Asian Americans; 1% international students; 8% of undergraduates 25 years of age or older.

1991 FRESHMAN DATA 446 students applied for fall 1991 admission; 97% were accepted; 67% of those accepted enrolled. 23% of freshmen were in top 10% of secondary school class, 46% were in top 25%, 73% were in top half.

ENROLLMENT PATTERNS 78% of fall 1990 freshmen returned for fall 1991 term. 50% of 1986 freshmen graduated within 5 years; 17% of students completing a bachelor's program went on for further study.

FRESHMAN ADMISSIONS Options: early entrance, deferred entrance. Required: high school transcript, SAT or ACT, TOEFL (for foreign students). Recommended: some high school foreign language. Required for some: interview. Test scores used for counseling/placement. Application deadline: 9/1. Notification date: continuous until 9/1. College's own assessment of entrance difficulty level: moderately difficult.

TRANSFER ADMISSIONS Required: high school transcript, college transcript, minimum 2.0 grade point average. Required for some: interview. Application deadline: 9/1. Notification date: continuous until 9/1.

EXPENSES (1992–93) Comprehensive fee of $11,170 includes full-time tuition ($8600) and college room and board ($2570). Part-time tuition: $360 per semester hour.

FINANCIAL AID College-administered aid for all 1991–92 undergraduates: 220 need-based scholarships (average $500); 970 non-need scholarships (average $1150); low-interest long-term loans from college funds (average $700), from external sources (average $3200); SEOG; College Work-Study; 1,000 part-time jobs. Supporting data: institutional form required; IRS required for some; FFS, FAF, AFSA/SAR acceptable. Priority application deadline: 4/15.

CAMPUS LIFE/STUDENT SERVICES Chapel; drama/theater; student-run newspaper; musical groups; special interest clubs; service organizations. Institution provides health clinic, career/placement services, personal/psychological counseling.

STUDY ABROAD SITES The Netherlands, Germany, Mexico, Costa Rica, Spain.

ATHLETICS Member NAIA. Intercollegiate sports: basketball M, W; golf M, W; ice hockey M; soccer M; softball W; swimming and diving M, W; tennis M, W; track and field M, W; volleyball W. Intramural sports: baseball, basketball, bowling, field hockey, gymnastics, ice hockey, soccer, swimming and diving, table tennis (Ping Pong), tennis, track and field, volleyball.

MAJORS Accounting; agricultural business; agricultural sciences; animal science; art/fine arts; biology/biological sciences; business administration/commerce/management; business education; chemistry; communication; communication: radio/TV; computer science; (pre)dentistry sequence; Dutch; education; elementary education; engineering (electrical emphasis); engineering (mechanical emphasis); engineering science; English; environmental sciences; German; history; journalism; (pre)law; management information systems; mathematics; medical technology; (pre)medicine sequence; music; music education; natural sciences; (pre)nursing; (pre)pharmacy; philosophy; physical education; (pre)physical therapy; physics; plant science; political science/government; psychology; secondary education; secretarial studies/office management; (pre)seminary; social studies; social work; sociology; Spanish; theater arts/drama; theology; (pre)veterinary medicine sequence. Most popular majors of class of 1991: education, business administration/commerce/management, social work.

SPECIAL NOTE FROM THE COLLEGE Dordt College does not adhere to the traditional distinctions between liberal arts and professional training. The College instead focuses on transmitting "serviceable insight," a biblically based understanding that encompasses both the structure of the created order and the nature and demands of a wide range of vocations and professions. This perspective on education is the reason why the College has majors such as agriculture, business, and computer science; why there are accredited programs in social work and engineering; and why every course at Dordt will challenge students to think about the real-world applications of their learning.

CONTACT Mr. Quentin Van Essen, Director of Admissions, Dordt College, 498 4th Avenue NE, Sioux Center, IA 51250, 712-722-6080 or toll-free 800-34-DORDT.

EASTERN COLLEGE

Saint Davids, Pennsylvania

Total Enrollment: 1,507

UG Enrollment: 1,213 (65% W)

Application Deadline: 8/15

Tuition & Fees: $9850

Room & Board: $4130

Entrance: moderately difficult

SAT ≥ 500: 35% V, 49% M

ACT ≥ 21: 80%

Denominational Affiliation: American Baptist

GENERAL INFORMATION Independent comprehensive coed institution. Founded 1932. Awards B, M. Primary accreditation: regional. Small-town setting, with easy access to Philadelphia; 100-acre campus. Total enrollment: 1,507. Faculty: 128 (43 full-time, 85 part-time); 70% of full-time faculty have terminal degrees; graduate assistants teach a few undergraduate courses. Library holdings: 104,946 bound volumes, 77,120 titles on microform, 784 periodical subscriptions, 2,295 records/tapes/CDs. Computer terminals/PCs available for student use: 45, located in computer center, classroom building.

UNDERGRADUATE PROFILE Fall 1991: 1,213 undergraduates (227 freshmen) from 36 states and territories and 13 foreign countries; 29% part-time; 70% state residents; 30% transfers; 47% financial aid recipients; 65% women; 11% African Americans; 1% Native Americans; 2% Hispanics; 1% Asian Americans; 2% international students; 45% of undergraduates 25 years of age or older.

1991 FRESHMAN DATA 556 students applied for fall 1991 admission; 83% were accepted; 49% of those accepted enrolled. 1 freshman was a National Merit Scholarship Finalist; 1 received a National Merit Scholarship. 14% of freshmen were in top 10% of secondary school class, 39% were in top 25%, 65% were in top half.

ENROLLMENT PATTERNS 71% of fall 1990 freshmen returned for fall 1991 term. 46% of 1986 freshmen graduated within 5 years.

FRESHMAN ADMISSIONS Options: early entrance, deferred entrance. Required: essay, high school transcript, 1 recommendation, SAT or ACT, TOEFL (for foreign students).

Recommended: 3 years of high school math and science, some high school foreign language, interview, English Composition Test. Test scores used for admission. Application deadline: rolling. Notification date: continuous. College's own assessment of entrance difficulty level: moderately difficult.

TRANSFER ADMISSIONS Required: essay, standardized test scores, high school transcript, 1 recommendation, college transcript, minimum 2.0 grade point average. Recommended: 3 years of high school math and science, some high school foreign language, interview. Application deadline: rolling. Notification date: continuous. College's own assessment of entrance difficulty level: moderately difficult.

EXPENSES (1992–93 estimated) Comprehensive fee of $13,980 includes full-time tuition ($9850) and college room and board ($4130). Part-time tuition: $235 per credit.

FINANCIAL AID College-administered aid for all 1991–92 undergraduates: 394 need-based scholarships; (average $3080); non-need scholarships; low-interest long-term loans from external sources (average $3300); SEOG; College Work-Study. Supporting data: IRS, institutional form required; FFS, FAF, AFSA/SAR acceptable. Priority application deadline: 6/1.

CAMPUS LIFE/STUDENT SERVICES Drama/theater group; student-run newspaper and radio station. Institution provides health clinic, personal/psychological counseling.

ATHLETICS Member NCAA (Division III). Intercollegiate sports: baseball M(s); basketball M(s), W(s); cross-country running M(s), W(s); field hockey W(s); lacrosse W(s); soccer M(s), W(s); softball w(s); tennis M, W; volleyball W(s). Intramural sports: baseball, basketball, bowling, football, soccer, softball, table tennis (Ping Pong), tennis, volleyball.

MAJORS Accounting; art history; astronomy; biblical studies; biology/biological sciences; business administration/commerce/management; chemistry; communication; creative writing; economics; elementary education; English communication for secondary education; English for secondary education; French; health and physical education; health services administration; history; literature; mathematics; medical technology; music; nursing; organizational management; philosophy; political science/government; psychology; religion-philosophy; school health services; secondary education; social work; sociology; Spanish; studio art; youth ministries. Most popular majors of class of 1991: organizational management, nursing, elementary education.

SPECIAL NOTE FROM THE COLLEGE Eastern College is known for its innovative academic programs, caring Christian community, commitment to social action, and exceptionally beautiful campus. Class sizes are kept small, and professors are both role models to their students and highly accomplished experts in their fields. In addition to integrating faith and learning, Eastern's creative academic programs encourage students to learn from many disciplines. The campus community is highly diverse, with a multiethnic student body that includes representatives from over 30 countries. A strong campus ministries program and Eastern's proximity to the city of Philadelphia provide many opportunities for Christian service. The life of the Eastern College community is firmly centered in Jesus Christ.

CONTACT Dr. Ronald L. Keller, Vice President for Enrollment Management, Eastern College, 10 Fairview Drive, Saint Davids, PA 19087-3696, 215-341-5967.

EASTERN MENNONITE COLLEGE

Harrisonburg, Virginia

Total Enrollment: 974 (all UG)

Women: 60%

Application Deadline: 8/1

Tuition & Fees: $8600

Room & Board: $3400

Entrance: moderately difficult

SAT ≥ 500: 39% V, 55% M

ACT ≥ 21: 76%

Denominational Affiliation: Mennonite

GENERAL INFORMATION Independent 4-year coed college. Administratively affiliated with Eastern Mennonite Seminary. Founded 1917. Awards A (college transfer and terminal), B. Primary accreditation: regional. Small-town setting; 90-acre campus. Total enrollment: 974. Faculty: 81 (64 full-time, 17 part-time); 57% of full-time faculty have terminal degrees; graduate assistants teach no undergraduate courses. Library holdings: 122,000 bound volumes, 40,900 titles on microform, 1,039 periodical subscriptions, 2,900 records/tapes/CDs. Computer terminals/PCs available for student use: 65, located in computer center, library, dormitories, science center.

UNDERGRADUATE PROFILE Fall 1991: 974 undergraduates (195 freshmen) from 34 states and territories and 16 foreign countries; 6% part-time; 33% state residents; 9% transfers; 92% financial aid recipients; 60% women; 2% African Americans; 0% Native Americans; 2% Hispanics; 1% Asian Americans; 3% international students; 3% of undergraduates 25 years of age or older.

1991 FRESHMAN DATA 355 students applied for fall 1991 admission; 97% were accepted; 57% of those accepted enrolled. 2 freshmen were National Merit Scholarship Finalists. 19% of freshmen were in top 10% of secondary school class, 41% were in top 25%, 69% were in top half.

ENROLLMENT PATTERNS 74% of fall 1990 freshmen returned for fall 1991 term. 60% of 1986 freshmen graduated within 5 years; 11% of students completing a bachelor's program went on for further study.

FRESHMAN ADMISSIONS Options: early entrance, deferred entrance. Required: essay, high school transcript, 2 recommendations, statement of commitment, SAT or ACT, TOEFL (for foreign students). Recommended: 3 years of high school math and science, 2 years of high school foreign language, interview. Test scores used for admission. Application deadline: 8/1. Notification date: continuous until 8/1. College's own assessment of entrance difficulty level: moderately difficult.

TRANSFER ADMISSIONS Required: essay, high school transcript, 2 recommendations, college transcript, minimum 2.0 grade point average, statement of commitment. Recommended: standardized test scores, 3 years of high school math and science, 2 years of high school foreign language, interview. Application deadline: 8/1. Notification date: continuous until 8/1. College's own assessment of entrance difficulty level: moderately difficult.

EXPENSES (1992–93) Comprehensive fee of $12,000 includes full-time tuition ($8600) and college room and board ($3400). Part-time tuition: $360 per semester hour.

FINANCIAL AID College-administered aid for all 1991–92 undergraduates: 630 need-based scholarships (average $1350); 900 non-need scholarships (average $826); low-interest long-term loans from college funds (average $1340), from external sources (average $3016); SEOG; College Work-Study; 158 part-time jobs. Supporting data: FAF, institutional form required; state form, IRS, AFSA/SAR required for some; FFS acceptable. Priority application deadline: 4/15.

CAMPUS LIFE/STUDENT SERVICES Mandatory chapel; drama/theater group; student-run newspaper and radio station. Institution provides health clinic, personal/psychological counseling.

STUDY ABROAD SITES Mexico, Costa Rica, Israel, Egypt, Germany, France, England, China, Spain, Japan, Commonwealth of Independent States (USSR).

ATHLETICS Member NCAA (Division III). Intercollegiate sports: baseball M; basketball M, W; cross-country running M, W; field hockey W; golf M; soccer M; softball W; tennis M, W; track and field M, W; volleyball W. Intramural sports: badminton, basketball, football, racquetball, soccer, softball, table tennis (Ping Pong), tennis, volleyball, weight lifting.

MAJORS Accounting; agricultural sciences; art/fine arts; biblical studies; biology/biological sciences; business administration/commerce/management; chemistry; community services; computer information systems; computer programming; computer science; data processing; (pre)dentistry sequence; dietetics; early childhood education; education; elementary education; (pre)engineering sequence; English; food services management; French; German; history; (pre)law sequence; liberal arts/general studies; mathematics; medical technology; (pre)medicine sequence; ministries; modern languages; music; music education; nursing; nutrition; paralegal studies; pastoral studies; peace studies; philosophy; physical education; psychology; recreation and leisure services; religious studies; science education; secondary education; social work; sociology; Spanish; special education; teacher aide studies; teaching English as a second language; theology; (pre)veterinary medicine sequence. Most popular majors of class of 1991: education, business administration/commerce/management, liberal arts/general studies.

SPECIAL NOTE FROM THE COLLEGE EMC students discover what it means to be a Christian and a world citizen. EMC's Global Village curriculum integrates the liberal arts and sciences with Christian values and personal contact with people of other cultures. Students spend a semester in the Middle East, Latin America, or Europe; a summer in China, Ireland, New Zealand, Appalachia, Mexico, South Africa, or Southeast Asia; or a year in Washington, DC, in a study-service program. Graduates are equipped with a distinctive intellectual framework and extraordinary, often life-transforming, experience in human relations. EMC alumni find that they are well prepared for advanced study and report that their careers and professional practice are profoundly enriched by a global perspective. Students come to see life as an opportunity for faithful Christian service and peacemaking in a needy world. All of this begins in a friendly campus community in the heart of the scenic and historic Shenandoah Valley of Virginia.

CONTACT Mrs. Ellen B. Miller, Director of Admissions, Eastern Mennonite College, 1200 Park Road, Harrisonburg, VA 22801, 703-732-4118 or toll-free 800-368-2665 (out-of-state).

EASTERN NAZARENE COLLEGE

Quincy, Massachusetts

Total Enrollment: 1,004

UG Enrollment: 820 (64% W)

Application Deadline: rolling

Tuition & Fees: $8200

Room & Board: $3300

Entrance: moderately difficult

SAT ≥ 500: 23% V, 36% M

ACT ≥ 21: N/R

Denominational Affiliation: Church of the Nazarene

GENERAL INFORMATION Independent comprehensive coed institution. Founded 1918. Awards A (college transfer and terminal), B, M. Primary accreditation: regional. Suburban setting, with easy access to Boston; 15-acre campus. Total enrollment: 1,004. Faculty: 63 (48 full-time, 15 part-time); 59% of full-time faculty have terminal degrees; graduate assistants teach no undergraduate courses. Library holdings: 112,750 bound volumes, 240 titles on microform, 550 periodical subscriptions, 530 records/tapes/CDs. Computer terminals/PCs available for student use: 70, located in computer center, library.

UNDERGRADUATE PROFILE Fall 1991: 820 undergraduates (187 freshmen) from 29 states and territories and 16 foreign countries; 5% part-time; 38% state residents; 18% transfers; 80% financial aid recipients; 64% women; 4% African Americans; 0% Native Americans; 2% Hispanics; 2% Asian Americans; 4% international students; 10% of undergraduates 25 years of age or older.

1991 FRESHMAN DATA 382 students applied for fall 1991 admission; 96% were accepted; 51% of those accepted enrolled. 16% of freshmen were in top 10% of secondary school class, 33% were in top 25%, 65% were in top half.

ENROLLMENT PATTERNS 75% of fall 1990 freshmen returned for fall 1991 term.

FRESHMAN ADMISSIONS Options: early entrance, deferred entrance. Required: high school transcript, 1 recommendation, SAT or ACT, TOEFL (for foreign students). Recommended: essay, 3 years of high school math and science, some high school foreign language, interview. Test scores used for counseling/

placement. Application deadline: rolling. Notification date: continuous. College's own assessment of entrance difficulty level: moderately difficult.

TRANSFER ADMISSIONS Required: standardized test scores, high school transcript, 1 recommendation, college transcript, minimum 2.0 grade point average. Recommended: interview. Application deadline: rolling. Notification date: continuous.

EXPENSES (1992–93) Comprehensive fee of $11,500 includes full-time tuition ($7735), mandatory fees ($465), and college room and board ($3300).

FINANCIAL AID College-administered aid for all 1991–92 undergraduates: 100 need-based scholarships (average $1500); 300 non-need scholarships; short-term loans (average $400); low-interest long-term loans from external sources (average $3800); SEOG; College Work-Study; 100 part-time jobs. Supporting data: FAF, IRS, state form, institutional form, AFSA/SAR required. Priority application deadline: 3/1.

CAMPUS LIFE/STUDENT SERVICES Mandatory chapel; drama/theater group; student-run newspaper and radio station. Institution provides health clinic, personal/psychological counseling.

STUDY ABROAD SITES Germany, Switzerland, Great Britain, France, Spain, Belize.

ATHLETICS Member NCAA (Division III). Intercollegiate sports: baseball M; basketball M, W; cross-country running M, W; soccer M; softball W; tennis M, W; volleyball M, W. Intramural sports: basketball, soccer, softball, volleyball.

MAJORS Aerospace engineering; biblical studies; biology/biological sciences; biomedical engineering; business administration/commerce/management; chemistry; communication; computer engineering; computer information systems; computer science; (pre)dentistry sequence; early childhood education; education; electrical engineering; elementary education; engineering physics; English; French; history; (pre)law sequence; liberal arts/general studies; manufacturing engineering; mathematics; mechanical engineering; (pre)medicine sequence; ministries; music; music education; pastoral studies; physical education; physics; psychology; religious education; religious studies; science; social science; social work; sociology; Spanish; systems engineering; (pre)veterinary medicine sequence. Most popular majors of class of 1991: business administration/commerce/management, education, psychology.

SPECIAL NOTE FROM THE COLLEGE Eastern Nazarene College offers a strong commitment to a liberal arts education in a small-school, Christian-oriented setting. ENC has been producing graduates in Quincy, Massachusetts, for over 70 years and has maintained a reputation for being a caring, yet academically demanding, school. Boston's libraries, universities, conservatories, museums, historic sights, and churches offer unsurpassed educational opportunities and abundant possibilities for employment and entertainment. ENC believes that the solid academic programs, supportive faculty, Christian values, and Boston area location provide students with unparalleled opportunities for personal growth. Moreover, Eastern Nazarene seeks to develop in each person a Christian world view and to encourage each person to become God's creative and redemptive agent in today's world.

CONTACT Mr. D. William Nichols, Director of Enrollment Management, Eastern Nazarene College, 23 East Elm Avenue, Quincy, MA 02170, 617-773-2373.

ERSKINE COLLEGE

Due West, South Carolina

Total Enrollment: 490 (all UG)

Women: 53%

Application Deadline: rolling

Tuition & Fees: $10,125

Room & Board: $3515

Entrance: moderately difficult

SAT ≥ 500: 40% V, 60% M

ACT ≥ 21: N/R

Denominational Affiliation: Associate Reformed Presbyterian Church

GENERAL INFORMATION Independent 4-year coed college. Founded 1839. Primary accreditation: regional. Small-town setting; 85-acre campus. Total enrollment: 490. Faculty: 46 (39 full-time, 7 part-time); 82% of full-time faculty have terminal degrees; graduate assistants teach no undergraduate courses. Library holdings: 220,000 bound volumes, 72,500 titles on microform, 1,100 periodical subscriptions, 1,050 records/tapes/CDs. Computer terminals/PCs available for student use: 204, located in computer center, library.

UNDERGRADUATE PROFILE Fall 1991: 490 undergraduates (102 freshmen) from 19 states and territories and 9 foreign countries; 4% part-time; 70% state residents; 7% transfers; 92% financial aid recipients; 53% women; 9% African Americans; 1% Native Americans; 2% Hispanics; 1% Asian Americans; 5% international students; 5% of undergraduates 25 years of age or older.

1991 FRESHMAN DATA 425 students applied for fall 1991 admission; 82% were accepted; 29% of those accepted enrolled. 2 freshmen were National Merit Scholarship Finalists. 46% of freshmen were in top 10% of secondary school class, 71% were in top 25%, 88% were in top half.

ENROLLMENT PATTERNS 80% of fall 1990 freshmen returned for fall 1991 term. 62% of 1986 freshmen graduated within 5 years.

FRESHMAN ADMISSIONS Preference given to members of Associate Reformed Presbyterian Church. Option: deferred entrance. Required: high school transcript, 1 recommendation, SAT or ACT, TOEFL (for foreign students). Recommended: 3 years of high school math and science, 2 years of high school foreign language. Required for some: campus interview. Test scores used for admission. Application deadline: rolling. Notification date: continuous. College's own assessment of entrance difficulty level: moderately difficult.

TRANSFER ADMISSIONS Required: 1 recommendation, college transcript, minimum 2.0 grade point average. Recommended: campus interview. Required for some: standardized test scores, high school transcript. Application deadline: rolling. College's own assessment of entrance difficulty level: moderately difficult.

EXPENSES (1992–93) Comprehensive fee of $13,640 includes full-time tuition ($9410), mandatory fees ($715), and college room and board ($3515). College room only: $1600. Part-time tuition: $225 per semester hour.

FINANCIAL AID College-administered aid for all 1991–92 undergraduates: 360 need-based scholarships (average $6000); 150 non-need scholarships (average $1900); short-term loans (average $47); low-interest long-term loans from college funds (average $2000), from external sources (average $2700); SEOG; College Work-Study; 140 part-time jobs. Supporting data: FAF, IRS, state form, institutional form, AFSA/SAR required; FFS acceptable. Priority application deadline: 4/1.

CAMPUS LIFE/STUDENT SERVICES Drama/theater group; student-run newspaper. Institution provides health clinic, personal/psychological counseling. Social organizations: 3 male literary societies, 3 female literary societies; 40% of eligible undergraduate men and 30% of eligible undergraduate women are members.

STUDY ABROAD SITES Scotland, England, France.

ATHLETICS Member NCAA (Division II). Intercollegiate sports: baseball M(s); basketball M(s), W(s); cross-country running M(s); golf M(s); soccer M(s), W(s); softball W(s); tennis M(s), W(s); volleyball W(s). Intramural sports: basketball, soccer, softball, tennis, volleyball.

MAJORS Accounting; behavioral sciences; biblical studies; biology/biological sciences; business administration/commerce/management; chemistry; early childhood education; elementary education; English; French; history; mathematics; music; music education; natural sciences; physical education; physics; piano/organ; psychology; religious education; sociology; Spanish; special education; sports management; voice. Most popular majors of class of 1991: business administration/commerce/management, history, English.

SPECIAL NOTE FROM THE COLLEGE Dr. Paul Sharp, distinguished former president of 4 universities and colleges, recently of Erskine College: "You have a remarkable academic village. . . . Your whole college is a neighborhood." Stating that "the greatest asset of Erskine is its quality faculty," Dr. Sharp praised Erskine's "commitment to teaching and commitment to students." Commitment to students extends beyond the classroom to responsibility for self-government. Students respond to this responsibility by conducting a business that raises funds for computers; building their own alcohol- and drug-free student club; helping Erskine plan through representation on a "Futures Council"; and maintaining Christian emphasis through a Student Christian Association.

CONTACT Mrs. Dot Carter, Director of Admissions and Financial Aid, Erskine College, P.O. Box 176, Due West, SC 29639, 803-379-8832.

EVANGEL COLLEGE

Springfield, Missouri

Total Enrollment: 1,440 (all UG)

Women: 54%

Application Deadline: 8/15

Tuition & Fees: $6480

Room & Board: $2960

Entrance: moderately difficult

SAT ≥ 500: N/R

ACT ≥ 21: 53%

Denominational Affiliation: Assemblies of God

GENERAL INFORMATION Independent 4-year coed college. Founded 1955. Awards A (terminal), B. Primary accreditation: regional. Urban setting; 80-acre campus. Total enrollment: 1,440. Faculty: 122 (86 full-time, 36 part-time); 47% of full-time faculty have terminal degrees; graduate assistants teach no undergraduate courses. Library holdings: 105,000 bound volumes, 23,000 titles on microform, 610 periodical subscriptions, 3,000 records/tapes/CDs. Computer terminals/PCs available for student use: 64, located in computer center, library, labs.

UNDERGRADUATE PROFILE Fall 1992: 1,440 undergraduates (332 freshmen) from 47 states and territories and 10 foreign countries; 7% part-time; 36% state residents; 8% transfers; 83% financial aid recipients; 54% women; 3% African Americans; 1% Hispanics; 2% international students; 1% of undergraduates 25 years of age or older.

1992 FRESHMAN DATA 438 students applied for fall 1992 admission; 95% were accepted; 80% of those accepted enrolled. 19% of freshmen were in top 10% of secondary school class, 45% were in top 25%, 77% were in top half.

ENROLLMENT PATTERNS 64% of fall 1991 freshmen returned for fall 1992 term. 51% of 1987 freshmen graduated within 5 years.

FRESHMAN ADMISSIONS Option: deferred entrance. Required: high school transcript, SAT or ACT, TOEFL (for foreign students). Recommended: 3 years of high school math and science, some high school foreign language. Test scores used for admission. Application deadline: 8/15. Notification date: continuous. College's own assessment of entrance difficulty level: moderately difficult.

TRANSFER ADMISSIONS Required: college transcript, minimum 2.0 grade point average. Required for some: high school transcript. Application deadline: 8/15. Notification date: continuous. College's own assessment of entrance difficulty level: moderately difficult.

EXPENSES (1992–93) Comprehensive fee of $9440 includes full-time tuition ($6320), mandatory fees ($160), and college room and board ($2960). College room only: $1410. Part-time tuition: $245 per credit hour. Part-time mandatory fees per semester: $48.

FINANCIAL AID College-administered aid for all 1992–93 undergraduates: need-based scholarships; 831 non-need scholarships (average $1605); low-interest long-term loans from college funds (average $1637), from external sources (average $2770); SEOG; College Work-Study; 129 part-time jobs. Supporting data: FAF, institutional form required; IRS required for some; AFSA/SAR acceptable. Priority application deadline: 4/1.

CAMPUS LIFE/STUDENT SERVICES Dress code; mandatory chapel; drama/theater group; student-run newspaper, radio and TV stations. Institution provides health clinic, personal/psychological counseling.

ATHLETICS Member NAIA. Intercollegiate sports: baseball M(s); basketball M(s), W(s); cross-country running M(s), W(s); football M(s); softball W; track and field M(s), W(s); volleyball W(s). Intramural sports: baseball, basketball, football, soccer, softball, volleyball.

MAJORS Accounting; art education; art/fine arts; behavioral sciences; biblical studies; biology/biological sciences; broadcasting; business administration/commerce/management; business education; chemistry; child care/child and family studies; communication; computer science; (pre)dentistry sequence; early childhood education; education; elementary education; English; history; journalism; laboratory technologies; (pre)law sequence; marketing/retailing/merchandising; mathematics; medical technology; (pre)medicine sequence; mental health/rehabilitation counseling; music; music education; physical education; political science/government; psychology; public administration; radio and television studies; recreation and leisure services; sacred music; science education; secondary education; secretarial studies/office management; social science; social work; sociology; Spanish; special education; speech/rhetoric/public address/debate; (pre)veterinary medicine sequence. Most popular majors of class of 1991: business administration/commerce/management, education, communication.

SPECIAL NOTE FROM THE COLLEGE As the national college of arts and sciences of the Assemblies of God, Evangel comes from a full gospel, charismatic heritage. It is a residential college—80% of students live on campus in modern residence halls—and draws from all 50 states and from several countries. Evangel offers over 30 academic majors, from business to engineering to journalism to premed, and is located near 6 other colleges and a seminary. The Student Development Department provides planned programs that contribute to students' intellectual, social, vocational, physical, emotional, and spiritual development. Finally, Springfield is the gateway to the Ozarks Mountain recreational haven and is close to numerous lakes, parks, the Silver Dollar City theme park, and the renowned country music performance capital—Branson, Missouri. Evangel believes recreation is a vital part of the total education process.

CONTACT Mr. David I. Schoolfield, Executive Director of Enrollment, Evangel College, 1111 North Glenstone, Springfield, MO 65802, 417-865-2811 Ext. 7202.

FRESNO PACIFIC COLLEGE

Fresno, California

Total Enrollment: 1,410

UG Enrollment: 589 (55% W)

Application Deadline: rolling

Tuition & Fees: $8800

Room & Board: $3400

Entrance: moderately difficult

SAT ≥ 500: 29% V, 42% M

ACT ≥ 21: N/R

Denominational Affiliation: Mennonite Brethren Church

GENERAL INFORMATION Independent comprehensive coed institution. Founded 1944. Awards A (college transfer), B, M. Primary accreditation: regional. Urban setting; 40-acre campus. Total enrollment: 1,410. Faculty: 79 (40 full-time, 39 part-time); 53% of full-time faculty have terminal degrees; graduate assistants teach a few undergraduate courses. Library holdings: 138,000 bound volumes, 150,000 titles on microform, 920 periodical subscriptions, 4,000 records/tapes/CDs. Computer terminals/PCs available for student use: 66, located in computer center, student center, library.

UNDERGRADUATE PROFILE Fall 1991: 589 undergraduates (100 freshmen) from 14 states and territories; 11% part-time; 85% state residents; 20% transfers; 86% financial aid recipients; 55% women; 2% African Americans; 0% Native Americans; 10% Hispanics; 2% Asian Americans; 5% international students; 25% of undergraduates 25 years of age or older.

1991 FRESHMAN DATA 271 students applied for fall 1991 admission; 80% were accepted; 46% of those accepted enrolled. 45% of freshmen were in top 10% of secondary school class, 81% were in top 25%, 95% were in top half.

ENROLLMENT PATTERNS 71% of fall 1990 freshmen returned for fall 1991 term. 38% of 1986 freshmen graduated within 5 years.

FRESHMAN ADMISSIONS Options: early entrance, deferred entrance. Required: essay, high school transcript, 1 recommendation, 2 years high school foreign language, SAT or ACT. Recommended: TOEFL (for foreign students). Required for some: interview. Test scores used for admission. Application

deadline: rolling. Notification date: continuous until 7/31. College's own assessment of entrance difficulty level: moderately difficult.

TRANSFER ADMISSIONS Required: essay, high school transcript, 1 recommendation, college transcript, minimum 2.0 grade point average. Recommended: minimum 3.0 grade point average. Required for some: standardized test scores, interview. Application deadline: rolling. Notification date: continuous until 7/31. College's own assessment of entrance difficulty level: moderately difficult.

EXPENSES (1992–93) Comprehensive fee of $12,631 includes full-time tuition ($8800), mandatory fees ($161), and college room and board ($3400). College room only: $1420. Part-time tuition: $315 per unit.

FINANCIAL AID College-administered aid for all 1991–92 undergraduates: 343 need-based scholarships (average $653); 930 non-need scholarships (average $1589); short-term loans (average $300); low-interest long-term loans from external sources (average $3151); SEOG; College Work-Study; 250 part-time jobs. Supporting data: FAF, institutional form, AFSA/SAR required; IRS required for some. Priority application deadline: 3/2.

CAMPUS LIFE/STUDENT SERVICES Mandatory chapel; drama/theater group; student-run newspaper. Institution provides health clinic, personal/psychological counseling.

STUDY ABROAD SITES Mexico, Germany, Spain, France, Israel, People's Republic of China, Costa Rica, England, Greece.

ATHLETICS Member NAIA. Intercollegiate sports: basketball M(s), W(s); cross-country running M(s), W(s); soccer M(s); track and field M(s), W(s); volleyball W. Intramural sports: baseball, basketball, bowling, cross-country running, football, racquetball, skiing (cross-country), skiing (downhill), soccer, tennis, track and field, volleyball.

MAJORS Accounting; biblical studies; biology/biological sciences; business administration/commerce/management; business education; child psychology/child development; communication; computer science; education; elementary education; English; history; humanities; (pre)law sequence; liberal arts/general studies; literature; management information systems; mathematics; (pre)medicine sequence; ministries; music; natural sciences; physical education; political science/government; psychology; religious studies; secondary education; social science; sociology; Spanish. Most popular majors of class of 1991: liberal arts, English, biblical studies.

SPECIAL NOTE FROM THE COLLEGE Fresno Pacific was named one of the 10 best regional liberal arts colleges in the West by *U.S. News & World Report*'s "America's Best Colleges 1992." With the College's tree-covered campus, which is located in the heart of the vast agricultural valley of central California, Fresno Pacific is just an hour's drive from its 5-acre retreat center in the High Sierra and a 2½-hour drive from Pacific Ocean beaches. Pacific's academic program includes a unique core-course sequence and practical Christian service and professional internships. At Fresno Pacific, special emphasis is placed upon developing responsible personal freedom and a strong Christian community. Prospective students should come for a campus visit and meet faculty members and students. It's people who make the difference at Fresno Pacific College.

CONTACT Mr. Cary W. Templeton, Director of Admissions, Fresno Pacific College, 1717 South Chestnut Avenue, Fresno, CA 93702, 209-453-2030 or toll-free 800-660-6089 (in state).

GENEVA COLLEGE

Beaver Falls, Pennsylvania

Total Enrollment: 1,362

UG Enrollment: 1,311 (50% W)

Application Deadline: rolling

Tuition & Fees: $8164

Room & Board: $3980

Entrance: moderately difficult

Denominational Affiliation: Reformed Presbyterian Church

GENERAL INFORMATION Independent comprehensive coed institution. Founded 1848. Awards A (college transfer and terminal), B, M. Primary accreditation: regional. Suburban setting, with easy access to Pittsburgh; 55-acre campus. Total enrollment: 1,362. Faculty: 104 (58 full-time, 46 part-time); 66% of full-time faculty have terminal degrees; graduate assistants teach no undergraduate courses. Library holdings: 146,045 bound volumes, 70,380 titles on microform, 722 periodical subscriptions, 10,040 records/tapes/CDs. Computer terminals/PCs available for student use: 100, located in computer center, library, education department.

UNDERGRADUATE PROFILE Fall 1991: 1,311 undergraduates (255 freshmen) from 32 states and territories and 6 foreign countries; 22% part-time; 79% state residents; 93% financial aid recipients; 50% women; 10% African Americans; 0% Native Americans; 0% Hispanics; 1% Asian Americans; 1% international students.

1991 FRESHMAN DATA 550 students applied for fall 1991 admission; 90% were accepted; 52% of those accepted enrolled. 16% of freshmen were in top 10% of secondary school class, 61% were in top half.

ENROLLMENT PATTERNS 76% of fall 1990 freshmen returned for fall 1991 term. 55% of 1986 freshmen graduated within 5 years; 15% of students completing a bachelor's program went on for further study.

FRESHMAN ADMISSIONS Options: early entrance, deferred entrance. Required: essay, high school transcript, 2 years of high school foreign language, recommendations, SAT or ACT, TOEFL (for foreign students). Required for some: interview. Test scores used for admission. Application deadline: rolling. Notification date: continuous. College's own assessment of entrance difficulty level: moderately difficult.

TRANSFER ADMISSIONS Required: essay, high school transcript, 2 years of high school foreign language, college transcript, minimum 2.0 grade point average. Required for some: standardized test scores, recommendations, interview. Application deadline: rolling. Notification date: continuous. College's own assessment of entrance difficulty level: moderately difficult.

EXPENSES (1992–93) Comprehensive fee of $12,144 includes full-time tuition ($8164), and college room and board ($3980). Part-time tuition: $240 per credit.

FINANCIAL AID College-administered aid for all 1991–92 undergraduates: 1,233 need-based scholarships (average $1037); 421 non-need scholarships (average $576); short-term loans (average $50); low-interest long-term loans from external sources (average $2643); SEOG; College Work-Study; 366 part-time jobs. Supporting data: institutional form required; FAF, IRS, state form required for some; FFS, AFSA/SAR acceptable. Priority application deadline: 4/15.

CAMPUS LIFE/STUDENT SERVICES Mandatory chapel; drama/theater group; student-run newspaper and radio station. Institution provides health clinic, personal/psychological counseling.

STUDY ABROAD SITES Europe, China, Commonwealth of Independent States (USSR).

ATHLETICS Member NAIA. Intercollegiate sports: baseball M(s); basketball M(s), W(s); cross-country running M(s), W(s); football M(s); soccer M(s), W(s); softball W(s); tennis M(s), W(s); track and field M(s), W(s); volleyball M(s), W(s). Intramural sports: basketball, bowling, football, ice hockey, racquetball, skiing (downhill), soccer, softball, volleyball.

MAJORS Accounting; applied mathematics; aviation administration; biblical studies; biology/biological sciences; broadcasting; business administration/commerce/management; business education; chemical engineering; chemistry; civil engineering; communication; computer science; economics; education; electrical engineering; elementary education; engineering (general); English; guidance and counseling; history; industrial engineering; journalism; Latin American studies; (pre)law sequence; management information systems; mathematics; mechanical engineering; medical technology; (pre)medicine sequence; ministries; music; music business; music education; pastoral studies; philosophy; physics; political science/government; psychology; radio and television studies; science; secondary education; sociology; Spanish; speech pathology and audiology; speech/rhetoric/public address/debate. Most popular majors of class of 1991: elementary education, engineering (general), business administration/commerce/management.

SPECIAL NOTE FROM THE COLLEGE Founded in 1848, Geneva is one of the oldest evangelical Christian colleges in the nation, the second oldest in the Christian College Coalition. It offers an education that articulates the implications of Christ's sovereignty over all his creation. Geneva is one of 14 model sites chosen for the Christian College Coalition Racial and Ethnic Diversity Project. Students of color are encouraged to explore educational opportunities at Geneva. Majors include engineering, speech pathology, and cardiovascular technology. Through a cooperative program, students can combine degrees in aviation, air traffic control, or aerospace management with a business degree. All students complete a core program, which integrates courses in history, music, art, literature, and culture with biblical Christianity. Cocurricular activities include intercollegiate programs in all major sports, theater, choir, an FM radio station, and marching and concert bands. Although Geneva seeks students with a biblical world/life view, all students are welcome.

CONTACT Dr. Bill Katip, Vice-President for Enrollment Management, Geneva College, 3200 College Avenue, Beaver Falls, PA 15010, 412-847-6506 or toll-free 800-847-2428 (in-state), 800-847-8255 (out-of-state).

GEORGE FOX COLLEGE

Newberg, Oregon

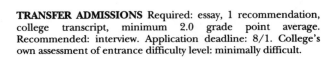

Total Enrollment: 1,222
UG Enrollment: 1,137 (56% W)
Application Deadline: 8/1
Tuition & Fees: $9940
Room & Board: $3600
Entrance: moderately difficult
SAT ≥ 500: 35% V, 39% M
ACT ≥ 21: N/R
Denominational Affiliation: Evangelical Friends

GENERAL INFORMATION Independent comprehensive coed institution. Founded 1891. Awards B, M, D. Primary accreditation: regional. Small-town setting, with easy access to Portland; 60-acre campus. Total enrollment: 1,222. Faculty: 88 (52 full-time, 36 part-time); 73% of full-time faculty have terminal degrees; graduate assistants teach no undergraduate courses. Library holdings: 113,000 bound volumes, 1,310 titles on microform, 557 periodical subscriptions, 1,042 records/tapes/CDs. Computer terminals/PCs available for student use: 83, located in computer center, library. New students receive an Apple Macintosh computer to use while a student and keep after they graduate.

UNDERGRADUATE PROFILE Fall 1991: 1,137 undergraduates (264 freshmen) from 22 states and territories and 16 foreign countries; 3% part-time; 72% state residents; 20% transfers; 86% financial aid recipients; 56% women; 1% African Americans; 1% Native Americans; 1% Hispanics; 1% Asian Americans; 4% international students; 30% of undergraduates 25 years of age or older.

1991 FRESHMAN DATA 5 freshmen were National Merit Scholarship Finalists; all received a National Merit Scholarship. 19% of freshmen were in top 10% of secondary school class, 42% were in top 25%, 78% were in top half.

ENROLLMENT PATTERNS 75% of fall 1990 freshmen returned for fall 1991 term. 40% of 1986 freshmen graduated within 5 years; 25% of students completing a degree program went on for further study.

FRESHMAN ADMISSIONS Options: early entrance, deferred entrance. Required: essay, high school transcript, 1 recommendation, SAT or ACT, TOEFL (for foreign students), WPCT. Recommended: 3 years of high school math and science, some high school foreign language. Required for some: interview. Test scores used for admission and counseling/placement. Application deadline: 8/1. College's own assessment of entrance difficulty level: moderately difficult.

TRANSFER ADMISSIONS Required: essay, 1 recommendation, college transcript, minimum 2.0 grade point average. Recommended: interview. Application deadline: 8/1. College's own assessment of entrance difficulty level: minimally difficult.

EXPENSES (1992–93) Comprehensive fee of $13,540 includes full-time tuition ($9800), mandatory fees ($140), and college room and board ($3600). Part-time tuition: $305 per semester hour.

FINANCIAL AID College-administered aid for all 1991–92 undergraduates: 398 need-based scholarships (average $1580); 987 non-need scholarships (average $773); low-interest long-term loans from external sources (average $2509); SEOG; College Work-Study; 119 part-time jobs. Supporting data: AFSA/SAR required; IRS required for some; FFS, FAF, state form, SINGLEFILE form of United Student Aid Funds acceptable. Priority application deadline: 8/1.

CAMPUS LIFE/STUDENT SERVICES Mandatory chapel; drama/theater group; student-run newspaper and radio station. Institution provides health clinic, personal/psychological counseling.

STUDY ABROAD SITES Egypt, Israel, Spain, Italy, Mexico, Guatemala, Australia, France, Greece, the Netherlands, Germany, Great Britain, Switzerland, Commonwealth of Independent States (USSR), Costa Rica, China, Japan.

ATHLETICS Member NAIA. Intercollegiate sports: baseball (M), basketball M(s), W(s); cross-country running M(s), W(s); soccer M(s), W(s); softball (W); track and field M(s), W(s); volleyball W(s). Intramural sports: badminton, basketball, football, racquetball, soccer, table tennis (Ping Pong), tennis, volleyball, weight lifting.

MAJORS Biblical studies; biology/biological sciences; broadcasting; business administration/commerce/management; business economics; chemistry; civil engineering; communication; computer engineering; computer information systems; computer science; (pre)dentistry sequence; economics; education; electrical engineering; elementary education; engineering (general); engineering sciences; English; history; home economics; home economics education; human resources; interdisciplinary studies; international studies; (pre)law sequence; liberal arts/general studies; literature; mathematics; (pre)medicine sequence; ministries; music; music education; physical education; psychology; religious studies; science; science education; secondary education; social work; sociology; sports medicine; telecommunications; (pre)veterinary medicine sequence. Most popular majors of class of 1991: education, business administration/management, sociology.

SPECIAL NOTE FROM THE COLLEGE Freedom or faith. A college decision may seem like a choice between the two: sacrifice your faith or put your mind on the shelf. At George Fox College, academic freedom and Christian faith go hand in hand. Students find faculty members who encourage questions, who value their uniqueness, and who challenge them to explore truth from a foundation of faith. Students find a community of friends who accept them as they are, not as they are "supposed to be." Graduates of George Fox leave with more than a competitive degree from a well-respected school. They leave with the ability to think critically, to express themselves, and to take their faith into today's world. At George Fox College, students have the freedom to think and the freedom to believe.

CONTACT Mr. Randy Comfort, Director of Admissions, George Fox College, Newberg, OR 97132, 503-538-8383 Ext. 235.

GORDON COLLEGE

Wenham, Massachusetts

Total Enrollment: 1,216 (all UG)

Women: 59%

Application Deadline: rolling

Tuition & Fees: $12,090

Room & Board: $3750

Entrance: moderately difficult

SAT ≥ 500: 46% V, 56% M

ACT ≥ 21: N/R

Denominational Affiliation: interdenominational

GENERAL INFORMATION Independent 4-year coed college. Founded 1889. Awards B. Primary accreditation: regional. Small-town setting, with easy access to Boston; 730-acre campus. Total enrollment: 1,216. Faculty: 101 (66 full-time, 35 part-time); 79% of full-time faculty have terminal degrees. Library holdings: 220,000 bound volumes, 22,500 titles on microform, 8,000 records/tapes/CDs. Computer terminals/PCs available for student use: 78, located in computer center, library.

UNDERGRADUATE PROFILE Fall 1991: 1,216 undergraduates (283 freshmen) from 41 states and territories and 10 foreign countries; 4% part-time; 36% state residents; 21% transfers; 80% financial aid recipients; 59% women; 3% African Americans; 0% Native Americans; 3% Hispanics; 4% Asian Americans; 3% international students; 1% of undergraduates 25 years of age or older.

1991 FRESHMAN DATA 555 students applied for fall 1991 admission; 91% were accepted; 56% of those accepted enrolled. 24% of freshmen were in top 10% of secondary school class, 63% were in top 25%, 85% were in top half.

ENROLLMENT PATTERNS 80% of fall 1990 freshmen returned for fall 1991 term. 61% of 1986 freshmen graduated within 5 years.

FRESHMAN ADMISSIONS Options: early entrance, early decision, deferred entrance. Required: essay, high school transcript, 1 recommendation, interview, SAT or ACT, TOEFL (for foreign students). Recommended: 3 years of high school math and science, 3 years of high school foreign language, Achievement Tests. Test scores used for admission. Application

deadlines: rolling, 12/15 for early decision. College's own assessment of entrance difficulty level: moderately difficult.

TRANSFER ADMISSIONS Required: essay, standardized test scores, 1 recommendation, interview, college transcript. Recommended: high school transcript, 3 years of high school math and science, 3 years of high school foreign language, minimum 2.0 grade point average. Application deadline: rolling. College's own assessment of entrance difficulty level: moderately difficult.

EXPENSES (1992–93) Comprehensive fee of $15,840 includes full-time tuition ($11,600), mandatory fees ($490), and college room and board ($3750). College room only: $2350 (minimum). Tuition prepayment plan available.

FINANCIAL AID College-administered aid for all 1991–92 undergraduates: 729 need-based scholarships (average $3758); 463 non-need scholarships (average $2669); short-term loans (average $50); low-interest long-term loans from external sources (average $2464); SEOG; College Work-Study; 220 part-time jobs. Supporting data: FAF, state form, institutional form, AFSA/SAR required; IRS required for some; FFS acceptable. Priority application deadline: 3/15.

CAMPUS LIFE/STUDENT SERVICES Mandatory chapel; drama/theater group; student-run newspaper. Institution provides health clinic, personal/psychological counseling.

STUDY ABROAD SITES Israel, Commonwealth of Independent States (USSR), France, Germany, Greece, Switzerland, Scandanavia, England, Belgium, Italy, Austria, Kenya, Spain, Japan.

ATHLETICS Member NCAA (Division III). Intercollegiate sports: baseball M; basketball M, W; cross-country running M, W; field hockey W; ice hockey M(c); lacrosse M(c); soccer M, W; softball W; tennis M, W; volleyball W. Intramural sports: basketball, football, ice hockey, skiing (cross-country), skiing (downhill), soccer, volleyball.

MAJORS Accounting; biblical studies; biology/biological sciences; business administration/commerce/management; business economics; chemistry; computer science; early childhood education; economics; education; elementary education; English; French; German; history; international affairs; (pre)law sequence; linguistics; mathematics; (pre)medicine sequence; ministries; music; music education; philosophy; physical fitness/human movement; physics; political science/government; psychology; recreation and leisure services; social work; sociology; Spanish; special education. Most popular majors of class of 1991: education, business administration/commerce/management, English.

SPECIAL NOTE FROM THE COLLEGE Gordon College, located on a wooded 730-acre campus 25 miles north of Boston, is New England's leading Christian liberal arts college. Described by *New York Times* education editor Edward B. Fiske as a "major intellectual bastion of Protestant evangelicalism," Gordon has won widespread recognition for quality. For example, Gordon's cooperative education program, through which students may alternate 6 months of study with 6 months of paid employment, has been ranked 2nd out of 381 such programs by the US Department of Education. The Academy for Educational Development has ranked Gordon's faculty development programs among the top 10 in the nation for attracting and retaining young, highly competent faculty members. Also, along with only 2 other Massachusetts schools, Gordon is profiled in Times Books' *The Best Buys in College Education*, a consumer's guide to 221 colleges that offer high-quality education at a reasonable cost.

CONTACT Mr. Mark Sylvester, Dean of Admissions and Financial Aid, Gordon College, 225 Grapevine Road, Wenham, MA 01984, 508-927-2306 Ext. 4217 or toll-free 800-343-1379.

GOSHEN COLLEGE

Goshen, Indiana

Total Enrollment: 1,117 (all UG)

Women: 55%

Application Deadline: rolling

Tuition & Fees: $8310

Room & Board: $3500

Entrance: moderately difficult

SAT ≥ 500: 43% V, 54% M

ACT ≥ 21: N/R

Denominational Affiliation: Mennonite

GENERAL INFORMATION Independent 4-year coed college. Founded 1894. Awards B. Primary accreditation: regional. Small-town setting; 135-acre campus. Total enrollment: 1,117. Faculty: 125 (85 full-time, 40 part-time); 63% of full-time faculty have terminal degrees. Library holdings: 120,000 bound volumes, 100 titles on microform, 800 periodical subscriptions, 1,500 records/tapes/CDs. Computer terminals/PCs available for student use: 75, located in computer center, dormitories.

UNDERGRADUATE PROFILE Fall 1991: 1,117 undergraduates (209 freshmen) from 35 states and territories and 29 foreign countries; 10% part-time; 41% state residents; 9% transfers; 86% financial aid recipients; 55% women; 5% African Americans; 0% Native Americans; 3% Hispanics; 1% Asian Americans; 7% international students; 14% of undergraduates 25 years of age or older.

1991 FRESHMAN DATA 442 students applied for fall 1991 admission; 88% were accepted; 51% of those accepted enrolled. 4 freshmen were National Merit Scholarship Finalists; all received a National Merit Scholarship. 25% of freshmen were in top 10% of secondary school class, 53% were in top 25%, 81% were in top half.

ENROLLMENT PATTERNS 81% of fall 1990 freshmen returned for fall 1991 term.

FRESHMAN ADMISSIONS Options: early entrance, deferred entrance. Required: high school transcript, 1 recommendation, SAT or ACT, TOEFL (for foreign students). Recommended: 3 years of high school math and science, some high school foreign language, interview. Test scores used for admission. Application deadline: rolling. Notification date: continuous. College's own assessment of entrance difficulty level: moderately difficult.

TRANSFER ADMISSIONS Required: high school transcript, 2 recommendations, college transcript, minimum 2.0 grade point

average. Recommended: 3 years of high school math and science, some high school foreign language, interview. Application deadline: rolling. Notification date: continuous. College's own assessment of entrance difficulty level: moderately difficult.

EXPENSES (1992–93) Comprehensive fee of $11,810 includes full-time tuition ($8310) and college room and board ($3500). College room only: $1660. Part-time tuition: ranges from $190 to $320 per credit hour.

FINANCIAL AID College-administered aid for all 1991–92 undergraduates: 781 need-based scholarships (average $770); 1,212 non-need scholarships (average $911); low-interest long-term loans from college funds (average $1518), from external sources (average $2020); SEOG; College Work-Study; 60 part-time jobs. Supporting data: FAF, institutional form required; IRS form required for some; FFS, AFSA/SAR acceptable. Priority application deadline: 3/1.

CAMPUS LIFE/STUDENT SERVICES Mandatory chapel; drama/theater group; student-run newspaper and radio station. Institution provides health clinic, personal/psychological counseling, women's center.

STUDY ABROAD SITES Dominican Republic, Germany, Costa Rica, Ivory Coast.

ATHLETICS Member NAIA. Intercollegiate sports: basketball M, W; cross-country running M, W; golf M; soccer M, W; softball W; tennis M, W; track and field M, W; volleyball W. Intramural sports: badminton, basketball, cross-country running, skiing (cross-country), soccer, softball, table tennis (Ping Pong), tennis, volleyball.

MAJORS Accounting; anthropology; art education; art/fine arts; art therapy; biblical studies; bilingual/bicultural education; biology/biological sciences; broadcasting; business administration/commerce/management; business education; chemistry; child care/child and family studies; communication; computer information systems; computer science; (pre)dentistry sequence; dietetics; early childhood education; economics; education; elementary education; English; family services; German; Hispanic studies; history; journalism; (pre)law sequence; liberal arts/general studies; mathematics; (pre)medicine sequence; music; music education; natural sciences; nursing; nutrition; physical education; physical sciences; physics; political science/government; psychology; religious studies; science education; secondary education; social work; sociology; Spanish; teaching English as a second language; theater arts/drama; (pre)veterinary medicine sequence. Most popular majors of class of 1991: business administration/commerce/management, nursing, elementary education.

SPECIAL NOTE FROM THE COLLEGE With its internationally recognized Study-Service Term, Goshen was the first college to require international education of all of its students. More than 80% of GC students spend 13 weeks on SST in a "significantly different" country, usually at the same cost as a term on campus. Students study the local culture, which is followed by service work that is often related to the student's major. GC is 1 of 3 schools with less than 1,200 students included in the Pew Science Program in Undergraduate Education. The Schrock Science Annex, with new laboratories and classrooms for all of the sciences, is also home to the Turner Precision X-Ray Laboratory, the first of its kind in the nation.

CONTACT Ms. Martha Hooley, Director of Admissions, Goshen College, 1700 South Main Street, Goshen, IN 46526, 219-535-7535 or toll-free 800-348-7422.

GRACE COLLEGE

Winona Lake, Indiana

Total Enrollment: 652 (all UG)

Women: 56%

Application Deadline: 8/1

Tuition & Fees: $7632

Room & Board: $3430

Entrance: moderately difficult

SAT ≥ 500: N/App

ACT ≥ 21: 66%

Denominational Affiliation: Fellowship of Grace Brethren Churches

GENERAL INFORMATION Independent 4-year coed college. Administratively affiliated with Grace Theological Seminary. Founded 1948. Awards A (terminal), B. Primary accreditation: regional. Small-town setting; 150-acre campus. Total enrollment: 652. Faculty: 61 (30 full-time, 31 part-time); graduate assistants teach a few undergraduate courses. Library holdings: 142,300 bound volumes, 600 periodical subscriptions, 6,750 records/tapes/CDs. Computer terminals/PCs available for student use: 38, located in computer center, library.

UNDERGRADUATE PROFILE Fall 1991: 652 undergraduates (127 freshmen) from 40 states and territories and 13 foreign countries; 15% part-time; 46% state residents; 7% transfers; 85% financial aid recipients; 56% women; 1% African Americans; 1% Native Americans; 0% Hispanics; 0% Asian Americans; 2% international students; 6% of undergraduates 25 years of age or older.

1991 FRESHMAN DATA 360 students applied for fall 1991 admission; 84% were accepted; 42% of those accepted enrolled. 23% of freshmen were in top 10% of secondary school class, 45% were in top 25%, 70% were in top half.

ENROLLMENT PATTERNS 69% of fall 1990 freshmen returned for fall 1991 term. 34% of 1986 freshmen graduated within 5 years.

FRESHMAN ADMISSIONS Options: early entrance, deferred entrance. Required: high school transcript, 3 recommendations, SAT or ACT. Recommended: some high school foreign language. Required for some: 3 years of high school math and science, interview. Test scores used for admission. Application deadline: 8/1. Notification date: continuous until 8/15. College's own assessment of entrance difficulty level: moderately difficult.

TRANSFER ADMISSIONS Required: high school transcript, 3 recommendations, college transcript, minimum 2.0 grade point average. Recommended: some high school foreign language. Required for some: 3 years of high school math and science, interview. Application deadline: 8/1. Notification date: continuous until 8/15. College's own assessment of entrance difficulty level: moderately difficult.

EXPENSES (1992–93) Comprehensive fee of $11,062 includes full-time tuition ($7312), mandatory fees ($320), and college room and board ($3430). Part-time tuition: ranges from $132 to $2522.

FINANCIAL AID College-administered aid for all 1991–92 undergraduates: 265 need-based scholarships (average $1650); non-need scholarships (average $1250); low-interest long-term loans from college funds (average $300), from external sources (average $2200); SEOG; College Work-Study; 220 part-time jobs. Supporting data: FAF, institutional form, AFSA/SAR required; FFS, IRS acceptable. Priority application deadline: 4/1.

CAMPUS LIFE/STUDENT SERVICES Dress code; mandatory chapel; drama/theater group; student-run newspaper. Institution provides health clinic, personal/psychological counseling.

STUDY ABROAD SITES France, Spain, Mexico, Germany.

ATHLETICS Member NAIA. Intercollegiate sports: baseball M(s); basketball M(s), W(s); golf M(s); soccer M(s); softball W(s); tennis M(s); volleyball W(s). Intramural sports: basketball, football, volleyball.

MAJORS Accounting; art education; art/fine arts; behavioral sciences; biblical languages; biblical studies; biology/biological sciences; business administration/commerce/management; commercial art; communication; criminal justice; elementary education; English; French; German; graphic arts; Greek; (pre)law sequence; mathematics; (pre)medicine sequence; music; music education; physical education; piano/organ; psychology; sacred music; science education; secretarial studies/office management; sociology; Spanish; speech/rhetoric/public address/debate. Most popular majors of class of 1991: psychology, elementary education, business administration/commerce/management.

SPECIAL NOTE FROM THE COLLEGE Grace College offers an opportunity for students to discover and develop personal interests and crucial, life-guiding values. Highly qualified professors, aggressive learning, and fully integrated biblical presuppositions are the foundation of Grace and lead to meaningful career/ministry action. The combination of a strong academic program and a host of creative on-campus activities aimed at cultivating proper interpersonal relationships serve to prepare students for life after college. Throughout each student's college experience, from personal assistance in receiving financial aid to careful help in career/ministry placement upon graduation, Grace College is dedicated to providing high-quality, personalized service.

CONTACT Mr. Ron Henry, Director of Enrollment Administration, Grace College, 200 Seminary Drive, Winona Lake, IN 46590, 219-372-5144 or toll-free 800-54 GRACE.

GRAND CANYON UNIVERSITY

Phoenix, Arizona

Total Enrollment: 1,745

UG Enrollment: 1,641 (61% W)

Application Deadline: rolling

Tuition & Fees: $6290 (estimated)

Room & Board: $2800 (estimated)

Entrance: moderately difficult

SAT ≥ 500: N/R

ACT ≥ 21: 38%

Denominational Affiliation: Southern Baptist

GENERAL INFORMATION Independent comprehensive coed institution. Founded 1949. Awards B, M. Primary accreditation: regional. Suburban setting; 70-acre campus. Total enrollment: 1,745. Faculty: 132 (66 full-time, 66 part-time); 53% of full-time faculty have terminal degrees; graduate assistants teach no undergraduate courses. Library holdings: 120,000 bound volumes, 34,200 titles on microform, 635 periodical subscriptions, 4,100 records/tapes/CDs. Computer terminals/PCs available for student use: 60, located in computer center, library, audiovisual lab.

UNDERGRADUATE PROFILE Fall 1991: 1,641 undergraduates (240 freshmen) from 35 states and territories and 6 foreign countries; 24% part-time; 87% state residents; 62% transfers; 85% financial aid recipients; 61% women; 4% African Americans; 3% Native Americans; 5% Hispanics; 1% Asian Americans; 3% international students; 17% of undergraduates 25 years of age or older.

1991 FRESHMAN DATA 1009 students applied for fall 1991 admission; 83% were accepted; 66% of those accepted enrolled. 20% of freshmen were in top 10% of secondary school class, 40% were in top 25%, 85% were in top half.

ENROLLMENT PATTERNS 85% of fall 1990 freshmen returned for fall 1991 term. 22% of 1986 freshmen graduated within 5 years.

FRESHMAN ADMISSIONS Option: early entrance. Required: essay, high school transcript, SAT or ACT, TOEFL (for foreign students). Recommended: 3 years of high school math and science, some high school foreign language. Required for some: 3 recommendations, campus interview. Test scores used for admission and counseling/placement. Application deadline: rolling. Notification date: continuous. College's own assessment of entrance difficulty level: moderately difficult.

TRANSFER ADMISSIONS Required: essay, college transcript, minimum 2.0 grade point average. Recommended: standardized test scores, high school transcript, 3 years of high school math and science, some high school foreign language. Required for some: 3 recommendations, campus interview. Application deadline: rolling. Notification date: continuous until 8/15. College's own assessment of entrance difficulty level: moderately difficult.

EXPENSES (1992–93 estimated) Comprehensive fee of $9090 includes full-time tuition ($5940), mandatory fees ($350), and college room and board ($2800). Part-time tuition: $198 per semester hour.

FINANCIAL AID College-administered aid for all 1991–92 undergraduates: 720 need-based scholarships (average $923); 459 non-need scholarships (average $2790); short-term loans (average $300); low-interest long-term loans from external sources (average $3237); SEOG; College Work-Study; 64 part-time jobs. Supporting data: institutional form, SINGLEFILE Form of United Student Aid Funds required; IRS required for some; FFS, FAF, state form, AFSA/SAR acceptable. Priority application deadline: 3/15.

CAMPUS LIFE/STUDENT SERVICES Mandatory chapel; drama/theater group; student-run newspaper. Institution provides health clinic, personal/psychological counseling.

STUDY ABROAD SITES China, Brazil, Spain, Hungary, Commonwealth of Independent States (USSR).

ATHLETICS Member NCAA (Division II). Intercollegiate sports: baseball M; basketball M(s), W(s); cross-country running M(s), W(s); golf M(s); soccer M(s); tennis W(s); volleyball W(s). Intramural sports: basketball, football, volleyball.

MAJORS Accounting; art education; art/fine arts; biblical studies; biology/biological sciences; business administration/commerce/management; business economics; business education; chemistry; communication; computer science; criminal justice; (pre)dentistry sequence; economics; elementary education; English; environmental biology; finance/banking; graphic arts; history; human resources; international business; (pre)law sequence; liberal arts/general studies; literature; marketing/retailing/merchandising; mathematics; (pre)medicine sequence; ministries; music; music business; music education; nursing; physical education; piano/organ; psychology; religious studies; sacred music; science education; secondary education; social science; sociology; Spanish; special education; speech/rhetoric/public address/debate; studio art; theater arts/drama; theology; (pre)veterinary medicine sequence; voice; wind and percussion instruments. Most popular majors of class of 1991: elementary education, nursing, psychology.

SPECIAL NOTE FROM THE COLLEGE Canyon just keeps getting better. Included in the University's top 10 for 1991–92: (1) it had its 3rd consecutive listing among *U.S. News & World Report*'s "Up and Coming" universities; (2) the University's women's tennis players became NCAA Division II doubles champs and the only western regional NCAA Division II academic all-Americans; (3) there was 100% placement of premed grads; (4) 100% of nursing grads passed the state licensing exam for the 5th straight year; (5) there was 95% placement of education grads; (6) there was an overwhelming response to the new MBA program; (7) international exchanges occurred with 10 countries; (8) 500 students and staff visited approximately 35 countries; (9) there were 3 conference/region coaches-of-the-year; (10) and there were 3 teams in national postseason play.

CONTACT Ms. Sherri Willborn, Director of Admissions and Enrollment Planning, Grand Canyon University, 3300 W. Camelback Road, P.O. Box 11097, Phoenix, AZ 85017, 602-589-2855.

GRAND RAPIDS BAPTIST COLLEGE AND SEMINARY

Grand Rapids, Michigan

Total Enrollment: 925

UG Enrollment: 787 (55% W)

Application Deadline: rolling

Tuition & Fees: $5920

Room & Board: $3738

Entrance: minimally difficult

SAT ≥ 500: N/App

ACT ≥ 21: 57%

Denominational Affiliation: Baptist

GENERAL INFORMATION Independent 4-year coed college. Founded 1941. Awards A (terminal), B, M. Primary accreditation: regional. Suburban setting; 132-acre campus. Total enrollment: 925. Faculty: 60 (34 full-time, 26 part-time); 35% of full-time faculty have terminal degrees; graduate assistants teach a few undergraduate courses. Library holdings: 89,542 bound volumes, 55 titles on microform, 652 periodical subscriptions, 3,200 records/tapes/CDs. Computer terminals/PCs available for student use: 34, located in computer center.

UNDERGRADUATE PROFILE Fall 1991: 787 undergraduates (208 freshmen) from 25 states and territories and 4 foreign countries; 10% part-time; 78% state residents; 11% transfers; 79% financial aid recipients; 55% women; 1% African Americans; 0% Native Americans; 1% Hispanics; 0% Asian Americans; 1% international students; 12% of undergraduates 25 years of age or older.

1991 FRESHMAN DATA 284 students applied for fall 1991 admission; 99% were accepted; 74% of those accepted enrolled. 2 freshmen were National Merit Scholarship Finalists, 1 received a National Merit Scholarship. 20% of freshmen were in top 10% of secondary school class, 45% were in top 25%, 74% were in top half.

ENROLLMENT PATTERNS 66% of fall 1990 freshmen returned for fall 1991 term. 31% of 1986 freshmen graduated within 5 years. 14% of students completing a bachelor's program went on for further study.

FRESHMAN ADMISSIONS Preference given to applicants with clear Christian testimony. Options: early entrance, deferred entrance. Required: essay, high school transcript, 1 recommendation, ACT, TOEFL (for foreign students). Recommended: 3 years of high school math and science, 2 years of high school foreign language, interview. Test scores used for admission and interview counseling/placement. Application deadline: rolling. College's own assessment of entrance difficulty level: minimally difficult.

TRANSFER ADMISSIONS Required: essay, standardized test scores, high school transcript, 1 recommendation, college transcript, minimum 2.0 grade point average. Recommended: 3 years of high school math and science, 2 years of high school foreign language, interview. Application deadline: rolling.

EXPENSES (1992–93) Comprehensive fee of $9658 includes full-time tuition ($5550), mandatory fees ($370), and college room and board ($3738). Part-time tuition: $213 per semester hour.

FINANCIAL AID College-administered aid for all 1991–92 undergraduates: 405 need-based scholarships (average $1361); 77 non-need scholarships (average $981); low-interest long-term loans from college funds (average $1540), from external sources (average $2226); SEOG; College Work-Study; 230 part-time jobs. Supporting data: FAF, IRS required; state form required for some; FFS, AFSA/SAR acceptable. Priority application deadline: 3/1.

CAMPUS LIFE/STUDENT SERVICES Dress code, mandatory chapel; drama/theater group; student-run newspaper, yearbook. Institution provides health clinic, personal/psychological counseling.

ATHLETICS Member NAIA and NCCAA. Intercollegiate sports: baseball M(s); basketball M(s), W(s); cross-country running M, W; golf M(s); soccer M(s); softball W(s); tennis M(s); volleyball W(s). Intramural sports: basketball, football, soccer, volleyball.

MAJORS Accounting; biblical languages; biblical studies; biology/ biological sciences; broadcasting; business administration/ commerce/management; business education; communication; computer information systems; education; elementary education; English; history; interdisciplinary studies; (pre)law sequence; marketing/retailing/merchandising; music; music education; pastoral studies; physical education; psychology; religious education; religious studies; science education; secondary education; secretarial studies/office management; social work; sociology; speech/rhetoric/public address/debate. Most popular majors of class of 1991: business administration/commerce/ management, biblical studies, education.

SPECIAL NOTE FROM THE COLLEGE Grand Rapids Baptist College is unique for its internships. While most colleges have internship programs for some majors, GRBC requires and arranges a practical internship for every student in all of its majors. The school's location as a small college in a large metropolitan area makes it possible for each student to have high-quality, on-the-job experience before graduation. A major aim of the internship program is to allow students the opportunity to put their Christianity into practice in real-world circumstances. This unique feature provides the student with excellent preparation for life and for work after graduation.

CONTACT Mrs. Kay Landrum, Director of Admissions, Grand Rapids Baptist College and Seminary, 1001 East Beltline Avenue, NE, Grand Rapids, MI 49505, 616-949-5300 Ext. 426 or toll-free 800-968-GRBC.

GREENVILLE COLLEGE

Greenville, Illinois

Total Enrollment: 893 (all UG)

Women: 45%

Application Deadline: rolling

Tuition & Fees: $8860

Room & Board: $3730

Entrance: moderately difficult

SAT ≥ 500: 54% V; 68% M

ACT ≥ 21: 49%

Denominational Affiliation: Free Methodist

GENERAL INFORMATION Independent 4-year coed college. Founded 1892. Awards B. Primary accreditation: regional. Small-town setting, with easy access to St. Louis; 12-acre campus. Total enrollment: 893. Faculty: 61 (54 full-time, 7 part-time); 47% of full-time faculty have terminal degrees; graduate assistants teach a few undergraduate courses. Library holdings: 114,059 bound volumes, 2,963 titles on microform, 545 periodical subscriptions, 1,702 records/tapes/CDs. Computer terminals/PCs available for student use: 48, located in computer center, library.

UNDERGRADUATE PROFILE Fall 1991: 893 undergraduates (201 freshmen) from 39 states and territories and 10 foreign countries; 8% part-time; 58% state residents; 10% transfers; 90% financial aid recipients; 45% women; 6% African Americans; 0% Native Americans; 1% Hispanics; 1% Asian Americans; 2% international students; 8% of undergraduates 25 years of age or older.

1991 FRESHMAN DATA 479 students applied for fall 1991 admission; 71% were accepted; 59% of those accepted enrolled. 22% of freshmen were in top 10% of secondary school class, 44% were in top 25%, 68% were in top half.

ENROLLMENT PATTERNS 70% of fall 1990 freshmen returned for fall 1991 term. 49% of 1986 freshmen graduated within 5 years; 20% of students completing a degree program went on for further study.

FRESHMAN ADMISSIONS Options: early entrance, deferred entrance. Required: high school transcript, 2 recommendations, agreement to code of conduct, SAT or ACT, TOEFL (for foreign students). Recommended: 3 years of high school foreign language. Required for some: interview. Test scores used for counseling/placement. Application deadline: rolling. College's own assessment of entrance difficulty level: moderately difficult.

TRANSFER ADMISSIONS Required: standardized test scores, 2 recommendations, college transcript, minimum 2.0 grade point average, agreement to code of conduct. Recommended: high school transcript, 3 years of high school foreign language. Required for some: interview. Application deadline: rolling. College's own assessment of entrance difficulty level: moderately difficult.

EXPENSES (1991–92) Comprehensive fee of $12,590 includes full-time tuition ($8740), mandatory fees ($120), and college room and board ($3730). Part-time tuition: $261 per credit hour.

FINANCIAL AID College-administered aid for all 1991–92 undergraduates: 665 need-based scholarships (average $2910); 83 non-need scholarships (average $1970); low-interest long-term loans from college funds (average $1500), from external sources (average $2830); SEOG; College Work-Study; 106 part-time jobs. Supporting data: FAF required; IRS required for some. Priority application deadline: 6/1.

CAMPUS LIFE/STUDENT SERVICES Mandatory chapel; drama/theater group; student-run newspaper and radio station. Institution provides personal/psychological counseling.

ATHLETICS Member NAIA. Intercollegiate sports: basketball M, W; cross-country running M, W; football M; golf M; soccer M, W; tennis M, W; track and field M, W; volleyball W. Intramural sports: badminton, basketball, football, table tennis (Ping Pong), volleyball.

MAJORS Accounting; art education; art/fine arts; biblical studies; biology/biological sciences; business administration/commerce/management; business education; chemistry; communication; computer science; (pre)dentistry sequence; early childhood education; economics; education; elementary education; English; French; gerontology; history; (pre)law sequence; liberal arts/general studies; management information systems; marketing/retailing/merchandising; mathematics; medical technology; (pre)medicine sequence; ministries; modern languages; music; music education; pastoral studies; philosophy; physical education; physics; political science/government; psychology; recreation and leisure services; religious studies; sacred music; secondary education; social work; sociology; Spanish; special education; speech/rhetoric/public address/debate; theater arts/drama; theology; (pre)veterinary medicine sequence. Most popular majors of class of 1991: education, business administration/commerce/management, biology/biological sciences.

SPECIAL NOTE FROM THE COLLEGE Greenville College is located just 50 minutes east of downtown St. Louis, in beautiful central Illinois. Established in 1892, Greenville is fully accredited. Greenville has structured a thoroughly evangelical environment that supports and encourages growth of the whole person—spiritually, academically, and socially. Greenville graduates excel. For example, alumnus James Buick is president of Zondervan Corporation; Bob Briner is president of ProServ Television; Chaz Corzine is vice president of Blanton/Herrell, Inc. (the talent management firm of Amy Grant and Michael W. Smith); Dr. Ernest Boyer, former US Commissioner of Education, is currently president of the Carnegie Foundation for the Advancement of Teaching; and hundreds of other graduates are teachers, doctors, businesspeople, missionaries, and laypeople in churches all over the world. Greenville College graduates are making a difference.

CONTACT Dr. Kent Krober, Dean of Admissions, Greenville College, 315 East College, Greenville, IL 62246, 618-664-1840 Ext. 218 or toll-free 800-248-2288 (in-state), 800-345-4440 (out-of-state).

HOUGHTON COLLEGE

Houghton, New York

Total Enrollment: 1,146 (all UG)

Women: 62%

Application Deadline: 8/1

Tuition & Fees: $9230

Room & Board: $3260

Entrance: moderately difficult

SAT ≥ 500: 50% V, 68% M

ACT ≥ 21: 76%

Denominational Affiliation: Wesleyan

GENERAL INFORMATION Independent 4-year coed college. Founded 1883. Awards A (college transfer), B. Primary accreditation: regional. Rural setting, with easy access to Buffalo and Rochester; 1,300-acre campus. Total enrollment: 1,146. Faculty: 100 (64 full-time, 36 part-time); 69% of full-time faculty have terminal degrees; graduate assistants teach no undergraduate courses. Library holdings: 206,731 bound volumes, 398 titles on microform, 624 periodical subscriptions, 5,842 records/tapes/CDs. Computer terminals/PCs available for student use: 130, located in computer center, library, dormitories, computer lab, divisional offices.

UNDERGRADUATE PROFILE Fall 1991: 1,146 undergraduates (247 freshmen) from 26 states and territories and 24 foreign countries; 4% part-time; 64% state residents; 5% transfers; 91% financial aid recipients; 62% women; 2% African Americans; 1% Native Americans; 1% Hispanics; 1% Asian Americans; 5% international students; 5% of undergraduates 25 years of age or older.

1991 FRESHMAN DATA 638 students applied for fall 1991 admission; 91% were accepted; 42% of those accepted enrolled. 4 freshmen were National Merit Scholarship Finalists. 29% of freshmen were in top 10% of secondary school class, 56% were in top 25%, 88% were in top half.

ENROLLMENT PATTERNS 88% of fall 1990 freshmen returned for fall 1991 term. 62% of 1986 freshmen graduated within 5 years; 18% of students completing a bachelor's program went on for further study.

FRESHMAN ADMISSIONS Preference given to evangelical Christians. Options: early entrance, deferred entrance. Required: essay, high school transcript, 1 recommendation, pastoral recommendation, SAT or ACT, TOEFL (for foreign students). Recommended: 3 years of high school math, some high school foreign language, interview. Test scores used for admission. Application deadline: 8/1. Notification date: continuous. College's own assessment of entrance difficulty level: moderately difficult.

TRANSFER ADMISSIONS Required: essay, high school transcript, 1 recommendation, college transcript, minimum 2.0 grade point average. Recommended: 3 years of high school math, some high school foreign language, interview. Required for some: standardized test scores. Application deadline: 8/1. Notification date: continuous. College's own assessment of entrance difficulty level: moderately difficult.

EXPENSES (1992–93 estimated) Comprehensive fee of $12,490 includes full-time tuition ($8870 minimum), mandatory fees ($360), and college room and board ($3260). College room only: $1470.

FINANCIAL AID College-administered aid for all 1991–92 undergraduates: 1,241 need-based scholarships (average $1292); 508 non-need scholarships (average $1313); short-term loans (average $500); low-interest long-term loans from external sources (average $2749); SEOG; College Work-Study; 219 part-time jobs. Supporting data: FAF, institutional form required; state form required for some; FFS acceptable. Priority application deadline: 3/15.

CAMPUS LIFE/STUDENT SERVICES Mandatory chapel; drama/theater group; student-run newspaper and radio station. Institution provides health clinic, personal/psychological counseling.

ATHLETICS Member NAIA. Intercollegiate sports: basketball M(s), W(s); cross-country running M(s), W(s); field hockey W(s); soccer M(s), W(s); track and field M(s), W(s); volleyball W(s). Intramural sports: basketball, equestrian sports, football, racquetball, skiing (cross-country), skiing (downhill), soccer, swimming and diving, table tennis (Ping Pong), tennis, volleyball, water polo, weight lifting.

MAJORS Accounting; art education; art/fine arts; biblical studies; biology/biological sciences; business administration/commerce/management; chemistry; communication; creative writing; (pre)dentistry sequence; early childhood education; education; elementary education; (pre)engineering sequence; English; French; history; humanities; international studies; (pre)law sequence; literature; mathematics; medical laboratory technology; medical technology; (pre)medicine sequence; ministries; music; music education; natural sciences; pastoral studies; philosophy; physical education; physical sciences; physics; piano/organ; political science/government; psychology; recreation and leisure services; religious education; religious studies; sacred music; science; science education; secondary education; social science; sociology; Spanish; stringed instruments; (pre)veterinary medicine sequence; voice; wind and percussion instruments. Most popular majors of class of 1991: elementary education, psychology, biblical studies.

SPECIAL NOTE FROM THE COLLEGE For over 100 years Houghton College has provided an educational experience that integrates high academic quality with the Christian faith. The College is fully accredited and rated highly by national college publications. Physical facilities at Houghton include an equestrian farm, comprehensive art studios, downhill and cross-country ski trails, an initiatives ropes course, and 4 major residence halls. Houghton offers 45 majors and programs on 2 campuses. The 1,300-acre Houghton campus in the beautiful countryside of western New York has 1,150 students. Students in programs calling for an urban focus may spend time on the 50-acre suburban campus near Buffalo. Programs in the sciences, education, music, and art are highly respected, and the religion department is rated among the best in the country. Over 100 international students and MKs (missionary's kids) come from over 30 countries to attend Houghton. Internships and study-abroad options are available.

CONTACT Mr. Timothy R. Fuller, Executive Director of Admissions and Alumni, Houghton College, P.O. Box 128, Houghton, NY 14744, 716-567-9353 or toll-free 800-777-2556.

HUNTINGTON COLLEGE

Huntington, Indiana

Total Enrollment: 614

UG Enrollment: 555 (51% W)

Application Deadline: 8/15

Tuition & Fees: $8730

Room & Board: $3480

Entrance: moderately difficult

SAT ≥ 500: 18% V, 21% M

ACT ≥ 21: 16%

Denominational Affiliation: Church of the United Brethren in Christ

GENERAL INFORMATION Independent comprehensive coed institution. Founded 1897. Awards A (college transfer and terminal), B, M. Primary accreditation: regional. Small-town setting; 100-acre campus. Total enrollment: 614. Faculty: 45 (38 full-time, 7 part-time); 66% of full-time faculty have terminal degrees; graduate assistants teach no undergraduate courses. Library holdings: 71,275 bound volumes, 29,352 titles on microform, 487 periodical subscriptions, 1,496 records/tapes/CDs. Computer terminals/PCs available for student use: 52, located in computer center.

UNDERGRADUATE PROFILE Fall 1991: 555 undergraduates (158 freshmen) from 18 states and territories and 13 foreign countries; 9% part-time; 65% state residents; 6% transfers; 92% financial aid recipients; 51% women; 1% African Americans; 0% Native Americans; 0% Hispanics; 1% Asian Americans; 8% international students; 13% of undergraduates 25 years of age or older.

1991 FRESHMAN DATA 721 students applied for fall 1991 admission; 78% were accepted; 28% of those accepted enrolled. 3 freshmen were National Merit Scholarship Finalists. 14% of freshmen were in top 10% of secondary school class, 39% were in top 25%, 77% were in top half.

ENROLLMENT PATTERNS 66% of fall 1990 freshmen returned for fall 1991 term. 70% of 1986 freshmen graduated within 5 years. 50% of students completing a college-transfer associate program went on to 4-year colleges; 12% of students completing a bachelor's program went on for further study.

FRESHMAN ADMISSIONS Options: early entrance, deferred entrance. Required: high school transcript, SAT or ACT, TOEFL (for foreign students). Recommended: 3 years of high school math and science, 1 year of high school foreign language. Test scores used for counseling/placement. Application deadline: 8/15. College's own assessment of entrance difficulty level: moderately difficult.

TRANSFER ADMISSIONS Required: standardized test scores, high school transcript, college transcript. Recommended: 3 years of high school math and science, 1 year of high school foreign language, interview, minimum 2.0 grade point average. Application deadline: 8/15. College's own assessment of entrance difficulty level: moderately difficult.

EXPENSES (1992–93) Comprehensive fee of $12,210 includes full-time tuition ($8480), mandatory fees ($250), and college room and board ($3480). Part-time tuition: $230 per semester hour.

FINANCIAL AID College-administered aid for all 1991–92 undergraduates: need-based scholarships; non-need scholarships; low-interest long-term loans from external sources (average $1500); SEOG; College Work-Study; part-time jobs. Supporting data: FAF, IRS, state form, AFSA/SAR required; FFS acceptable. Priority application deadline: 3/1.

CAMPUS LIFE/STUDENT SERVICES Mandatory chapel; drama/theater group; student-run newspaper. Institution provides health clinic, personal/psychological counseling. Social organizations: 1 national fraternity, 1 national sorority; 7% of eligible undergraduate men and 10% of eligible undergraduate women are members.

STUDY ABROAD SITES Jamaica, Costa Rica, England.

ATHLETICS Member NAIA, NCCAA, and MCC. Intercollegiate sports: baseball M; basketball M(s), W(s); cross-country running M(s), W(s); golf M(s); soccer M(s); softball W; tennis M(s), W(s); track and field M(s), W(s); volleyball W(s). Intramural sports: basketball, football, soccer, tennis, volleyball.

MAJORS Accounting; art/fine arts; biblical studies; biology/biological sciences; business administration/commerce/management; business economics; business education; chemistry; communication; computer science; (pre)dentistry sequence; economics; education; elementary education; (pre)engineering sequence; English; exercise science; fitness management; graphic arts; history; (pre)law sequence; mathematics; medical technology; (pre)medicine sequence; ministries; music; music education; natural resource management; office management; philosophy; physical education; piano/organ; psychology; recreation and leisure services; religious studies; science; science education; secondary education; sociology; special education; theater arts/drama; theology; (pre)veterinary medicine sequence; voice. Most popular majors of class of 1991: business administration/commerce/management, theology, elementary education.

SPECIAL NOTE FROM THE COLLEGE Huntington College is the only public or private college or university in the state of Indiana that allows students to freeze tuition. Through the Huntington Plan, a guaranteed tuition program, students pay a one-time fee equal to 10% of the current year's tuition to lock in tuition at that rate through graduation. The program is designed to help students obtain a college degree while controlling college costs.

CONTACT Mr. Chantler Thompson, Dean of Enrollment Management, Huntington College, 2303 College Avenue, Huntington, IN 46750, 219-356-6000 Ext. 1016, 219-356-7930, or toll-free 800-642-6493.

INDIANA WESLEYAN UNIVERSITY

Marion, Indiana

Total Enrollment: 2,773

UG Enrollment: 2,022 (50% W)

Application Deadline: rolling

Tuition & Fees: $8120

Room & Board: $3528

Entrance: moderately difficult

SAT ≥ 500: 10% V, 26% M

ACT ≥ 21: 44%

Denominational Affiliation: Wesleyan

GENERAL INFORMATION Independent comprehensive coed institution. Founded 1920. Awards A (college transfer and terminal), B, M. Primary accreditation: regional. Small-town setting, with easy access to Indianapolis; 75-acre campus. Total enrollment: 2,773. Faculty: 105 (67 full-time, 38 part-time); 50% of full-time faculty have terminal degrees; graduate assistants teach no undergraduate courses. Library holdings: 119,808 bound volumes, 7,592 titles on microform, 750 periodical subscriptions, 18,604 records/tapes/CDs. Computer terminals/PCs available for student use: 50, located in computer center, library, writing center, learning center.

UNDERGRADUATE PROFILE Fall 1991: 2,022 undergraduates (347 freshmen) from 38 states and territories and 6 foreign countries; 15% part-time; 83% state residents; 5% transfers; 79% financial aid recipients; 50% women; 4% African Americans; 0% Native Americans; 1% Hispanics; 1% Asian Americans; 3% international students, 62% of undergraduates 25 years of age or older.

1991 FRESHMAN DATA 900 students applied for fall 1991 admission; 67% were accepted; 58% of those accepted enrolled. 20% of freshmen were in top 10% of secondary school class, 28% were in top 25%, 75% were in top half.

FRESHMAN ADMISSIONS Options: early entrance, deferred entrance. Required: essay, high school transcript, 1 recommendation, SAT or ACT, TOEFL (for foreign students). Recommended: interview. Required for some: interview. Test scores used for admission and counseling/placement. Application deadline: rolling. Notification date: continuous. College's own assessment of entrance difficulty level: moderately difficult.

TRANSFER ADMISSIONS Required: essay, high school transcript, 1 recommendation, college transcript, minimum 2.0 grade point average. Recommended: standardized test scores, interview. Required for some: interview. Application deadline: rolling. Notification date: continuous. College's own assessment of entrance difficulty level: moderately difficult.

EXPENSES (1992–93) Comprehensive fee of $11,648 includes full-time tuition ($8120) and college room and board ($3528). Part-time tuition and fees per semester (1 to 11 semester hours) range from $175 to $3190.

FINANCIAL AID College-administered aid for all 1991–92 undergraduates: 686 need-based scholarships (average $1500); 1,100 non-need scholarships (average $900); low-interest long-term loans from college funds (average $1500), from external sources (average $2000); SEOG; College Work-Study; 300 part-time jobs, athletic scholarships. Supporting data: FAF, institutional form, AFSA/SAR required; IRS required for some; FFS acceptable. Priority application deadline: 4/1.

CAMPUS LIFE/STUDENT SERVICES Dress code; mandatory chapel; drama/theater group; student-run newspaper and radio station. Institution provides health clinic, personal/psychological counseling.

ATHLETICS Member NAIA. Intercollegiate sports: baseball M(s); basketball M(s), W(s); cross-country running M(s), W(s); golf M(s); soccer M(s), W(s); softball W(s); tennis M(s), W(s); track and field M(s), W(s); volleyball W(s). Intramural sports: badminton, basketball, bowling, football, golf, racquetball, soccer, table tennis (Ping Pong), tennis, volleyball, weight lifting.

MAJORS Accounting; art education; art/fine arts; biblical studies; biology/biological sciences; business administration/commerce/management; chemistry; communication; computer information systems; creative writing; criminal justice; (pre)dentistry sequence; economics; education; elementary education; (pre)engineering sequence; English; finance/banking; history; law enforcement/police sciences; (pre)law sequence; liberal arts/general studies; mathematics; medical laboratory technology; medical technology; (pre)medicine sequence; mental health/rehabilitation counseling; ministries; music; music business; music education; nursing; pastoral studies; philosophy; physical education; physical sciences; piano/organ; political science/government; psychology; recreation and leisure services; recreation management; religious education; religious studies; sacred music; science; science education; secondary education; social science; social work; sociology; Spanish; studio art; theology; (pre)veterinary medicine sequence; voice; wind and percussion instruments.

SPECIAL NOTE FROM THE COLLEGE Uniqueness, a distinctly Christian approach, and dynamic growth characterize Indiana Wesleyan University. IWU's uniqueness is demonstrated by its academic programs, which include Addictions Counseling, Athletic Training, Criminal Justice, Medical Laboratory Technology, Nursing, Recreation Management, and Social Work. Integration of biblical principles and faith in Christ occurs in classrooms, athletics, and extracurricular activities. Bible classes and chapel along with accountability, discipleship, and Bible study groups also enhance spiritual growth. New residence halls, a new art/communications classroom building, new academic majors, and significant campus development have produced dynamic enrollment growth as the freshman class has increased from 218 students in 1987 to 348 students in 1991.

CONTACT Mr. Charles Mealy, Director of Admissions, Indiana Wesleyan University, 4201 South Washington Street, Marion, IN 46953, 317-677-2138 or toll-free 800-332-6901.

JOHN BROWN UNIVERSITY

Siloam Springs, Arkansas

Total Enrollment: 1,044 (all UG)

Women: 53%

Application Deadline: rolling

Tuition & Fees: $5930

Room & Board: $3210

Entrance: moderately difficult

SAT ≥ 950: 63% V, 74% M

ACT ≥ 22: 68%

Denominational Affiliation: nondenominational

GENERAL INFORMATION Independent 4-year coed college. Founded 1919. Awards A (college transfer and terminal), B. Primary accreditation: regional. Rural setting; 200-acre campus. Total enrollment: 1,044. Faculty: 79 (59 full-time, 20 part-time); 60% of full-time faculty have terminal degrees; graduate assistants teach no undergraduate courses. Library holdings: 92,000 bound volumes, 125 titles on microform, 620 periodical subscriptions, 2,400 records/tapes/CDs. Computer terminals/PCs available for student use: 70, located in computer center, classrooms.

UNDERGRADUATE PROFILE Fall 1991: 1,044 undergraduates (255 freshmen) from 44 states and territories and 30 foreign countries; 13% part-time; 32% state residents; 13% transfers; 81% financial aid recipients; 53% women; 1% African Americans; 1% Native Americans; 2% Hispanics; 1% Asian Americans; 10% international students; 8% of undergraduates 25 years of age or older.

1991 FRESHMAN DATA 530 students applied for fall 1991 admission; 68% were accepted; 71% of those accepted enrolled. 1 freshman was a National Merit Scholarship Finalist and received a National Merit Scholarship. 21% of freshmen were in top 10% of secondary school class, 40% were in top 25%, 75% were in top half.

ENROLLMENT PATTERNS 75% of fall 1990 freshmen returned for fall 1991 term. 43% of 1986 freshmen graduated within 5 years; 18% of students completing a bachelor's program went on for further study.

FRESHMAN ADMISSIONS Options: early entrance, deferred entrance. Required: high school transcript, 3 years of high school math, 2 recommendations, SAT or ACT, TOEFL (for foreign students). Recommended: 3 years of high school science, some high school foreign language. Required for some: essay, interview, 4 years of high school science for engineering majors. Test scores

used for admission. Application deadline: rolling. College's own assessment of entrance difficulty level: moderately difficult.

TRANSFER ADMISSIONS Required: 2 recommendations, college transcript, minimum 2.0 grade point average. Required for some: essay, standardized test scores, high school transcript, 3 years of high school math and science, interview. College's own assessment of entrance difficulty level: moderately difficult.

EXPENSES (1992–93) Comprehensive fee of $9140 includes full-time tuition ($5820), mandatory fees ($110), and college room and board ($3210). Part-time tuition: $250 per semester hour. Tuition prepayment plan available.

FINANCIAL AID College-administered aid for all 1991–92 undergraduates: 710 need-based scholarships (average $600); 550 non-need scholarships (average $1435); low-interest long-term loans from college funds (average $2000), from external sources (average $2770); SEOG; College Work-Study; 240 part-time jobs. Supporting data: IRS required; FFS, state form required for some; FAF, AFSA/SAR acceptable. Priority application deadline: 4/1.

CAMPUS LIFE/STUDENT SERVICES Mandatory chapel; drama/theater group; student-run newspaper and radio station. Institution provides health clinic, personal/psychological counseling.

ATHLETICS Member NAIA. Intercollegiate sports: basketball M(s), W(s); soccer M(s); swimming and diving M(s), W(s); tennis M(s), W(s); volleyball W(s). Intramural sports: basketball, cross-country running, football, racquetball, rugby, soccer, softball, tennis, volleyball.

MAJORS Accounting; art/fine arts; athletic training; biblical studies; biology/biological sciences; broadcasting; business administration/commerce/management; business education; chemistry; commercial art; communications; construction engineering; construction management; early childhood education; education; electrical engineering; elementary education; engineering (general); engineering management; engineering technology; English; graphic arts; health education; health services administration; history; interdisciplinary studies; journalism; liberal arts/general studies; mathematics; mechanical engineering; medical technology; (pre)medicine sequence; middle school education; ministries; music; music education; pastoral studies; physical education; physical fitness/human movement; piano/organ; psychology; public relations; radio and television studies; recreational facilities management; religious education; religious studies; secondary education; secretarial studies/office management; social science; special education; sports medicine; theology; voice. Most popular majors of class of 1991: business administration/commerce/management, elementary education, psychology.

SPECIAL NOTE FROM THE COLLEGE The most distinctive feature of John Brown University is its career orientation. This orientation is reflected in some of JBU's programs: engineering, broadcasting, building construction, and office administration. It is also the cornerstone of traditional programs: business, teacher education, and science. At JBU, career orientation is found in more than its programs—it is an attitude. JBU wants it graduates to be successful in their careers—no matter what career—no matter how they define success. JBU's second most distinctive feature is its intercultural perspective. With 120 international students and over 80 Third World culture missionary's kids, JBU offers a global approach to Christian higher education right in northwest Arkansas.

CONTACT Mr. Don Crandall, Director of Enrollment Management, John Brown University, 2000 West University Street, Siloam Springs, AR 72761, 501-524-3131 Ext. 150 or toll-free 800-634-6969.

JUDSON COLLEGE

Elgin, Illinois

Total Enrollment: 619 (all UG)

Women: 56%

Application Deadline: 8/15

Tuition & Fees: $8780

Room & Board: $4294

Entrance: moderately difficult

SAT ≥ 500: N/R

ACT ≥ 21: N/R

Denominational Affiliation: Baptist

GENERAL INFORMATION Independent 4-year coed college. Founded 1963. Awards B. Primary accreditation: regional. Suburban setting, with easy access to Chicago; 80-acre campus. Total enrollment: 619. Faculty: 70 (29 full-time, 41 part-time); 50% of full-time faculty have terminal degrees; graduate assistants teach no undergraduate courses. Library holdings: 75,000 bound volumes, 28,000 titles on microform, 425 periodical subscriptions, 6,200 records/tapes/CDs. Computer terminals/PCs available for student use: 50, located in computer center, library.

UNDERGRADUATE PROFILE Fall 1991: 619 undergraduates (125 freshmen) from 21 states and territories and 7 foreign countries; 10% part-time; 69% state residents; 11% transfers; 97% financial aid recipients; 56% women; 7% African Americans; 1% Hispanics; 1% Asian Americans; 2% international students; 15% of undergraduates 25 years of age or older.

1991 FRESHMAN DATA 600 students applied for fall 1991 admission; 50% were accepted; 42% of those accepted enrolled. 13% of freshmen were in top 10% of secondary school class, 29% were in top 25%, 60% were in top half.

ENROLLMENT PATTERNS 70% of fall 1990 freshmen returned for fall 1991 term.

FRESHMAN ADMISSIONS Option: deferred entrance. Required: essay, high school transcript, SAT or ACT, TOEFL (for foreign students). Required for some: 1 recommendation, campus interview. Test scores used for admission. Application deadline: 8/15. Notification date: continuous. College's own assessment of entrance difficulty level: moderately difficult.

TRANSFER ADMISSIONS Required: essay, college transcript, minimum 2.0 grade point average. Required for some: standardized test scores, high school transcript, 1 recommendation, campus interview. Application deadline: 8/15. Notification date: continuous. College's own assessment of entrance difficulty level: moderately difficult.

EXPENSES (1992–93) Comprehensive fee of $13,074 includes full-time tuition ($8380), mandatory fees ($400), and college room and board ($4294). Part-time tuition: $273 per semester hour.

FINANCIAL AID College-administered aid for all 1991–92 undergraduates: 345 need-based scholarships (average $1112); 604 non-need scholarships (average $1086); low-interest long-term loans from external sources (average $2610); SEOG; College Work-Study; 70 part-time jobs. Supporting data: FAF required; FFS, IRS, AFSA/SAR acceptable. Priority application deadline: 5/1.

CAMPUS LIFE/STUDENT SERVICES Mandatory chapel; drama/theater group; student-run radio station. Institution provides health clinic, personal/psychological counseling.

ATHLETICS Member NAIA. Intercollegiate sports: basketball M(s), W(s); soccer M(s); tennis M(s), W; volleyball M, W(s). Intramural sports: badminton, basketball, football, soccer, tennis, volleyball.

MAJORS Accounting; anthropology; art/fine arts; biblical studies; biology/biological sciences; business administration/commerce/management; chemistry; communication; computer information systems; computer science; education; elementary education; English; history; (pre)law sequence; linguistics; literature; mathematics; (pre)medicine sequence; music; nursing; painting/drawing; philosophy; physical education; physical sciences; psychology; religious studies; science; social science; sociology; speech/rhetoric/public address/debate; theater arts/drama; voice.

SPECIAL NOTE FROM THE COLLEGE The Judson community experience is designed to equip graduates to be decisive leaders and active participants in church and society, articulate proponents of biblical Christianity, honest advocates for the sovereignty of God over all life, and ambassadors for Christ to a troubled world. Judson is committed to a broad-based liberal arts education based on a Christian world view—educating the spirit, mind, and body. Courses are taught by a highly qualified and competent Christian faculty that encourages students to claim ideas and concepts that can sharpen their insights and establish the pattern for a lifelong quest for learning. The curriculum is designed to prepare graduates for a vocation and/or graduate study. The College is close to Chicago, which provides exciting cultural opportunities for ministry, education, and recreation.

CONTACT Mr. Matthew Osborne, Director of Admissions, Judson College, 1151 North State Street, Elgin, IL 60123, 708-695-2500 Ext. 160.

KING COLLEGE

Bristol, Tennessee

Total Enrollment: 540 (all UG)

Women: 58%

Application Deadline: 8/1

Tuition & Fees: $7400

Room & Board: $3050

Entrance: moderately difficult

SAT ≥ 500: 39% V, 55% M

ACT ≥ 21: 77%

Denominational Affiliation: Presbyterian

GENERAL INFORMATION Independent 4-year coed college. Founded 1867. Awards B. Primary accreditation: regional. Suburban setting; 135-acre campus. Total enrollment: 540. Faculty: 60 (40 full-time, 20 part-time); 66% of full-time faculty have terminal degrees; graduate assistants teach no undergraduate courses. Library holdings: 92,300 bound volumes, 428 titles on microform, 559 periodical subscriptions, 1,200 records/tapes/CDs. Computer terminals/PCs available for student use: 46, located in computer center, library, classroom buildings, multi-media network.

UNDERGRADUATE PROFILE Fall 1991: 540 undergraduates (197 freshmen) from 27 states and territories and 14 foreign countries; 8% part-time; 37% state residents; 8% transfers; 90% financial aid recipients; 58% women; 1% African Americans; 0% Native Americans; 2% Hispanics; 0% Asian Americans; 7% international students; 3% of undergraduates 25 years of age or older.

1991 FRESHMAN DATA 479 students applied for fall 1991 admission; 62% were accepted; 66% of those accepted enrolled. 28% of freshmen were in top 10% of secondary school class, 65% were in top 25%, 85% were in top half.

ENROLLMENT PATTERNS 64% of fall 1990 freshmen returned for fall 1991 term. 30% of 1986 freshmen graduated within 5 years; 15% of students completing a degree program went on for further study.

FRESHMAN ADMISSIONS Option: early entrance. Required: essay, high school transcript, SAT or ACT. Recommended: 3 years of high school math and science, some high school foreign language, interview, TOEFL (for foreign students). Required for some: recommendations, interview. Test scores used for admission. Application deadline: 8/1. College's own assessment of entrance difficulty level: moderately difficult.

TRANSFER ADMISSIONS Required: essay, high school transcript, college transcript, minimum 2.0 grade point average. Recommended: standardized test scores, 3 years of high school math and science, some high school foreign language, interview. Required for some: interview. Application deadline: 8/1. College's own assessment of entrance difficulty level: moderately difficult.

EXPENSES (1992–93) Comprehensive fee of $10,450 includes full-time tuition ($6700), mandatory fees ($700), and college room and board ($3050). College room only: $1500. Part-time tuition: ranges from $125 to $250 per hour.

FINANCIAL AID College-administered aid for all 1991–92 undergraduates: 337 need-based scholarships (average $3862); 145 non-need scholarships (average $3096); low-interest long-term loans from college funds (average $964), from external sources (average $2709); SEOG; College Work-Study; 203 part-time jobs. Supporting data: FAF, IRS, institutional form, AFSA/SAR required; Financial Aid Transcript required for some. Priority application deadline: 3/15.

CAMPUS LIFE/STUDENT SERVICES Mandatory chapel; drama/theater group; student-run newspaper. Institution provides health center, personal/psychological counseling.

STUDY ABROAD SITES The Netherlands, Israel, France, Mexico, Morocco, Africa, New Guinea, Korea, Spain, Germany, Great Britain, Commonwealth of Independent States (USSR), Costa Rica.

ATHLETICS Member NAIA. Intercollegiate sports: basketball M(s), W(s); cross-country running M, W; golf M, W; soccer M(s); softball W; tennis M, W; volleyball W(s). Intramural sports: basketball, football, golf, skiing (downhill), soccer, swimming and diving, table tennis (Ping Pong), tennis, volleyball, weight lifting.

MAJORS Accounting; art/fine arts; biblical studies; biology/biological sciences; business administration/commerce/management; business economics; chemistry; (pre)dentistry sequence; economics; education; elementary education; English; French; history; international business; (pre)law sequence; mathematics; medical technology; (pre)medicine sequence; music; physics; political science/government; psychology; religious studies; science; theater arts/drama; (pre)veterinary medicine sequence. Most popular majors of class of 1991: English, economics, psychology.

SPECIAL NOTE FROM THE COLLEGE King College prepares students for leadership as Christian professionals. Programs are designed to produce individuals grounded in faith and character and qualified both personally and professionally to make an impact on the world. Renowned for its preprofessional programs, over 80% of students apply for advanced studies, entering the university of their choice. The Carnegie Foundation rates King as a highly selective liberal arts college. A state-of-the-art computer network offers advanced preparation, and campus-life programs create a meaningful spectrum of activities and events that foster an atmosphere for personal growth and achievement.

CONTACT Director of Admissions, King College, 1350 King College Road, Bristol, TN 37620-2699, 615-652-4861 or toll-free 800-362-0014.

THE KING'S COLLEGE

Briarcliff Manor, New York

Total Enrollment: 459 (all UG)

Women: 61%

Application Deadline: rolling

Tuition & Fees: $8310

Room & Board: $3920

Entrance: moderately difficult

SAT ≥ 500: 22% V, 36% M

ACT ≥ 21: N/R

Denominational Affiliation: nondenominational

GENERAL INFORMATION Independent 4-year coed college. Founded 1938. Awards A (college transfer), B. Primary accreditation: regional. Suburban setting, with easy access to New York City; 80-acre campus. Total enrollment: 459. Faculty: 48 (41 full-time, 17 part-time); 49% of full-time faculty have terminal degrees; graduate assistants teach no undergraduate courses. Library holdings: 100,000 bound volumes, 135,000 titles on microform, 600 periodical subscriptions, 1,500 records/tapes/ CDs. Computer terminals/PCs available for student use: 50, located in computer center, library, dormitories, some faculty offices. Offers an English Language Institute year-round.

UNDERGRADUATE PROFILE Fall 1991: 459 undergraduates (110 freshmen) from 25 states and territories and 10 foreign countries; 4% part-time; 45% state residents; 24% transfers; 87% financial aid recipients; 61% women; 7% African Americans; 1% Native Americans; 6% Hispanics; 7% Asian Americans; 4% international students; 5% of undergraduates 25 years of age or older.

1991 FRESHMAN DATA 340 students applied for fall 1991 admission; 86% were accepted; 38% of those accepted enrolled. 14% of freshmen were in top 10% of secondary school class, 38% were in top 25%, 79% were in top half.

ENROLLMENT PATTERNS 76% of fall 1990 freshmen returned for fall 1991 term.

FRESHMAN ADMISSIONS Options: early entrance, deferred entrance. Required: high school transcript, 2 recommendations, SAT or ACT, TOEFL (for foreign students). Recommended:

essay, 3 years of high school math and science, 1 year foreign language. Required for some: campus interview. Test scores used for admission. Application deadline: rolling. College's own assessment of entrance difficulty level: moderately difficult.

TRANSFER ADMISSIONS Required: 2 recommendations, college transcript, minimum 2.0 grade point average. Recommended: essay, 3 years of high school math and science, 1 year foreign language. Required for some: standardized test scores, high school transcript, campus interview. Application deadline: rolling. College's own assessment of entrance difficulty level: moderately difficult.

EXPENSES (1992–93) Comprehensive fee of $12,230 includes full-time tuition ($8190), mandatory fees ($120), and college room and board ($3920). College room only: $1928. Part-time tuition: $260 per semester hour.

FINANCIAL AID College-administered aid for all 1991–92 undergraduates: 312 need-based scholarships (average $1552); 317 non-need scholarships (average $990); low-interest long-term loans from external sources (average $2488); SEOG; College Work-Study; 234 part-time jobs. Supporting data: FAF, IRS, institutional form required; state form required for some; FFS, AFSA/SAR acceptable. Priority application deadline: 3/1.

CAMPUS LIFE/STUDENT SERVICES Mandatory chapel; drama/theater group; student-run newspaper. Institution provides health clinic, personal/psychological counseling. Outreach groups, Mu Kappa, MENC, FCEA, political committee.

STUDY ABROAD SITES France, Spain, Germany, England, Dominican Republic.

ATHLETICS Member NAIA. Intercollegiate sports: baseball M; basketball M(s), W(s); cross-country running M(s), W(s); soccer M(s), W(s); softball W; volleyball W(s). Intramural sports: basketball, football, volleyball, weight lifting. Men's volleyball club.

MAJORS Accounting; biblical studies; biology/biological sciences; business administration; chemistry; communications; computer science; early childhood education; education; elementary education; English; French; history; mathematics; medical technology; modern languages; music; music education; nursing; physical education; psychology; religious education; religious studies; secondary education; sociology, Spanish; youth ministry. Most popular majors of class of 1991: elementary education, business administration, physical education.

SPECIAL NOTE FROM THE COLLEGE The King's College is relocating in the fall of 1993 to a picturesque, lakeside campus in Tuxedo, New York. The new facilities are located on 310 acres in Orange County—just an hour's ride from midtown Manhattan. King's prepares students to apply Christian values to daily life. Faculty members are distinguished, academic programs are strong, and curriculums are diverse. Eighty-six percent of King's students receive some form of financial aid. King's is committed to forming a "partnership" with students to work together with them to provide the money needed to afford a high-quality, Christian education.

CONTACT Ms. Cheryl Burdick, Director of Admissions and Financial Aid, The King's College, 150 Lodge Road, Briarcliff Manor, NY 10510, 914-944-5650 or toll-free 800-344-4926.

THE KING'S COLLEGE

Edmonton, Alberta, Canada

Total Enrollment: 425 (all UG)

Women: 56%

Application Deadline: rolling

Tuition & Fees: $3400

Room Only: $1520

Entrance: moderately difficult

Denominational Affiliation: nondenominational

GENERAL INFORMATION Independent 3-year coed college. Founded 1979. Awards B. Primary accreditation: provincial charter. Urban setting; 1-acre campus. Total enrollment: 425. Faculty: 59 (23 full-time, 36 part-time); Library holdings: 55,000 bound volumes, 280 periodical subscriptions, 1,800 records/tapes/CDs. Computer terminals/PCs available for student use: 21, located in computer lab.

UNDERGRADUATE PROFILE Fall 1991: 425 undergraduates (220 freshmen) from 7 provinces and territories and 10 foreign countries; 8% part-time; 90% province residents; 14% transfers; 50% financial aid recipients; 56% women; 2% African Canadians; 1% Native Canadians; 0% Hispanics; 9% Asian Canadians; 4% international students; 14% of undergraduates 25 years of age or older.

1991 FRESHMAN DATA 452 students applied for fall 1991 admission; 58% were accepted; 85% of those accepted enrolled.

ENROLLMENT PATTERNS 69% of fall 1990 freshmen returned for fall 1991 term.

FRESHMAN ADMISSIONS Required: high school transcript, 1 recommendation, TOEFL (for foreign students). Test scores used for admission. Application deadline: rolling. Notification date: continuous until 8/15. College's own assessment of entrance difficulty level: moderately difficult.

TRANSFER ADMISSIONS Required: high school transcript, 1 recommendation, college transcript, minimum 2.0 grade point average. Required for some: campus interview. Application deadline: rolling. Notification date: continuous until 8/15. College's own assessment of entrance difficulty level: minimally difficult.

EXPENSES (1992–93) Tuition: $3300 full-time, $330 per course part-time. Mandatory fees: $100. College room only: $1520.

FINANCIAL AID College-administered aid for all 1991–92 undergraduates: 17 need-based scholarships (average $520); 39 non-need scholarships (average $347); low-interest long-term loans from external sources (average $600); 18 part-time jobs. Supporting data: institutional form required; government form required for some. Application deadline: 3/31.

CAMPUS LIFE/STUDENT SERVICES Drama/theater group; student-run newspaper. Institution provides personal/psychological counseling.

ATHLETICS Intercollegiate sports: basketball M, W; ice hockey M; volleyball M, W.

MAJORS Biology/biological sciences; chemistry; English; history; music; philosophy; psychology; social science.

SPECIAL NOTE FROM THE COLLEGE The King's College is an independent, Christian liberal arts college located in an urban setting in one of western Canada's major cities. Christian students learn how to be "in the world, but not of the world" through an education that integrates the Christian faith with life and learning, with an emphasis on the unique task of the Christian in a secular society. The College is within commuting distance of the University of Alberta, one of Canada's largest, allowing for significant interaction with that institution. At the same time, the College's small size and highly qualified faculty contribute to a caring and intellectually stimulating environment for learning and personal growth. Continued development of degree programs and plans to move to a new campus in 1993 combine to project exciting years of growth for the College and its students.

CONTACT Mr. Fred Woudstra, Director of Liaison, The King's College, 10766 97th Street, Edmonton, AB T5H 2M1, Canada, 403-428-0727 Ext. 218.

LEE COLLEGE

Cleveland, Tennessee

Total Enrollment: 1,827 (all UG)

Women: 51%

Application Deadline: rolling

Tuition & Fees: $4128

Room & Board: $3000

Entrance: minimally difficult

SAT ≥ 500: N/R

ACT ≥ 21: 50%

Denominational Affiliation: Church of God

GENERAL INFORMATION Independent 4-year coed college. Founded 1918. Awards B. Primary accreditation: regional. Small-town setting; 60-acre campus. Total enrollment: 1,827. Faculty: 157 (88 full-time, 69 part-time); 50% of full-time faculty have terminal degrees; graduate assistants teach a few undergraduate courses. Library holdings: 126,392 bound volumes, 20,278 titles on microform, 330 periodical subscriptions, 2,467 records/tapes/CDs. Computer terminals/PCs available for student use: 38, located in computer center.

UNDERGRADUATE PROFILE Fall 1991: 1,827 undergraduates (544 freshmen) from 46 states and territories and 27 foreign countries; 6% part-time; 75% state residents; 13% transfers; 85% financial aid recipients; 51% women; 2% African Americans; 1% Native Americans; 5% Hispanics; 2% Asian Americans; 3% international students; 15% of undergraduates 25 years of age or older.

1991 FRESHMAN DATA 731 students applied for fall 1991 admission; 90% were accepted; 83% of those accepted enrolled.

ENROLLMENT PATTERNS 60% of fall 1990 freshmen returned for fall 1991 term.

FRESHMAN ADMISSIONS Options: early entrance, deferred entrance. Required: high school transcript, SAT or ACT, TOEFL (for foreign students). Required for some: 1 recommendation. Test scores used for counseling/placement. Application deadline: rolling. College's own assessment of entrance difficulty level: minimally difficult.

TRANSFER ADMISSIONS Required: college transcript, minimum 2.0 grade point average. Application deadline: rolling. College's own assessment of entrance difficulty level: minimally difficult.

EXPENSES (1992–93) Comprehensive fee of $7282 includes full-time tuition ($4128), mandatory fees ($154), and college room and board ($3000). College room only: $1500. Part-time tuition: $172 per semester hour.

FINANCIAL AID College-administered aid for all 1991–92 undergraduates: 675 need-based scholarships (average $500); non-need scholarships; short-term loans (average $150); low-interest long-term loans from external sources (average $2800); SEOG; College Work-Study; part-time jobs. Supporting data: FFS, institutional form required; IRS required for some; AFSA/SAR acceptable. Priority application deadline: 4/15.

CAMPUS LIFE/STUDENT SERVICES Dress code; mandatory chapel; student-run newspaper. Institution provides health clinic, personal/psychological counseling. Social organizations: 3 local fraternities, 2 local sororities; 20% of eligible undergraduate men and 20% of eligible undergraduate women are members.

STUDY ABROAD SITES England, Germany, China, Ukraine.

ATHLETICS Member NAIA. Intercollegiate sports: basketball M(s), W(s); golf M(s); soccer M(s), W(s); softball W(s); tennis M(s), W(s); volleyball W(s). Intramural sports: basketball, football, racquetball, soccer, softball, table tennis (Ping Pong), tennis, volleyball.

MAJORS Accounting; biblical studies; biology/biological sciences; business administration/commerce/management; business education; chemistry; communication; computer information systems; education; elementary education; English; health education; history; mathematics; medical technology; modern languages; music; music education; natural sciences; pastoral studies; physical education; piano/organ; psychology; religious education; secondary education; secretarial studies/office management; social science; sociology; theater arts/drama; theology; voice. Most popular majors of class of 1991: elementary education, biblical studies, business administration/commerce/management.

SPECIAL NOTE FROM THE COLLEGE Nestled on 60 acres in the beauty of the Southeast is Lee College. In this day of declining student populations, Lee has realized a 40% increase since 1983. This results in a student population that is alive and excited about the future. A Pentecostal/Charismatic institution, Lee is among the least expensive of the Coalition schools. In addition, Lee graduates post an exceptionally high acceptance rate into medical and other graduate schools. Combine all this with 1,800 students who live together in the shadow of the Great Smoky Mountains, and Lee becomes one of the most attractive options in higher education a Christian student can consider.

CONTACT Ms. Davonna Kier, Admissions Office Coordinator, Lee College, 1120 North Ocoee Street, Cleveland, TN 37311, 615-478-7316 Ext. 316 or toll-free 800-LEE-9930.

LeTourneau University

Longview, Texas

Total Enrollment: 1570 (all UG)

Women: 26%

Application Deadline: 8/15

Tuition & Fees: $7940

Room & Board: $3860

Entrance: moderately difficult

SAT ≥ 500: 42% V, 72% M

ACT ≥ 21: 64%

Denominational Affiliation: nondenominational

GENERAL INFORMATION Independent 4-year coed college. Founded 1946. Awards A (terminal), B. Primary accreditation: regional. Small town setting. 162-acre campus. Total enrollment: 1570. Faculty: 114 (49 full-time, 65 part-time); 65% of full-time faculty have terminal degrees; graduate assistants teach no undergraduate courses. Library holdings: 98,641 bound volumes, 38,520 titles on microform, 435 periodical subscriptions, 2,670 records/tapes/CDs, 114,450 non-book items. Computer terminals/PCs available for student use: 200, located in computer center, library.

UNDERGRADUATE PROFILE Fall 1991: 1570 undergraduates (210 freshmen) from 52 states and territories and 24 foreign countries; 7% part-time; 45% state residents; 30% transfers; 80% financial aid recipients; 26% women; 4% African Americans; 1% Native Americans; 2% Hispanics; 1% Asian Americans; 6% international students; 15% of undergraduates 25 years of age or older.

1991 FRESHMAN DATA 411 students applied for fall 1991 admission; 95% were accepted; 54% of those accepted enrolled. 1 freshman was a National Merit Scholarship Finalist and received a National Merit Scholarship. 26% of freshmen were in top 10% of secondary school class, 48% were in top 25%, 77% were in top half.

ENROLLMENT PATTERNS 64% of fall 1990 freshmen returned for fall 1991 term.

FRESHMAN ADMISSIONS Options: early entrance, deferred entrance. Required: essay, high school transcript, 2 recommendations, SAT or ACT, TOEFL (for foreign students). Recommended: 3 years of high school science. Required for some: 3 years of high school math, campus interview. Test scores used for admission and counseling/placement. Application deadline: 8/15. Notification date: continuous. College's own assessment of entrance difficulty level: moderately difficult.

TRANSFER ADMISSIONS Required: essay, 2 recommendations, college transcript, minimum 2.0 grade point average. Required for some: standardized test scores, high school transcript, campus interview. Application deadline: 8/15. Notification date: continuous. College's own assessment of entrance difficulty level: moderately difficult.

EXPENSES (1992–93) Comprehensive fee of $11,800 includes full-time tuition ($7830), mandatory fees ($110), and college room and board ($3860). Part-time tuition and fees per semester (1 to 11 semester hours) range from $90 to $3310.

FINANCIAL AID College-administered aid for all 1991–92 undergraduates: 632 need-based scholarships (average $1070); 336 non-need scholarships (average $1066); low-interest long-term loans from college funds (average $1350), from external sources (average $2530); SEOG; College Work-Study; 190 part-time jobs. Supporting data: FAF, AFSA/SAR required; IRS required for some; FFS acceptable. Priority application deadline: 2/15.

CAMPUS LIFE/STUDENT SERVICES Mandatory chapel; drama/theater group; student-run newspaper. Institution provides health clinic, personal/psychological counseling. Social organizations: 5 local housing societies; 13% of eligible undergraduate men are members.

ATHLETICS Member NAIA. Intercollegiate sports: baseball M; basketball M; cross-country running M, W; soccer M; track and field M, W; volleyball W. Intramural sports: badminton, basketball, bowling, cross-country running, field hockey, football, golf, racquetball, soccer, softball, swimming and diving, table tennis (Ping Pong), tennis, track and field, volleyball, weight lifting, wrestling.

MAJORS Accounting; aircraft and missile maintenance; automotive technologies; aviation technology; biblical studies; biology/biological sciences; business administration/commerce/management; chemistry; computer engineering; computer science; computer technologies; (pre)dentistry sequence; drafting and design; electrical engineering; electrical engineering technology; engineering (general); engineering technology; English; flight training; history; industrial administration; (pre)law sequence; marketing/retailing/merchandising; mathematics; mechanical engineering; mechanical engineering technology; medical technology; (pre)medicine sequence; natural sciences; physical education; psychology; public administration; sports administration; (pre)veterinary medicine sequence; welding engineering; welding technology. Most popular majors of class of 1991: aviation technology, engineering (general), mechanical engineering.

SPECIAL NOTE FROM THE COLLEGE Set apart by a special "spirit of ingenuity," LeTourneau University continues to expand on the excellence and inventive zeal of its heritage. Always striving to excell, LeTourneau was the first evangelical Christian college to receive professional accreditation by the Accreditation Board for Engineering and Technology (ABET). The University provides solid programs in more than 40 majors, with special emphasis on aviation, business, engineering, and technology. Set in the beautiful pine woods and lakes of East Texas, the spacious contemporary campus is home to innovative students from all 50 states and more than 20 nations. At LeTourneau, "Faith brings us together, ingenuity sets us apart."

CONTACT Mr. Howard Wilson, Director of Admissions, LeTourneau University, P.O. Box 7001, Longview, TX 75607, 903-753-0231 Ext. 240 or toll-free 800-759-8811.

MALONE COLLEGE

Canton, Ohio

Total Enrollment: 1,702

UG Enrollment: 1,601 (64% W)

Application Deadline: rolling

Tuition & Fees: $8490

Room & Board: $3150

Entrance: moderately difficult

SAT ≥ 500: 15% V, 44% M

ACT ≥ 21: 54%

Denominational Affiliation: Evangelical Friends Church, Eastern Region

GENERAL INFORMATION Independent comprehensive coed institution. Founded 1892. Awards A (terminal), B, M. Primary accreditation: regional. Urban setting, with easy access to Cleveland; 78-acre campus. Total enrollment: 1,702. Faculty: 117 (70 full-time, 47 part-time); 49% of full-time faculty have terminal degrees; graduate assistants teach no undergraduate courses. Library holdings: 123,339 bound volumes, 237,944 titles on microform, 1,003 periodical subscriptions, 11,328 records/tapes/CDs. Computer terminals/PCs available for student use: 50, located in computer center, library.

UNDERGRADUATE PROFILE Fall 1991: 1,601 undergraduates (326 freshmen) from 14 states and territories and 6 foreign countries; 17% part-time; 97% state residents; 4% transfers; 84% financial aid recipients; 64% women; 5% African Americans; 1% Native Americans; 1% Hispanics; 1% Asian Americans; 1% international students; 30% of undergraduates 25 years of age or older.

1991 FRESHMAN DATA 546 students applied for fall 1991 admission; 95% were accepted; 63% of those accepted enrolled. 23% of freshmen were in top 10% of secondary school class, 50% were in top 25%, 77% were in top half.

ENROLLMENT PATTERNS 73% of fall 1990 freshmen returned for fall 1991 term. 43% of 1986 freshmen graduated within 5 years; 9% of students completing a bachelor's program went on for further study.

FRESHMAN ADMISSIONS Options: early entrance, deferred entrance. Required: essay, high school transcript, SAT or ACT, TOEFL (for foreign students). Recommended: 3 years of high school math and science, some high school foreign language. Required for some: 2 recommendations, interview. Test scores used for counseling/placement. Application deadline: rolling. Notification date: continuous until 8/29. College's own assessment of entrance difficulty level: moderately difficult.

TRANSFER ADMISSIONS Required: essay, 1 recommendation, college transcript, minimum 2.0 grade point average. Recommended: essay, 3 years of high school math and science, some high school foreign language. Required for some: standardized test scores, high school transcript, interview. Application deadline: rolling. Notification date: continuous until 8/29. College's own assessment of entrance difficulty level: moderately difficult.

EXPENSES (1992–93) Comprehensive fee of $11,640 includes full-time tuition ($8370), mandatory fees ($120), and college room and board ($3150). Part-time tuition: $195 per credit hour.

FINANCIAL AID College-administered aid for all 1991–92 undergraduates: 1,311 need-based scholarships (average $1350); 1,882 non-need scholarships (average $1019); low-interest long-term loans from college funds (average $1500), from external sources (average $2617); SEOG; College Work-Study; 110 part-time jobs. Supporting data: FAF, institutional form, AFSA/SAR required; IRS, state form required for some. Application deadline: continuous to 4/15.

CAMPUS LIFE/STUDENT SERVICES Mandatory chapel; drama/theater group; student-run newspaper and radio station. Institution provides health clinic, personal/psychological counseling.

STUDY ABROAD SITES Guatemala, Hong Kong, Costa Rica, Africa.

ATHLETICS Member NAIA. Intercollegiate sports: baseball M(s); basketball M(s), football M(s), W(s); cross-country running M(s), W(s); golf M(s); soccer M(s); softball W(s); tennis M(s), W(s); track and field M(s), W(s); volleyball W(s). Intramural sports: baseball, basketball, bowling, cross-country running, football, golf, racquetball, skiing (cross-country), skiing (downhill), soccer, softball, table tennis (Ping Pong), tennis, volleyball, weight lifting.

MAJORS Accounting; anesthesiology; art; biblical studies; biology/biological sciences; broadcasting; business administration/commerce/management; business education; chemistry; commercial music technology; communication; computer science; (pre)dentistry sequence; early childhood education; education; elementary education; (pre)engineering sequence; English; health education; history; journalism; (pre)law sequence; liberal arts/general studies; mathematics; medical technology; (pre)medicine sequence; ministries; music; music education; nursing; physical education; psychology; radio and television studies; radiological sciences; religious education; sacred music; science; science education; secondary education; social science; social work; Spanish; special education; sports medicine; theater arts/drama; theology; (pre)veterinary medicine sequence. Most popular majors of class of 1991: elementary education, business administration/commerce/management, science.

SPECIAL NOTE FROM THE COLLEGE Malone College, located in Canton, Ohio, and only minutes from the professional Football Hall of Fame, offers prospective students the opportunity to put their faith and careers into motion by combining classroom work with hands-on experience through internships and cooperative work experience. In addition, students can participate in a variety of campus activities ranging from mission trips to movie nights and huge banana-split parties. And if it's the athletic life students desire, Malone's nationally ranked teams have a record for winning. The competition brings the college's teams head-to-head with the nation's best.

CONTACT Mr. Leland J. Sommers, Dean of Admissions, Malone College, 515 25th Street, NW, Canton, OH 44709, 216-471-8100 or toll-free 800-521-1146.

THE MASTER'S COLLEGE

Santa Clarita, California

Total Enrollment: 1,011

UG Enrollment: 850 (52% W)

Application Deadline: rolling

Tuition & Fees: $7790

Room & Board: $4160

Entrance: moderately difficult

SAT ≥ 500: 27% V, 42% M

ACT ≥ 21: 22%

Denominational Affiliation: nondenominational

GENERAL INFORMATION Independent comprehensive coed institution. Founded 1927. Awards B, M. Primary accreditation: regional. Suburban setting, with easy access to Los Angeles; 110-acre campus. Total enrollment: 1,011. Faculty: 87 (48 full-time, 39 part-time); 42% of full-time faculty have terminal degrees; graduate assistants teach no undergraduate courses. Library holdings: 150,000 bound volumes, 1,500 titles on microform, 452 periodical subscriptions, 3,000 records/tapes/CDs. Computer terminals/PCs available for student use: 20, located in computer center, library, business center.

UNDERGRADUATE PROFILE Fall 1991: 850 undergraduates (186 freshmen) from 37 states and territories and 11 foreign countries; 9% part-time; 71% state residents; 12% transfers; 91% financial aid recipients; 52% women; 3% African Americans; 1% Native Americans; 3% Hispanics; 3% Asian Americans; 2% international students; 10% of undergraduates 25 years of age or older.

1991 FRESHMAN DATA 325 students applied for fall 1991 admission; 85% were accepted; 68% of those accepted enrolled. 2 freshmen were National Merit Scholarship Finalists and received a National Merit Scholarship.

ENROLLMENT PATTERNS 74% of fall 1990 freshmen returned for fall 1991 term. 40% of 1986 freshmen graduated within 5 years; 35% of students completing a degree program went on for further study.

FRESHMAN ADMISSIONS Option: deferred entrance. Required: essay, high school transcript, 3 years of high school math, 2 years of high school foreign language, 2 recommendations, SAT or ACT, TOEFL (for foreign students). Recommended: interview, Achievement Tests, English Composition Test. Test scores used for admission. Application deadline: rolling. Notification date: continuous until 9/7. College's own assessment of entrance difficulty level: moderately difficult.

TRANSFER ADMISSIONS Required: essay, 2 recommendations, college transcript, minimum 2.0 grade point average. Recommended: interview. Required for some: standardized test scores, high school transcript. Application deadline: rolling. Notification date: continuous until 9/7.

EXPENSES (1992–93) Comprehensive fee of $11,950 includes full-time tuition ($7370), mandatory fees ($420), and college room and board ($4160). Part-time tuition: $275 per unit.

FINANCIAL AID College-administered aid for all 1991–92 undergraduates: 415 need-based scholarships (average $1716); 396 non-need scholarships (average $2502); low-interest long-term loans from external sources (average $3021); SEOG; College Work-Study; part-time jobs. Supporting data: FAF, IRS, institutional form required; AFSA/SAR required for some; FFS acceptable. Application deadline: continuous to 8/1.

CAMPUS LIFE/STUDENT SERVICES Dress code; mandatory chapel; drama/theater group. Institution provides health clinic, personal/psychological counseling.

ATHLETICS Member NAIA. Intercollegiate sports: baseball M(s); basketball M(s), W(s); cross-country running M(s), W(s); soccer M(s); volleyball W(s). Intramural sports: basketball, football, volleyball.

MAJORS Accounting; biblical languages; biblical studies; biology/biological sciences; business administration/commerce/management; communication; English; history; home economics; liberal arts/general studies; mathematics; ministries; music; music education; natural sciences; physical education; political science/government; radio and television studies; theology. Most popular majors of class of 1991: biblical studies, liberal arts/general studies, business administration/management.

SPECIAL NOTE FROM THE COLLEGE Located in a rural country setting within an hour of white-sand beaches, ski mountains, and the cultural advantages of Los Angeles, the Master's College has a beautiful 110-acre campus in sunny southern California. Personalized scholarship and personalized discipleship are at the heart of academic and spiritual development for every student. Powerful chapels and campus ministry teams combine with vision-building opportunities that include a World Prayer Center and Summer Missions Program (designed with the eventual goal of having every student spend a summer ministering overseas before graduation). Beginning with a foundation of 18 Bible units, students can go on to 1 of 15 diverse majors, including Bible and theology, business administration, and teacher education, at a moderate cost.

CONTACT Mr. Don Gilmore, Director of Admissions, Master's College, 21726 Placerita Canyon Road, Newhall, CA 91322, 805-259-3540 Ext. 347 or toll-free 800-568-6248.

MESSIAH COLLEGE

Grantham, Pennsylvania

Total Enrollment: 2,259 (all UG)

Women: 59%

Application Deadline: rolling

Tuition & Fees: $9070

Room & Board: $4550

Entrance: competitive

SAT ≥ 500: 77% V, 95% M

ACT ≥ 21: 100%

Denominational Affiliation: Brethren in Christ Church

GENERAL INFORMATION Independent 4-year coed college. Founded 1909. Awards B. Primary accreditation: regional. Small-town setting; 310-acre campus. Total enrollment: 2,259. Faculty: 182 (127 full-time, 55 part-time); 66% of full-time faculty have terminal degrees; graduate assistants teach no undergraduate courses. Library holdings: 180,000 bound volumes, 5,000 titles on microform, 1,000 periodical subscriptions, 5,500 records/tapes/CDs. Computer terminals/PCs available for student use: 250, located in computer center, library.

UNDERGRADUATE PROFILE Fall 1991: 2,259 undergraduates (560 freshmen) from 34 states and territories and 21 foreign countries; 3% part-time; 49% state residents; 5% transfers; 84% financial aid recipients; 59% women; 4% African Americans; 0% Native Americans; 3% Hispanics; 3% Asian Americans; 1% international students; 2% of undergraduates 25 years of age or older.

1991 FRESHMAN DATA 1,456 students applied for fall 1991 admission; 81% were accepted; 48% of those accepted enrolled. 48% of freshmen were in top 10% of secondary school class, 86% were in top 25%, 99% were in top half. 4 freshmen were National Merit Scholarship Finalists and all received a National Merit Scholarship.

ENROLLMENT PATTERNS 86% of fall 1990 freshmen returned for fall 1991 term. 70% of 1986 freshmen graduated within 5 years.

FRESHMAN ADMISSIONS Options: early entrance, deferred entrance. Required: essay, high school transcript, 2 recommendations, SAT or ACT. Recommended: 3 years of high school math and science. Required for some: some high school foreign language. Test scores used for admission. Application deadline: rolling. Notification date: continuous. College's own assessment of entrance difficulty level: moderately difficult.

TRANSFER ADMISSIONS Required: essay, 2 recommendations, college transcript, minimum 2.5 grade point average. Application deadline: rolling. Notification date: continuous. College's own assessment of entrance difficulty level: competitive.

EXPENSES (1992–93) Comprehensive fee of $13,530 includes full-time tuition ($9070), mandatory fees ($80), and college room and board ($4550). College room only: $2270. Part-time tuition: $380 per credit.

FINANCIAL AID College-administered aid for all 1991–92 undergraduates: 1,036 need-based scholarships (average $1500); 1,200 non-need scholarships (average $1275); low-interest long-term loans from external sources (average $2500); SEOG; College Work-Study; 1,000 part-time jobs. Supporting data: state form required for some; FAF acceptable. Priority application deadline: 4/1.

CAMPUS LIFE Mandatory chapel; drama/theater group; student-run newspaper and radio station.

STUDY ABROAD SITES England, Germany, France, Spain, Greece, Israel, China, Kenya, Japan, Colombia.

ATHLETICS Member NCAA (Division III). Intercollegiate sports: baseball M; basketball M, W; cross-country running M, W; field hockey W; golf M; soccer M, W; softball W; tennis M, W; track and field M, W; volleyball W; wrestling M. Intramural sports: baseball, basketball, cross-country running, field hockey, football, golf, gymnastics, soccer, softball, tennis, track and field, volleyball, wrestling.

MAJORS Accounting; art/fine arts; art history; behavioral sciences; biblical studies; business administration/commerce/management; chemistry; civil engineering technology; clinical psychology; communication; computer information systems; computer science; dietetics; early childhood education; education; elementary education; English; experimental psychology; family services; French; geography; German; history; home economics; humanities; human resources; journalism; (pre)law sequence; liberal arts/general studies; marketing/retailing/merchandising; mathematics; medical technology; (pre)medicine sequence; modern languages; music; music education; natural sciences; nursing; pastoral studies; physical education; physics; psychology; radio and television studies; religious education; religious studies; secondary education; social science; social work; sociology; Spanish; sports medicine; theology; (pre)veterinary medicine sequence; voice. Most popular majors of class of 1991: business administration/commerce/management, natural sciences, education.

SPECIAL NOTE FROM THE COLLEGE Messiah College is a 4-year, residential Christian college of the arts and sciences. The size of the enrollment (2,300) provides numerous advantages, including personal contact between students and faculty. Located in Grantham, Pennsylvania, 10 miles south of Harrisburg, Messiah's 310-acre campus is easily accessible by interstate highways, Harrisburg International Airport, and train and bus lines. Messiah offers more than 40 majors, including traditional liberal arts curricula and professional and preprofessional programs in business, computer science, education, engineering, medicine, and nursing. Cooperative education, internships, and international service opportunities are also available at Messiah. Most of Messiah's excellent facilities have been constructed within the past 15 years, enabling the College to offer a high-quality education in an ever-changing world.

CONTACT Mr. Ron E. Long, Vice President for Admissions, Financial Aid, and Communications, Messiah College, Grantham, PA 17027, 717-766-2511 Ext. 6000 or toll-free 800-382-1349 (in-state), 800-233-4220 (out-of-state).

MIDAMERICA NAZARENE COLLEGE

Olathe, Kansas

Total Enrollment: 1,370

UG Enrollment: 1,349 (58% W)

Application Deadline: rolling

Tuition & Fees: $6006

Room & Board: $3316

Entrance: noncompetitive

SAT ≥ 500: N/R

ACT ≥ 21: 48%

Denominational Affiliation: Church of the Nazarene

GENERAL INFORMATION Independent comprehensive coed institution. Founded 1966. Awards A (college transfer and terminal), B, M (in education and management only). Primary accreditation: regional. Suburban setting, with easy access to Kansas City; 112-acre campus. Total enrollment: 1,370. Faculty: 97 (54 full-time, 43 part-time); 39% of full-time faculty have terminal degrees; graduate assistants teach no undergraduate courses. Library holdings: 79,297 bound volumes, 17,527 titles on microform, 400 periodical subscriptions, 993 records/tapes/CDs. Computer terminals/PCs available for student use: 100, located in computer center, library.

UNDERGRADUATE PROFILE Fall 1991: 1,349 undergraduates (183 freshmen) from 40 states and territories and 10 foreign countries; 20% part-time; 64% state residents; 44% transfers; 90% financial aid recipients; 58% women; 4% African Americans; 1% Native Americans; 1% Hispanics; 1% Asian Americans; 3% international students; 35% of undergraduates 25 years of age or older.

1991 FRESHMAN DATA 405 students applied for fall 1991 admission; 100% were accepted; 45% of those accepted enrolled.

ENROLLMENT PATTERNS 70% of fall 1990 freshmen returned for fall 1991 term. 44% of 1986 freshmen graduated within 5 years.

FRESHMAN ADMISSIONS Open admissions. Options: early entrance, deferred entrance. Required: high school transcript, 2 recommendations, ACT, TOEFL (for foreign students). Test scores used for counseling/placement. Notification date: continuous. College's own assessment of entrance difficulty level: noncompetitive.

TRANSFER ADMISSIONS Required: college transcript. Required for some: standardized test scores. Application deadline: rolling. Notification date: continuous.

EXPENSES (1992–93) Comprehensive fee of $9322 includes full-time tuition ($5610), mandatory fees ($396), and college room and board ($3316). Part-time tuition: $187 per semester hour.

FINANCIAL AID College-administered aid for all 1991–92 undergraduates: need-based scholarships; 625 non-need scholarships (average $700); low-interest long-term loans from external sources (average $2625); SEOG; College Work-Study; part-time jobs. Supporting data: FFS, IRS, institutional form, AFSA/SAR required; state form required for some; FAF acceptable. Priority application deadline: 3/1.

CAMPUS LIFE/STUDENT SERVICES Dress code; mandatory chapel; drama/theatre group; student-run newspaper. Institution provides health clinic, personal/psychological counseling.

ATHLETICS Member NAIA. Intercollegiate sports: baseball M(s); basketball M(s), W(s); cross-country running M(s), W(s); football M(s); track and field M(s), W(s); volleyball W(s). Intramural sports: baseball, basketball, football, track and field, volleyball, wrestling.

MAJORS Accounting; agricultural business; athletic training; biology/biological sciences; business administration/commerce/management; business education; chemistry; communication; computer science; early childhood education; elementary education; English; health education; history; human resources; international business; liberal arts/general studies; mathematics; ministries; modern languages; music; music education; nursing; physical education; physics; psychology; public relations; religious education; religious studies; sacred music; secondary education; Spanish.

SPECIAL NOTE FROM THE COLLEGE MidAmerica Nazarene College is a private, holiness college in the Wesleyan tradition. It is a coeducational, career-oriented, undergraduate college of liberal arts. New programs include management of human resources and a master's in education. The campus is located 19 miles southwest of downtown Kansas City, on 112 acres. The College has as its purpose the Christian education of individuals in a liberal arts context for personal development, service to God and humanity, and career preparation. MANC places importance on guiding the student in the development of a sense of self-worth and achievement predicated on acceptance of the inspiration of the Bible, with the life of Christian holiness as a guide.

CONTACT Mr. Dennis Troyer, Director of Admissions, MidAmerica Nazarene College, 2030 College Way, Olathe, KS 66062, 913-791-3380.

MILLIGAN COLLEGE

Milligan College, Tennessee

Total Enrollment: 764

UG Enrollment: 719 (55% W)

Application Deadline: rolling

Tuition & Fees: $6712

Room & Board: $2874

Entrance: moderately difficult

SAT ≥ 500: 43% V, 61% M

ACT ≥ 21: 65%

Denominational Affiliation: nondenominational

GENERAL INFORMATION Independent comprehensive coed institution. Founded 1866. Awards A (terminal), B, M. Primary accreditation: regional. Rural setting; 145-acre campus. Total enrollment: 764. Faculty: 73 (48 full-time, 25 part-time); 54% of full-time faculty have terminal degrees; graduate assistants teach no undergraduate courses. Library holdings: 87,714 bound volumes, 140,886 titles on microform, 550 periodical subscriptions, 2,487 records/tapes/CDs. Computer terminals/PCs available for student use: 40, located in computer center, classroom buildings.

UNDERGRADUATE PROFILE Fall 1991: 719 undergraduates (205 freshmen) from 44 states and territories and 6 foreign countries; 9% part-time; 29% state residents; 12% transfers; 80% financial aid recipients; 55% women; 1% African Americans; 1% Native Americans; 1% Hispanics; 1% Asian Americans; 1% international students; 20% of undergraduates 25 years of age or older.

1991 FRESHMAN DATA 515 students applied for fall 1991 admission; 66% were accepted; 60% of those accepted enrolled.

ENROLLMENT PATTERNS 63% of fall 1990 freshmen returned for fall 1991 term.

FRESHMAN ADMISSIONS Options: early entrance, deferred entrance. Required: high school transcript, 2 recommendations, SAT or ACT, TOEFL (for foreign students). Recommended: 3 years of high school math, 2 years of high school foreign language. Required for some: interview. Test scores used for admission. Application deadline: rolling. Notification date: continuous. College's own assessment of entrance difficulty level: moderately difficult.

TRANSFER ADMISSIONS Required: high school transcript, 2 recommendations, college transcript, minimum 2.0 grade point average. Recommended: 3 years of high school math, 2 years of high school foreign language. Required for some: interview. Application deadline: rolling. Notification date: continuous. College's own assessment of entrance difficulty level: moderately difficult.

EXPENSES (1991–92) Comprehensive fee of $9586 includes full-time tuition ($6622), mandatory fees ($90), and college room and board ($2874). College room only: $1372. Part-time tuition per semester (1 to 11 semester hours) ranges from $221.50 to $3003.

FINANCIAL AID College-administered aid for all 1991–92 undergraduates: need-based scholarships (average $750); non-need scholarships (average $1200); short-term loans (average $2000); low-interest long-term loans from external sources (average $2625); SEOG; College Work-Study; part-time jobs. Supporting data: institutional form required; IRS, state form required for some; FFS, FAF, AFSA/SAR acceptable. Priority application deadline: 5/1.

CAMPUS LIFE/STUDENT SERVICES Dress code; mandatory chapel; drama/theater group; student-run newspaper. Institution provides health clinic, personal/psychological counseling.

STUDY ABROAD SITE England.

ATHLETICS Member NAIA. Intercollegiate sports: basketball M(s), W(s); golf M(s); soccer M(s); tennis M(s), W(s); volleyball W(s). Intramural sports: basketball, field hockey, football, table tennis (Ping Pong), tennis, volleyball.

MAJORS Accounting; biblical studies; biology/biological sciences; business administration/commerce/management; chemistry; communication; computer science; (pre)dentistry sequence; early childhood education; elementary education; English; health education; health services administration; history; humanities; human services; mathematics; (pre)medicine sequence; ministries; music; music education; paralegal studies; physical education; psychology; religious education; sacred music; secretarial studies/office management A,; social work; sociology; special education; (pre)veterinary medicine sequence. Most popular majors of class of 1991: business administration/commerce/management, communication.

SPECIAL NOTE FROM THE COLLEGE Milligan College combines the 3 areas of learning: God's world (taught through science), God's man (taught through the humanities), and God Himself (taught through revelation). Christ is central at Milligan College—both in its curriculum and in campus life. Milligan is a Christian liberal arts college dedicated to the integration of faith and learning in all facets of its college program. Milligan's mission is to prepare today's young people for a complicated world, and to do it in a Christian environment. Milligan's motto is "Christian education: the hope of the world!"

CONTACT Mr. Mike Johnson, Director of Admissions, Milligan College, Milligan College, TN 37682, 615-461-8736.

MISSISSIPPI COLLEGE

Clinton, Mississippi

Total Enrollment: 3,771

UG Enrollment: 2,545 (61% W)

Application Deadline: rolling

Tuition & Fees: $5310

Room & Board: $2620

Entrance: moderately difficult

SAT ≥ 500: N/R

ACT ≥ 21: N/R

Denominational Affiliation: Southern Baptist

GENERAL INFORMATION Independent comprehensive coed institution. Founded 1826. Awards B, M, D. Primary accreditation: regional. Small-town setting; 320-acre campus. Total enrollment: 3,771. Faculty: 234 (149 full-time, 85 part-time); 67% of full-time faculty have terminal degrees; graduate assistants teach a few undergraduate courses. Library holdings: 230,000 bound volumes, 14,000 titles on microform, 768 periodical subscriptions, 10,576 records/tapes/CDs. Computer terminals/PCs available for student use: 67, located in computer center.

UNDERGRADUATE PROFILE Fall 1991: 2,545 undergraduates (247 freshmen) from 40 states and territories and 6 foreign countries; 24% part-time; 87% state residents; 25% transfers; 80% financial aid recipients; 61% women; 15% African Americans; 1% Native Americans; 1% Hispanics; 1% Asian Americans; 1% international students; 44% of undergraduates 25 years of age or older.

1991 FRESHMAN DATA 479 students applied for fall 1991 admission; 80% were accepted; 63% of those accepted enrolled. 13 freshmen were National Merit Scholarship Finalists; all received a National Merit Scholarship. 25% of freshmen were in top 10% of secondary school class, 66% were in top 25%, 89% were in top half.

ENROLLMENT PATTERNS 90% of fall 1990 freshmen returned for fall 1991 term. 45% of students completing a degree program went on for further study.

FRESHMAN ADMISSIONS Option: early entrance. Required: high school transcript, SAT or ACT, TOEFL (for foreign students). Test scores used for admission. Application deadline: rolling. Notification date: continuous. College's own assessment of entrance difficulty level: moderately difficult.

TRANSFER ADMISSIONS Required: college transcript, minimum 2.0 grade point average. Application deadline: rolling. Notification date: continuous. College's own assessment of entrance difficulty level: moderately difficult.

EXPENSES (1992–93) Comprehensive fee of $7930 includes full-time tuition ($5010), mandatory fees ($300), and college room and board ($2620). College room only: $1150. Part-time tuition: $167 per credit hour.

FINANCIAL AID College-administered aid for all 1991–92 undergraduates: need-based scholarships; 550 non-need scholarships (average $1000); short-term loans (average $100); low-interest long-term loans from college funds (average $1500), from external sources (average $2500); SEOG; College Work-Study; 250 part-time jobs. Supporting data: FAF, institutional form required. Priority application deadline: 4/1.

CAMPUS LIFE/STUDENT SERVICES Dress code; mandatory chapel; drama/theater group; student-run newspaper and radio station. Institution provides health clinic, personal/psychological counseling. Social organizations: 3 local fraternities, 4 local sororities; 17% of eligible undergraduate men and 33% of eligible undergraduate women are members.

STUDY ABROAD SITES Germany, England.

ATHLETICS Member NCAA (Division II). Intercollegiate sports: basketball M(s), W(s); cross-country running M(s); football M(s); golf M(s); tennis M(s), W(s); track and field M(s); volleyball W(s). Intramural sports: basketball, cross-country running, football, golf, soccer, tennis, track and field, volleyball.

MAJORS Accounting; applied art; art education; art/fine arts; biblical studies; biology/biological sciences; business administration/commerce/management; chemistry; communication; computer science; criminal justice; data processing; (pre)dentistry sequence; early childhood education; economics; education; elementary education; English; history; home economics; home economics education; interior design; journalism; law enforcement/police sciences; (pre)law sequence; marketing/retailing/merchandising; mathematics; medical technology; (pre)medicine sequence; modern languages; music; music education; nursing; nutrition; occupational therapy; paralegal studies; physics; piano/organ; political science/government; psychology; public administration; religious education; religious studies; retail management; sacred music; science education; secretarial studies/office management; social science; social work; sociology; Spanish; special education; speech pathology and audiology. Most popular majors of class of 1991: business administration/commerce/management, elementary education, nursing.

SPECIAL NOTE FROM THE COLLEGE Mississippi College is a private, 4-year college affiliated with the Mississippi Baptist Convention. Founded in 1826, it is located 5 miles west of Jackson, in Clinton, Mississippi. Recognized as the oldest institution of higher learning in the state, it is the second-oldest Baptist college in the nation and was one of the first coeducational colleges in the country to grant degrees to women. In addition to its outstanding liberal arts program, it is recognized for its graduate school and School of Law programs. The College won the 1989 NCAA Division II national championship in football.

CONTACT Mrs. Jennifer Trussell, Director of Admissions, Mississippi College, Clinton, MS 39058, 601-925-3240.

MONTREAT-ANDERSON COLLEGE

Montreat, North Carolina

Total Enrollment: 398 (all UG)

Women: 49%

Application Deadline: 8/20

Tuition & Fees: $6512

Room & Board: $3242

Entrance: minimally difficult

SAT ≥ 500: N/R

ACT ≥ 21: N/R

Denominational Affiliation: Presbyterian (USA)

GENERAL INFORMATION Independent 4-year coed college. Founded 1916. Awards A (college transfer), B. Primary accreditation: regional. Small-town setting; 100-acre campus. Total enrollment: 398. Faculty: 36 (27 full-time, 9 part-time); 46% of full-time faculty have terminal degrees; graduate assistants teach no undergraduate courses. Library holdings: 60,559 bound volumes, 415 titles on microform, 417 periodical subscriptions, 1,799 records/tapes/CDs. Computer terminals/PCs available for student use: 30, located in computer center, student center, library, dormitories.

UNDERGRADUATE PROFILE Fall 1991: 398 undergraduates (131 freshmen) from 21 states and territories and 10 foreign countries; 5% part-time; 60% state residents; 14% transfers; 85% financial aid recipients; 49% women; 8% African Americans; 1% Native Americans; 1% Hispanics; 1% Asian Americans; 4% international students; 7% of undergraduates 25 years of age or older.

1991 FRESHMAN DATA 371 students who applied for fall 1991 admission, 71% were accepted; 49% of those accepted enrolled.

ENROLLMENT PATTERNS 70% of fall 1990 freshmen returned for fall 1991 term. 94% of students completing a college-transfer associate program went on to 4-year colleges. 28% of students completing a degree program went on for further study.

FRESHMAN ADMISSIONS Options: early entrance, deferred entrance. Required: essay, high school transcript, SAT or ACT, TOEFL (for foreign students). Recommended: 3 years of high school math and science, some high school foreign language, 1 recommendation. Required for some: interview. Test scores used for admission. Application deadline: 8/20. Notification date: continuous. College's own assessment of entrance difficulty level: minimally difficult.

TRANSFER ADMISSIONS Required: essay, standardized test scores, high school transcript, college transcript. Recommended: 3 years of high school math and science, some high school foreign language, 1 recommendation, minimum 2.0 grade point average. Required for some: interview. Application deadline: 8/20. Notification date: continuous. College's own assessment of entrance difficulty level: minimally difficult.

EXPENSES (1992–93) Comprehensive fee of $9754 includes full-time tuition ($6136), mandatory fees ($376), and college room and board ($3242). Part-time tuition: $70 per semester hour.

FINANCIAL AID College-administered aid for all 1991–92 undergraduates: 242 need-based scholarships (average $4000); 89 non-need scholarships (average $1500); short-term loans (average $1000); low-interest long-term loans from college funds (average $1000), from external sources (average $1800); SEOG; College Work-Study; 20 part-time jobs. Supporting data: FAF, IRS, institutional form required; state form required for some; FFS, AFSA/SAR acceptable. Priority application deadline: 3/15.

CAMPUS LIFE/STUDENT SERVICES Mandatory chapel; drama/theater group; student-run newspaper, yearbook and literary magazine. Institution provides health clinic, personal/psychological counseling.

ATHLETICS Member NAIA. Intercollegiate sports: baseball M(s); basketball M(s), W(s); soccer M(s); tennis W; volleyball W(s). Intramural sports: badminton, basketball, football, skiing (cross-country), skiing (downhill), table tennis (Ping Pong), tennis, volleyball.

MAJORS Business administration/accounting/economics/marketing; cultural studies/child and family studies; English; environmental studies; history; human services; liberal arts/general studies; ministries; outdoor recreation and leisure services; religious studies; science; secondary education; social science, math. Most popular majors of class of 1991: business administration, outdoor recreation, human services, religious studies.

SPECIAL NOTE FROM THE COLLEGE Montreat-Anderson College is firm in its commitment to Christian education. Its sense of Christian community is one of the most distinctive features of campus life. The small but vibrant campus creates a close-knit and personal atmosphere—an atmosphere that encourages involvement and participation from all segments of the student body. The campus is surrounded by the Blue Ridge Mountains, wooded hiking trails, mountain streams, and a mountain lake. M-AC takes advantage of this inspiring location by offering one of the most challenging and unique outdoor-recreation programs in the country. The Business Administration Program has one of the best liberal arts and professional curriculums. M-AC offers students a meditative mountain setting; small, challenging classes; friendly, enthusiastic students; and a variety of degree programs plus the warmth, security, and moral structure that only a Christ-centered school can provide.

CONTACT Mr. Charles Lance, Director of Admissions, Montreat-Anderson College, P.O. Box 1267, Montreat, NC 28757, 704-669-8011 Ext. 229 or toll-free 800-627-1750.

MOUNT VERNON NAZARENE COLLEGE

Mount Vernon, Ohio

Total Enrollment: 1,044

UG Enrollment: 1,027 (56% W)

Application Deadline: rolling

Tuition & Fees: $6575

Room & Board: $3090

Entrance: moderately difficult

SAT ≥ 500: N/App

ACT ≥ 21: 53%

Denominational Affiliation: Church of the Nazarene

GENERAL INFORMATION Independent 4-year comprehensive coed institution. Founded 1964. Awards A (college transfer and terminal), B, M. Primary accreditation: regional. Small-town setting, with easy access to Columbus; 210-acre campus. Total enrollment: 1,044. Faculty: 67 (51 full-time, 16 part-time); 55% of full-time faculty have terminal degrees; graduate assistants teach no undergraduate courses. Library holdings: 82,154 bound volumes, 3,294 titles on microform, 526 periodical subscriptions, 3,317 records/tapes/CDs. Computer terminals/PCs available for student use: 128, located in academic center, business center.

UNDERGRADUATE PROFILE Fall 1991: 1,027 undergraduates (244 freshmen) from 19 states and territories and 5 foreign countries; 9% part-time; 83% state residents; 6% transfers; 93% financial aid recipients; 56% women; 1% African Americans; 0% Native Americans; 1% Hispanics; 1% Asian Americans; 1% international students; 5% of undergraduates 25 years of age or older.

1991 FRESHMAN DATA 395 students applied for fall 1991 admission; 91% were accepted; 68% of those accepted enrolled. 19% of freshmen were in top 10% of secondary school class, 41% were in top 25%, 69% were in top half.

ENROLLMENT PATTERNS 68% of fall 1990 freshmen returned for fall 1991 term.

FRESHMAN ADMISSIONS Options: early entrance, deferred entrance. Required: essay, high school transcript, 2 recommendations, ACT, TOEFL (for foreign students). Recommended: 3 years of high school math and science, 2 years of high school foreign language, interview. Test scores used for counseling/placement. Application deadline: rolling. Notification date: continuous. College's own assessment of entrance difficulty level: moderately difficult.

TRANSFER ADMISSIONS Required: essay, high school transcript, 2 recommendations, college transcript, minimum 2.0 grade point average. Recommended: 3 years of high school math and science, 2 years of high school foreign language, interview. Required for some: standardized test scores. Application deadline: rolling. Notification date: continuous.

EXPENSES (1992–93) Comprehensive fee of $9665 includes full-time tuition ($6230), mandatory fees ($345), and college room and board ($3090). Part-time tuition: $222 per credit hour, part-time fees: $10 per credit hour.

FINANCIAL AID College-administered aid for all 1991–92 undergraduates: 188 need-based scholarships (average $675); 615 non-need scholarships (average $1050); low-interest long-term loans from external sources (average $2000); SEOG; College Work-Study; 210 part-time jobs. Supporting data: FAF, IRS, institutional form, AFSA/SAR required; state form required for some; FFS acceptable. Priority application deadline: 4/15.

CAMPUS LIFE/STUDENT SERVICES Dress code; mandatory chapel; drama/theater group; student-run newspaper and radio station. Institution provides health clinic, personal/psychological counseling.

ATHLETICS Member NAIA. Intercollegiate sports: baseball M(s); basketball M(s), W(s); golf M(s); soccer M(s); softball W(s); tennis M(s), W(s); volleyball W(s). Intramural sports: basketball, bowling, golf, skiing (downhill), soccer, softball, table tennis (Ping Pong), tennis, volleyball.

MAJORS Accounting; applied art; art education; art/fine arts; biblical studies; biochemistry; biology/biological sciences; broadcasting; business administration/commerce/management; business education; chemistry; communication; computer science; computer technologies; criminal justice; data processing; (pre)dentistry sequence; early childhood education; education; elementary education; (pre)engineering sequence; English; health science; history; home economics; home economics education; human services; (pre)law sequence; liberal arts/general studies; literature; marketing/retailing/merchandising; mathematics; medical technology; (pre)medicine sequence; modern languages; music; music education; natural resource management; philosophy; physical education; piano/organ; psychology; religious education; religious studies; sacred music; science; science education; secondary education; secretarial studies/office management; social science; social work; sociology; Spanish; special education; sports administration; sports medicine; theater arts/drama; theology; (pre)veterinary medicine sequence; voice; wind and percussion instruments. Most popular majors of class of 1991: business administration/commerce/management, social science, education.

SPECIAL NOTE FROM THE COLLEGE Mount Vernon Nazarene College exists to "train servant leaders for the 21st Century." A closer look at MVNC reveals not only a Christ-centered education but a service-oriented outlook on life. Students invest themselves in a variety of missions and ministry projects during the school year, during the January term, and during the summer in places across the state, around the nation, and throughout the world. MVNC's rural setting, apartment-style living, and comprehensive campus-ministries program headed by the College's full-time chaplain/campus pastor, promote a sense of family. A 4-1-4 calendar allows off-campus classes midyear. An extensive high-quality academic program and abundant extracurricular activities in a peaceful country setting make MVNC a wonderful place to live and grow.

CONTACT Rev. Bruce Oldham, Director, Admissions and Student Recruitment, Mount Vernon Nazarene College, 800 Martinsburg Road, Mount Vernon, OH 43050, 614-397-1244 Ext. 4500 or toll-free 800-782-2435.

NORTH PARK COLLEGE

Chicago, Illinois

Total Enrollment: 1,189
UG Enrollment: 987 (54% W)
Application Deadline: rolling
Tuition & Fees: $11,295
Room & Board: $4140
Entrance: moderately difficult
SAT ≥ 500: 37% V, 56% M
ACT ≥ 21: 61%
Denominational Affiliation: Evangelical Covenant Church of America

GENERAL INFORMATION Independent comprehensive coed institution. Founded 1891. Awards B, M. Primary accreditation: regional. Urban setting; 30-acre campus. Total enrollment: 1,189. Faculty: 158; 82% of full-time faculty have terminal degrees; graduate assistants teach no undergraduate courses. Library holdings: 207,000 bound volumes, 3,300 titles on microform, 1,000 periodical subscriptions, 5,000 records/tapes/CDs. Computer terminals/PCs available for student use: 60, located in computer center, student center, library, classrooms.

UNDERGRADUATE PROFILE Fall 1991: 987 undergraduates (212 freshmen) from 40 states and territories and 6 foreign countries; 9% part-time; 56% state residents; 15% transfers; 85% financial aid recipients; 54% women; 5% African Americans; 0% Native Americans; 5% Hispanics; 5% Asian Americans; 6% international students; 4% of undergraduates 25 years of age or older.

1991 FRESHMAN DATA Of the students who applied for fall, 1991 admission, 70% were accepted. 17% of freshmen were in top 10% of secondary school class, 36% were in top 25%, 70% were in top half. 5 freshmen were National Merit Scholarship Finalists; all received a National Merit Scholarship.

ENROLLMENT PATTERNS 84% of fall 1990 freshmen returned for fall 1991 term.

FRESHMAN ADMISSIONS Option: early entrance. Required: essay, high school transcript, recommendations, SAT or ACT, TOEFL (for foreign students). Recommended: 3 years of high school math and science, some high school foreign language. Test scores used for admission. Application deadline: rolling.

Notification date: continuous. College's own assessment of entrance difficulty level: moderately difficult.

TRANSFER ADMISSIONS Required: essay, recommendations, college transcript, minimum 2.0 grade point average. Recommended: 3 years of high school math and science, some high school foreign language. Required for some: standardized test scores, high school transcript. Application deadline: rolling. Notification date: continuous. College's own assessment of entrance difficulty level: moderately difficult.

EXPENSES (1992–93) Comprehensive fee of $15,435 includes full-time tuition ($11,295) and college room and board ($4140).

FINANCIAL AID College-administered aid for all 1991–92 undergraduates: 600 need-based scholarships (average $4100); 110 non-need scholarships (average $1200); low-interest long-term loans from external sources (average $2250); SEOG; College Work-Study; 100 part-time jobs. Supporting data: FAF, IRS, institutional form required; state form, AFSA/SAR required for some; FFS acceptable. Priority application deadline: 8/15.

CAMPUS LIFE/STUDENT SERVICES Drama/theater group; student-run newspaper, music ministry team, Urban Outreach. Institution provides health clinic, personal/psychological counseling.

STUDY ABROAD SITES Sweden, Mexico, Israel.

ATHLETICS Member NCAA (Division III). Intercollegiate sports: baseball M; basketball M, W; cross-country running M, W; football M; soccer M; softball W; tennis M, W; track and field M, W; volleyball M, W. Intramural sports: basketball, football, volleyball, weight lifting.

MAJORS Accounting; anthropology; art education; art/fine arts; biblical studies; biology/biological sciences; business administration; business and society; chemistry; communication; (pre)dentistry sequence; early childhood education; economics; education; elementary education; English/writing; exercise science; finance; French; German; history; international affairs; international studies; (pre)law sequence; literature; marketing; mathematics; medical technology; (pre)medicine sequence; music; music education; natural science; nursing; philosophy; physical education; physics; political science/government; psychology; science; secondary education; social science; sociology; Spanish; speech; sports medicine; Swedish; theological studies; urban studies; (pre)veterinary medicine sequence. Most popular majors of class of 1991: business administration, education, nursing, psychology.

SPECIAL NOTE FROM THE COLLEGE North Park is the only member of the Christian College Coalition located in a world-class city. North Park is also the only residential liberal arts college in the city of Chicago. On account of this unique identity, North Park draws students from across America and around the world who wish to study on a Christian campus in a dynamic urban environment. From internships with major corporations to volunteer service with inner-city ministries to internationally renowned museums and theater to 6 professional sports teams, North Park offers a world of opportunities for learning and living.

CONTACT Mr. Randy Tumblin, Director of Admissions, North Park College, 3225 West Foster Avenue, Chicago, IL 60625, 312-583-2700 Ext. 4500 or toll-free 800-888-NPC8.

NORTHWEST CHRISTIAN COLLEGE

Eugene, Oregon

Total Enrollment: 282

UG Enrollment: 253 (48% W)

Application Deadline: rolling

Tuition & Fees: $6639

Room & Board: $3514

Entrance: minimally difficult

SAT ≥ 500: 26% V, 48% M

ACT ≥ 21: N/R

Denominational Affiliation: interdenominational

GENERAL INFORMATION Independent comprehensive coed institution. Founded 1895. Awards A (college transfer), B, M. Primary accreditation: regional. Small town setting; 10-acre campus. Total enrollment: 282. Faculty: 34 (11 full-time, 16 part-time); 55% of full-time faculty have terminal degrees; graduate assistants teach no undergraduate courses. Library holdings: 51,876 bound volumes, 551 titles on microform, 230 periodical subscriptions, 1,576 records/tapes/CDs. Computer terminals/PCs available for student use: 9, located in library.

UNDERGRADUATE PROFILE Fall 1991: 253 undergraduates (61 freshmen) from 10 states and territories and 4 foreign countries; 10% part-time; 79% state residents; 41% transfers; 80% financial aid recipients; 48% women; 1% African Americans; 0% Native Americans; 1% Hispanics; 2% Asian Americans; 3% international students; 23% of undergraduates 25 years of age or older.

1991 FRESHMAN DATA 76 students applied for fall 1991 admission; 98% were accepted; 80% of those accepted enrolled.

ENROLLMENT PATTERNS 64% of fall 1990 freshmen returned for fall 1991 term.

FRESHMAN ADMISSIONS Option: deferred entrance. Required: essay, high school transcript, 2 recommendations, SAT or ACT, TOEFL (for foreign students). Application deadline: rolling. Notification date: continuous. College's own assessment of entrance difficulty level: minimally difficult.

TRANSFER ADMISSIONS Required: 2 recommendations, college transcript. Recommended: minimum 2.0 grade point average. Application deadline: rolling. Notification date: continuous. College's own assessment of entrance difficulty level: minimally difficult.

EXPENSES (1992–93) Comprehensive fee of $10,153 includes full-time tuition ($6480), mandatory fees ($159), and college room and board ($3514). Part-time tuition: $72 per quarter hour.

FINANCIAL AID College-administered aid for all 1991–92 undergraduates: 87 need-based scholarships (average $961); 51 non-need scholarships (average $729); low-interest long-term loans from external sources (average $2993); SEOG; College Work-Study; 47 part-time jobs. Supporting data: FFS, FAF, institutional form, AFSA/SAR acceptable. Priority application deadline: 2/15.

CAMPUS LIFE/STUDENT SERVICES Mandatory chapel; student-run newspaper; musical groups; student government. Institution provides health clinic, personal/psychological counseling.

STUDY ABROAD SITE Israel.

ATHLETICS Intercollegiate sport: basketball M. Intramural sports: basketball, football, racquetball, volleyball.

MAJORS Biblical studies; business administration/commerce/management; communication; interdisciplinary studies; liberal arts/general studies; ministries; pastoral studies; religious studies; sacred music; theology.

SPECIAL NOTE FROM THE COLLEGE Northwest Christian College's small academic community is uniquely situated to help students clarify their faith, identify their strengths, and develop their professional potential. A strong core curriculum in the arts and sciences challenges students to grow in their knowledge of the world. Northwest Christian's scholarly and reverent study of the Bible encourages students to examine their faith in light of biblical revelation and apply it to all of life. An emphasis across the curriculum in evaluative thinking and effective communication, both written and spoken, help develop the skills students need for successful leadership and service. The College's combination program with the University of Oregon, which is just across the street, provides students with additional opportunities in nearly 30 academic and career areas. Finally, the campus provides a Christian environment where students can practice their faith through personal devotions, campus worship, community service, and planned ministries.

CONTACT Dr. Randolph P. Jones, Director of Admissions, Northwest Christian College, 828 East 11th Avenue, Eugene, OR 97401, 503-343-1641 Ext. 20.

Northwest College of the Assemblies of God

Kirkland, Washington

Total Enrollment: 658 (all UG)

Women: 49%

Application Deadline: rolling

Tuition & Fees: $6173

Room & Board: $3000

Entrance: minimally difficult

SAT ≥ 500: N/R

ACT ≥ 21: N/R

Denominational Affiliation: Assemblies of God

GENERAL INFORMATION Independent 4-year coed college. Founded 1934. Awards A (college transfer and terminal), B. Primary accreditation: regional. Suburban setting, with easy access to Seattle; 60-acre campus. Total enrollment: 658. Faculty: 55 (30 full-time, 25 part-time); 50% of full-time faculty have terminal degrees; graduate assistants teach no undergraduate courses. Library holdings: 84,000 bound volumes, 596 periodical subscriptions, 1,300 records/tapes/CDs. Computer terminals/PCs available for student use: 16, located in computer center, library.

UNDERGRADUATE PROFILE Fall 1991: 658 undergraduates (125 freshmen) from 29 states and territories and 10 foreign countries; 16% part-time; 65% state residents; 15% transfers; 65% financial aid recipients; 49% women; 1% African Americans; 2% Native Americans; 2% Hispanics; 6% Asian Americans; 4% international students; 24% of undergraduates 25 years of age or older.

1991 FRESHMAN DATA 160 students applied for fall 1991 admission; 100% were accepted; 78% of those accepted enrolled.

FRESHMAN ADMISSIONS Options: early entrance, early decision, deferred entrance. Required: essay, high school transcript, 2 recommendations, SAT or ACT, TOEFL (for foreign students). Recommended: some high school foreign language. Required for some: interview. Test scores used for counseling/placement. Application deadline: rolling, 11/15 for early decision. College's own assessment of entrance difficulty level: minimally difficult.

TRANSFER ADMISSIONS Required: essay, high school transcript, 2 recommendations, college transcript. Recommended: some high school foreign language, minimum 2.0 grade point average. Required for some: standardized test scores, interview. Application deadline: rolling, 12/1 for early decision. College's own assessment of entrance difficulty level: minimally difficult.

EXPENSES (1992–93) Comprehensive fee of $9173 includes full-time tuition ($5520), mandatory fees ($653), and college room and board ($3000). Part-time tuition: $230 per semester hour.

FINANCIAL AID College-administered aid for all 1991–92 undergraduates: need-based scholarships; non-need scholarships; short-term loans; low-interest long-term loans; SEOG; College Work-Study; part-time jobs. Supporting data: FAF, IRS, institutional form, AFSA/SAR required. Priority application deadline: 3/1.

CAMPUS LIFE/STUDENT SERVICES Dress code; mandatory chapel; drama/theater group, student-run radio station. Institution provides health clinic, personal/psychological counseling.

ATHLETICS Intercollegiate sports: basketball M, W; soccer M; volleyball W. Intramural sports: basketball, football, tennis, volleyball.

MAJORS Behavioral sciences; biblical studies; business administration/commerce/management; business machine technologies; elementary education; health sciences preparation; interdisciplinary studies; liberal arts/general studies; ministries; missions; pastoral ministries; pastoral studies; philosophy; religious education; religious studies; sacred music; teaching English as a second language; youth ministries. Most popular majors of class of 1991: elementary education, behavioral sciences, ministries.

SPECIAL NOTE FROM THE COLLEGE The educational experience at Northwest is designed around a professional curriculum geared toward today's job market. New majors in business management and administration, health sciences preparation, and teaching English as a second language are examples of program development that ensure the relevancy of the curriculum into the 21st century. Secondary education with content majors in English, history, and psychology will be offered beginning fall 1993. Northwest is located in the greater metropolitan Seattle area but is still within easy access of mountains, lakes, forests, and parks. It's an ideal location for skiing, hiking, boating, and sporting and cultural events.

CONTACT Dr. Calvin L. White, Director of Enrollment Services, Northwest College of the Assemblies of God, P.O. Box 579, Kirkland, WA 98083, 800-669-3781 Ext. 209.

NORTHWESTERN COLLEGE

Orange City, Iowa

Total Enrollment: 1,040
UG Enrollment: 1,021 (55% W)
Application Deadline: rolling
Tuition & Fees: $8700
Room & Board: $2900
Entrance: moderately difficult
SAT ≥ 500: N/R
ACT ≥ 21: 61%
Denominational Affiliation: Reformed Church in America

GENERAL INFORMATION Independent comprehensive coed institution. Founded 1882. Awards A (terminal), B, M. Primary accreditation: regional. Rural setting; 40-acre campus. Total enrollment: 1,040. Faculty: 94 (58 full-time, 36 part-time); 65% of full-time faculty have terminal degrees; graduate assistants teach no undergraduate courses. Library holdings: 98,000 bound volumes, 505 periodical subscriptions, 2,800 records/tapes/CDs. Computer terminals/PCs available for student use: 95, located in computer center, dormitories, classrooms.

UNDERGRADUATE PROFILE Fall 1991: 1,021 undergraduates (260 freshmen) from 29 states and territories and 15 foreign countries; 5% part-time; 70% state residents; 5% transfers; 95% financial aid recipients; 55% women; 2% African Americans; 0% Native Americans; 0% Hispanics; 6% international students.

1991 FRESHMAN DATA 685 students applied for fall 1991 admission; 86% were accepted; 44% of those accepted enrolled. 4 freshmen were National Merit Scholarship Finalists; all received a National Merit Scholarship. 28% of freshmen were in top 10% of secondary school class, 57% were in top 25%, 86% were in top half.

ENROLLMENT PATTERNS 87% of fall 1990 freshmen returned for fall 1991 term. 56% of 1986 freshmen graduated within 5 years; 15% of students completing a bachelor's program went on for further study.

FRESHMAN ADMISSIONS Option: deferred entrance. Required: high school transcript, 1 recommendation, SAT or ACT, TOEFL (for foreign students). Recommended: 3 years of high school math and science, interview. Test scores used for admission and counseling/placement. Application deadline: rolling. Notification

date: continuous until 8/30. College's own assessment of entrance difficulty level: moderately difficult.

TRANSFER ADMISSIONS Required: 1 recommendation, college transcript, minimum 2.0 grade point average. Recommended: interview. Application deadline: rolling. Notification date: continuous until 8/30.

EXPENSES (1992–93) Comprehensive fee of $11,600 includes full-time tuition ($8700) and college room and board ($2900). College room only: $1225. Part-time tuition per semester (1 to 11 credit hours) ranges from $175 to $3850.

FINANCIAL AID College-administered aid for all 1991–92 undergraduates: 790 need-based scholarships (average $1990); 296 non-need scholarships (average $2632); low-interest long-term loans from college funds (average $1240); from external sources (average $2386); SEOG; College Work-Study; 245 part-time jobs. Supporting data: institutional form required; IRS, AFSA/SAR required for some; FFS, FAF acceptable. Priority application deadline: 4/1.

CAMPUS LIFE/STUDENT SERVICES Mandatory chapel; drama/theater group; student-run newspaper and radio station. Institution provides health clinic, personal/psychological counseling.

STUDY ABROAD SITES Costa Rica, France, the Netherlands, Spain.

ATHLETICS Member NAIA. Intercollegiate sports: baseball M(s); basketball M(s), W(s); cross-country running M(s), W(s); football M(s); golf M(s), W(s); softball W(s); tennis M(s), W(s); track and field M(s), W(s); volleyball W(s); wrestling M(s). Intramural sports: badminton, basketball, bowling, cross-country running, football, golf, racquetball, soccer, softball, table tennis (Ping Pong), tennis, volleyball.

MAJORS Accounting; art education; biology/biological sciences; business administration/commerce/management; business education; chemistry; communication; computer science; criminal justice; (pre)dentistry sequence; early childhood education; economics; education; elementary education; English; French; health science; history; humanities; (pre)law sequence; literature; mathematics; medical technology; (pre)medicine sequence; music; music education; natural sciences; philosophy; physical education; physics; political science/government; psychology; recreation and leisure services; religious studies; secondary education; secretarial studies/office management; social work; sociology; Spanish; special education; theater arts/drama; theology; (pre)veterinary medicine sequence. Most popular majors of class of 1991: business administration/commerce/management, elementary education, biology/biological sciences.

SPECIAL NOTE FROM THE COLLEGE Northwestern College offers students and faculty members an academic journey that reflects on what it means to be a reformed, evangelical Christian in today's society. The academic program nurtures the development of a biblical perspective. Student development programs provide opportunities for holistic growth and Christian service. The College's newest facilities include Christ Chapel and DeWitt Music Hall, winner of numerous design awards. Other facilities include an outstanding student center featuring an art gallery, a theater, a game room, and a large fitness center; a learning resource center with newly enhanced computer and audiovisual equipment; and an innovative Business/Education Center housing the 2 largest academic departments.

CONTACT Mr. Ronald K. DeJong, Director of Admissions, Northwestern College, 101 Seventh Street, SW, Orange City, IA 51041-1996, 712-737-4821 Ext. 137.

NORTHWESTERN COLLEGE

St. Paul, Minnesota

Total Enrollment: 1,176 (all UG)

Women: 58%

Application Deadline: 8/15

Tuition & Fees: $9825

Room & Board: $2745

Entrance: moderately difficult

SAT ≥ 500: N/R

ACT ≥ 21: 64%

Denominational Affiliation: nondenominational

GENERAL INFORMATION Independent 4-year coed college. Founded 1902. Awards A (college transfer and terminal), B. Primary accreditation: regional. Suburban setting, with easy access to Minneapolis; 95-acre campus. Total enrollment: 1,176. Faculty: 112 (59 full-time, 52 part-time); 52% of full-time faculty have terminal degrees; graduate assistants teach no undergraduate courses. Library holdings: 75,000 bound volumes, 44,000 titles on microform, 550 periodical subscriptions, 4,500 records/tapes/CDs. Computer terminals/PCs available for student use: 58, located in computer center, classrooms.

UNDERGRADUATE PROFILE Fall 1991: 1,176 undergraduates (280 freshmen) from 36 states and territories and 13 foreign countries; 5% part-time; 66% state residents; 10% transfers; 85% financial aid recipients; 58% women; 1% African Americans; 0% Native Americans; 0% Hispanics; 1% Asian Americans; 2% international students; 10% of undergraduates 25 years of age or older.

1991 FRESHMAN DATA 433 students applied for fall 1991 admission; 98% were accepted; 66% of those accepted enrolled. 5 freshmen were National Merit Scholarship Finalists. 25% of freshmen were in top 10% of secondary school class, 52% were in top 25%, 77% were in top half.

ENROLLMENT PATTERNS 79% of fall 1990 freshmen returned for fall 1991 term. 17% of students completing a bachelor's program went on for further study.

FRESHMAN ADMISSIONS Options: early entrance, deferred entrance. Required: essay, high school transcript, 2 recommendations, lifestyle agreement, statement of Christian faith, SAT or ACT, TOEFL (for foreign students), PSAT. Recommended: 4 years of high school English, 3 years of high school math and science, 2 years of high school foreign language.

Required for some: campus interview. Test scores used for counseling/placement. Application deadline: 8/15. Notification date: continuous until 9/1. College's own assessment of entrance difficulty level: moderately difficult.

TRANSFER ADMISSIONS Required: essay, 2 recommendations, high school transcript, college transcript, lifestyle agreement, statement of Christian faith. Recommended: 2 years of high school foreign language, minimum 2.0 grade point average. Required for some: standardized test scores, campus interview. Application deadline: 8/15. Notification date: continuous until 9/1. College's own assessment of entrance difficulty level: moderately difficult.

EXPENSES (1992–93) Comprehensive fee of $12,570 includes full-time tuition ($9825) and college room and board ($2745). College room only: $1650. Part-time tuition: $275 per credit.

FINANCIAL AID College-administered aid for all 1991–92 undergraduates: 629 need-based scholarships (average $1449); 723 non-need scholarships (average $857); low-interest long-term loans from external sources (average $2450); SEOG; College Work-Study; 172 part-time jobs. Supporting data: IRS, AFSA/SAR required; institutional form required for some; FFS, FAF acceptable. Priority application deadline: 3/1.

CAMPUS LIFE/STUDENT SERVICES Dress code; mandatory chapel; drama/theater group; student-run newspaper and radio station. Institution provides health clinic, personal/psychological counseling.

STUDY ABROAD SITE Israel.

ATHLETICS Intercollegiate sports: baseball M(s); basketball M(s), W(s); cross-country running M(s), W(s); football M(s); golf M(s), W(s); soccer M(s); softball W(s); tennis M(s), W(s); track and field M(s), W(s); volleyball W(s); wrestling M(s). Intramural sports: badminton, basketball, bowling, broomball, football, racquetball, softball, table tennis (Ping Pong), volleyball.

MAJORS Accounting; adult and continuing education; agricultural business; art education; art/fine arts; biblical studies; broadcasting; business administration/commerce/management; communication; computer information systems; education; elementary education; (pre)engineering sequence; English; finance/banking; graphic arts; human resources; international business; journalism; legal secretarial studies; liberal arts/general studies; literature; marketing/retailing/merchandising; mathematics; ministries; music; music education; pastoral studies; physical education; psychology; religious education; science; secondary education; secretarial studies/office management; social science; theater arts/drama; theology. Most popular majors of class of 1991: elementary education, psychology, marketing/retailing/merchandising.

SPECIAL NOTE FROM THE COLLEGE Northwestern College is the only private, nondenominational Christian liberal arts college in the state of Minnesota. Northwestern students have 2 majors. Every bachelor's degree program requires 45 credits of Bible-related courses in addition to those obtained from 1 of 28 additional majors. The warm, friendly campus; challenging academic programs; and superb facilities offer each student the environment to develop as an individual both academically and spiritually.

CONTACT Mr. Ralph D. Anderson, Dean of Admissions, Northwestern College, 3003 North Snelling Avenue, St. Paul, MN 55113, 612-631-5111 or toll-free 800-827-6827.

NORTHWEST NAZARENE COLLEGE

Northwest Nazarene
College

Nampa, Idaho

Total Enrollment: 1,497
UG Enrollment: 1,107 (52% W)
Application Deadline: 9/20
Tuition & Fees: $8160
Room & Board: $2590
Entrance: moderately difficult
Denominational Affiliation: Church of the Nazarene

GENERAL INFORMATION Independent comprehensive coed institution. Founded 1913. Awards A (college transfer and terminal), B, M. Primary accreditation: regional. Suburban setting; 83-acre campus. Total enrollment: 1,497. Faculty: 101 (70 full-time, 31 part-time); 55% of full-time faculty have doctoral degrees; graduate assistants teach no undergraduate courses. Library holdings: 127,200 bound volumes, 47,319 titles on microform, 736 periodical subscriptions, 2,721 records/tapes/CDs.

UNDERGRADUATE PROFILE Fall 1992: 1,107 undergraduates (328 freshmen) from 26 states and territories and 7 foreign countries; 7% part-time; 32% state residents; 9% transfers, 95% financial aid recipients; 52% women; 1% African Americans; 1% Native Americans; 2% Hispanics; 1% Asian Americans; 1% international students; 13% of undergraduates 25 years of age or older.

1992 FRESHMAN DATA 436 students applied for admission; 80% were accepted; 70% of those accepted enrolled. 1 freshman was a National Merit Scholarship Finalist. 24% of freshmen were in top 10% of secondary school class, 45% were in top 25%, 80% were in top half.

ENROLLMENT PATTERNS 76% of fall 1990 freshmen returned for fall 1992 term. 25% of students completing bachelor's degree went on for further study.

FRESHMAN ADMISSIONS Options: early entrance, deferred entrance. Required: high school transcript, recommendations, TOEFL (for foreign students). Recommended: SAT or ACT,

WPCT. Test scores used for counseling/placement. Application deadline: 9/19. Notification date: continuous. College's own assessment of entrance difficulty level: moderately difficult.

TRANSFER ADMISSIONS Required: recommendations, college transcript. Required for some: standardized test scores, high school transcript. Application deadline: 9/19. Notification date: continuous. College's own assessment of entrance difficulty level: moderately difficult.

EXPENSES (1992–93) Comprehensive fee of $10,750 includes full-time tuition ($7821), mandatory fees ($339), and college room and board ($2590). Part-time tuition: $225 per credit.

FINANCIAL AID College-administered aid for all 1991–92 undergraduates: 230 need-based scholarships; non-need scholarships (average $1100); low-interest long-term loans from external sources (average $2500); SEOG; College Work-Study; 420 part-time jobs. Supporting data: FAF, institutional form, AFSA/SAR required. Priority deadline: 3/1.

CAMPUS LIFE/STUDENT SERVICES Mandatory chapel; drama/theater group; student-run newspaper. Institution provides health clinic, personal/psychological counseling.

ATHLETICS Member NAIA. Intercollegiate sports: baseball M; basketball M, W; soccer M; tennis W; track and field M, W; volleyball W.

MAJORS Accounting; art; athletic training; biological science; business; chemistry; child care management; compassionate ministry; computer (business); computer science; curriculum and instruction; (pre)dental; (pre)dietetics; drama; educationally handicapped; elementary education; engineering physics technology; English; entrepreneurship; fashion merchandising; finance; general studies; health; history; home economics; human services; individualized major; international studies; (pre)law; liberal studies; management; marketing; mathematics; mathematics and natural science; (pre)medical; ministry; music; natural science; (pre)nursing; office; (pre)optometry; philosophy; philosophy and religion; physical education; physical science; physical therapy; physics; political science; psychology; public policy; recreation; religion; religious education; seminary studies; science technology; social work; sociology; Spanish; special ministries; speech and hearing pathology; speech—communications; (pre)veterinary medicine.

SPECIAL NOTE FROM THE COLLEGE Northwest Nazarene College is proud of the fact that it has been selected to be among the top 10 liberal arts colleges in the western United States for 2 years in a row by *U.S. News & World Report*. Northwest Nazarene is a unique blend of academic excellence and a strong spiritual commitment. As expressed by Rick Heib, a NASA astronaut and 1977 graduate: "The solid academic preparation is important and the personal involvement of the faculty with students is something crucial to scholastic development. . . . I think of NNC experiences, ranging from music, athletics, and student body activities to community involvement, all in the overall framework of putting others ahead of oneself."

CONTACT Mr. Terrence A. Blom, Director of Enrollment Management, Northwest Nazarene College, Nampa, ID 83686, toll-free 800-NNC-4-YOU.

Nyack College

Nyack, New York

Total Enrollment: 699

UG Enrollment: 513 (59% W)

Application Deadline: rolling

Tuition & Fees: $7860

Room & Board: $3600

Entrance: moderately difficult

SAT ≥ 500: 24% V, 29% M

ACT ≥ 21: 20%

Denominational Affiliation: The Christian and Missionary Alliance

GENERAL INFORMATION Independent comprehensive coed institution. Founded 1882. Awards A (college transfer), B, M. Primary accreditation: regional. Small-town setting, with easy access to New York City; 64-acre campus. Total enrollment: 699. Faculty: 57 (46 full-time, 11 part-time); 60% of full-time faculty have terminal degrees; graduate assistants teach no undergraduate courses. Library holdings: 77,000 bound volumes, 420 titles on microform, 614 periodical subscriptions. Computer terminals/PCs available for student use: 25, located in computer center.

UNDERGRADUATE PROFILE Fall 1991: 513 undergraduates (183 freshmen) from 31 states and territories and 3 foreign countries; 9% part-time; 55% state residents; 11% transfers; 85% financial aid recipients; 59% women; 9% African Americans; 1% Native Americans; 7% Hispanics; 14% Asian Americans; 1% international students; 19% of undergraduates 25 years of age or older.

1991 FRESHMAN DATA 425 students applied for fall 1991 admission; 65% were accepted; 66% of those accepted enrolled.

ENROLLMENT PATTERNS 72% of fall 1990 freshmen returned for fall 1991 term. 77% of 1986 freshmen graduated within 5 years.

FRESHMAN ADMISSIONS Options: early entrance, deferred entrance. Required: essay, high school transcript, 3 recommendations, TOEFL (for foreign students). Recommended: 3 years of high school math and science, some high school foreign language. Required for some: interview, SAT or ACT. Test scores used for admission. Application deadline: rolling. Notification date: continuous. College's own assessment of entrance difficulty level: moderately difficult.

TRANSFER ADMISSIONS Required: essay, 3 recommendations, college transcript, minimum 2.0 grade point average. Recommended: some high school foreign language. Required for some: standardized test scores, high school transcript, interview. Application deadline: rolling. Notification date: continuous. College's own assessment of entrance difficulty level: moderately difficult.

EXPENSES (1992–93) Comprehensive fee of $11,460 includes full-time tuition ($7500), mandatory fees ($360), and college room and board ($3600). College room only: $1550. Part-time tuition: $320 per credit hour. Part-time mandatory fees per semester (1 to 11 credit hours) range from $35 to $58.

FINANCIAL AID College-administered aid for all 1992–93 undergraduate need-based and non-need-based scholarships. College participates in the following federal programs: Pell, Perkins, SEOG, College Work-Study, Stafford & SLS Loans, VA. State programs include TAP & HEOP. Application: The Nyack College Financial Aid Application (NCFAA), and the Financial Aid Form (FAF) for CSS (FSS acceptable) state form may be required. Priority application deadline 5/6.

CAMPUS LIFE/STUDENT SERVICES Mandatory chapel; drama/theater group; student-run newspaper and radio station. Institution provides health clinic, personal/psychological counseling.

STUDY ABROAD SITE England.

ATHLETICS Member NAIA. Intercollegiate sports: baseball M(s), softball W(s); basketball M(s), W(s); soccer M(s), W(s); volleyball W. Intramural sports: basketball, soccer.

MAJORS Adult and continuing education; biblical studies; business administration/commerce/management; early childhood education; education; elementary education; English; history; interdisciplinary studies; liberal arts/general studies; ministries; music; music education; nursing; pastoral studies; philosophy; piano/organ; psychology; religious education; religious studies; sacred music; secondary education; social science; voice. Most popular majors of class of 1991: elementary education, psychology, business administration/commerce/management; communications.

SPECIAL NOTE FROM THE COLLEGE Beautifully situated in a suburban community on the Hudson River, Nyack College partakes of the rich cultural and ethnic diversity of suburban New York. An excellent school of music and a new performing arts and communications division, along with a bustling seminary located on the campus, enrich the College atmosphere. Founded in 1882 for missionaries and ministers, Nyack has a long tradition of providing education that blends scholarship and service. Nyack College's participation as a model site college for the Christian College Coalition Minority Concerns Project will further enhance that tradition. Though today's curriculum is more diverse, ranging from business to missiology, a sound education and a thorough grounding in the faith still characterize the Nyack graduate.

CONTACT Mr. Dennis Whalen, Director of Admissions, Nyack College, Nyack, NY 10960, 914-358-1710 Ext. 350 or toll-free 800-33-NYACK.

OLIVET NAZARENE UNIVERSITY

Kankakee, Illinois

Total Enrollment: 1,898

UG Enrollment: 1,746 (55% W)

Application Deadline: 8/1

Tuition & Fees: $7048

Room & Board: $3826

Entrance: minimally difficult

SAT ≥ 500: N/App

ACT ≥ 21: 48%

Denominational Affiliation: Church of the Nazarene

GENERAL INFORMATION Independent comprehensive coed institution. Founded 1907. Awards A (college transfer and terminal), B, M. Primary accreditation: regional. Suburban setting, with easy access to Chicago; 168-acre campus. Total enrollment: 1,898. Faculty: 112 (92 full-time, 20 part-time); 50% of full-time faculty have terminal degrees; graduate assistants teach no undergraduate courses. Library holdings: 150,352 bound volumes, 49,575 titles on microform, 850 periodical subscriptions, 4,750 records/tapes/CDs. Computer terminals/PCs available for student use: 300, located in computer center, library, various departments.

UNDERGRADUATE PROFILE Fall 1991: 1,746 undergraduates (559 freshmen) from 36 states and territories and 16 foreign countries; 8% part-time; 44% state residents; 20% transfers; 80% financial aid recipients; 55% women; 4% African Americans; 0% Native Americans; 1% Hispanics; 1% Asian Americans; 4% international students; 10% of undergraduates 25 years of age or older.

1991 FRESHMAN DATA 660 students applied for fall 1991 admission; 96% were accepted; 60% of those accepted enrolled. 20% of freshmen were in top 10% of secondary school class, 40% were in top 25%, 71% were in top half.

ENROLLMENT PATTERNS 70% of fall 1990 freshmen returned for fall 1991 term.

FRESHMAN ADMISSIONS Options: early entrance, deferred entrance. Required: high school transcript, 2 recommendations, ACT, TOEFL (for foreign students). Recommended: 3 years of high school science, interview. Required for some: 3 years of high school math, some high school foreign language. Test scores used for counseling/placement. Application deadline: 8/1. Notification date: continuous. College's own assessment of entrance difficulty level: minimally difficult.

TRANSFER ADMISSIONS Required: 3 recommendations, college transcript, minimum 2.0 grade point average.

Recommended: interview. Required for some: high school transcript. Application deadline: 8/1. Notification date: continuous. College's own assessment of entrance difficulty level: minimally difficult.

EXPENSES (1992–93) Comprehensive fee of $10,874 includes full-time tuition ($6924), mandatory fees ($124), and college room and board ($3826). Part-time tuition: $289 per semester hour. Part-time mandatory fees per semester (1 to 11 semester hours) range from $10 to $62.

FINANCIAL AID College-administered aid for all 1991–92 undergraduates: need-based scholarships; non-need scholarships (average $650); low-interest long-term loans from external sources (average $2500); SEOG; College Work-Study; 650 part-time jobs. Supporting data: FAF, institutional form, AFSA/SAR required; IRS, state form required for some; FFS acceptable. Priority application deadline: 4/1.

CAMPUS LIFE/STUDENT SERVICES Dress code; mandatory chapel. Institution provides health clinic, personal/psychological counseling.

ATHLETICS Member NAIA. Intercollegiate sports: baseball M(s); basketball M(s), W(s); cross-country running M(s), W(s); football M(s); golf M; soccer M; softball W(s); tennis M, W; track and field M, W; volleyball W; wrestling M(s). Intramural sports: basketball, cross-country running, football, golf, soccer, softball, tennis, volleyball, wrestling.

MAJORS Accounting; art education; art/fine arts; biblical studies; biology/biological sciences; broadcasting; business administration/commerce/management; business economics; chemistry; child care/child and family studies; communication; computer information systems; computer science; criminal justice; (pre)dentistry sequence; dietetics; early childhood education; earth science; economics; education; elementary education; engineering (general); engineering sciences; English; family services; fashion merchandising; finance/banking; food services management; geology; history; home economics; home economics education; interdisciplinary studies; journalism; (pre)law sequence; liberal arts/general studies; literature; marketing/retailing/merchandising; mathematics; medical technology; (pre)medicine sequence; ministries; modern languages; music; music education; natural sciences; nursing; pastoral studies; physical education; physical sciences; piano/organ; psychology; radio and television studies; religious education; religious studies; Romance languages; sacred music; science; science education; secondary education; social science; social work; sociology; speech/rhetoric/public address/debate; stringed instruments; teacher aide studies; textiles and clothing; theology; (pre)veterinary medicine sequence; voice; wind and percussion instruments. Most popular majors of class of 1991: business administration/commerce/management, education, nursing, psychology.

SPECIAL NOTE FROM THE COLLEGE Olivet Nazarene University, 60 miles south of Chicago's Loop, offers students a high-quality liberal arts education based on Christian values. The scenic 160-acre campus includes a planetarium, a 35,000-watt FM radio station, and a new 4,000-seat convocation/athletic center. There are 29 major buildings. Five years after graduation, 85% of Olivet's alumni report employment in an area related to their college major. Internships are available in most majors. Four choirs, a concert band, a symphony orchestra, and other ensembles involve 400 students. Ten spiritual life organizations provide opportunities for service and ministry both on and off campus. Olivet specializes in campus visits as its best recruitment feature. Prospective students are welcome.

CONTACT Rev. John Mongerson, Director of Admissions, Olivet Nazarene University, P.O. Box 592, Kankakee, IL 60901, 815-939-5217.

PALM BEACH ATLANTIC COLLEGE

West Palm Beach, Florida

Total Enrollment: 1,500

UG Enrollment: 1,375 (53% W)

Application Deadline: 8/1

Tuition & Fees: $6300

Room & Board: $3100

Entrance: moderately difficult

GENERAL INFORMATION Independent comprehensive coed college. Founded 1968. Awards B, M (Master's in business only). Primary accreditation: regional. Urban setting, with easy access to Miami; 25-acre campus. Total enrollment: 1,500. Faculty: 100 (65 full-time, 35 part-time); 80% of full-time faculty have terminal degrees; graduate assistants teach no undergraduate courses. Library holdings: 60,000 bound volumes, 350 periodical subscriptions. Computer terminals/PCs available for student use: 75, located in computer center, library, and learning center.

UNDERGRADUATE PROFILE Fall 1991: 1,375 undergraduates (237 freshmen) from 35 states and territories and 23 foreign countries; 10% part-time; 70% state residents; 35% transfers; 85% financial aid recipients; 53% women; 5% African Americans; 1% Native Americans; 5% Hispanics; 2% Asian Americans; 5% international students.

1991 FRESHMAN DATA 510 students applied for fall 1991 admission; 53% were accepted; 86% of those accepted enrolled.

FRESHMAN ADMISSIONS Options: early entrance, deferred entrance. Required: essay, high school transcript, 2 recommendations, SAT or ACT, TOEFL (for foreign students). Recommended: 3 years of high school math and science, some high school foreign language, interview. Test scores used for counseling/placement. Application deadline: 8/1. Notification date: continuous. College's own assessment of entrance difficulty level: moderately difficult.

TRANSFER ADMISSIONS Required: essay, 2 recommendations, college transcript, minimum 2.0 grade point average.

Recommended: standardized test scores, 3 years of high school math and science, some high school foreign language, interview, minimum 3.0 grade point average. Application deadline: 8/1. Notification date: continuous. College's own assessment of entrance difficulty level: moderately difficult.

EXPENSES (1992–93) Comprehensive fee of $9400 includes full-time tuition ($6300) and college room and board ($3100). Part-time tuition: ranges from $185 to $195 per credit hour.

FINANCIAL AID College-administered aid for all 1991–92 undergraduates: need-based scholarships; non-need scholarships; low-interest long-term loans from external sources; SEOG; College Work-Study. Supporting data: IRS, institutional form required for some; FFS, FAF, AFSA/SAR acceptable. Priority application deadline: 5/1.

CAMPUS LIFE/STUDENT SERVICES Over forty clubs and organizations; required chapel; drama/theater group; student-run newspaper. Institution provides health clinic, personal/psychological counseling.

STUDY ABROAD SITES Europe, Latin America.

ATHLETICS Intercollegiate sports: baseball M(s); basketball M(s); soccer M(s); volleyball W(s). Intramural sports: basketball; bowling; football; golf M, W; racquetball; softball; table tennis; tennis M, W; volleyball.

MAJORS Accounting; art education; art/fine arts; biology/biological sciences; business administration/commerce/management; computer information system; (pre)dentistry sequence; early childhood education; economics; education; elementary education; English; finance/banking; history; international business; (pre)law sequence; mathematics; (pre)medicine sequence; music; music education; physical education; political science/government; psychology; religious studies; science; secondary education; speech/rhetoric/public address/debate.

SPECIAL NOTE FROM THE COLLEGE Palm Beach Atlantic is a 4-year, coeducational, liberal arts college in the Christian tradition. PBA attracts students who desire the benefits of a college committed to academic excellence within a Christian environment. The campus is an attractive mixture of the old and new and is in the early stages of a $100-million expansion program. It has built upon a rich heritage, adapting to the needs of students and faculty. Located in one of the fastest-growing cities in the country and one of the fastest-growing counties in the nation, it is ideally situated on beautiful Lake Worth, across from Palm Beach and 1 mile from the Atlantic Ocean. PBA provides educational opportunities through a scholarship program to many deserving students who might not otherwise be able to attend college.

CONTACT Mr. Rich Grimm, Director of Admissions, Palm Beach Atlantic College, 901 South Flager Drive, P.O. Box 24708, West Palm Beach, FL 33416-4708, 407-835-4309 or toll-free, 800-238-3998.

POINT LOMA NAZARENE COLLEGE

San Diego, California

Total Enrollment: 2,349

UG Enrollment: 1,909 (57% W)

Application Deadline: rolling

Tuition & Fees: $8838

Room & Board: $3830

Entrance: moderately difficult

SAT ≥ 500: 41% V, 21% M

ACT ≥ 21: 57%

Denominational Affiliation: Church of the Nazarene

GENERAL INFORMATION Independent comprehensive coed institution. Founded 1902. Awards B, M. Primary accreditation: regional. Suburban setting; 88-acre campus. Total enrollment: 2,349. Faculty: 132 (113 full-time, 19 part-time); 60% of full-time faculty have terminal degrees; graduate assistants teach no undergraduate courses. Library holdings: 150,100 bound volumes, 32,500 titles on microform, 642 periodical subscriptions, 1,610 records/tapes/CDs. Computer terminals/PCs available for student use: 60, located in computer center.

UNDERGRADUATE PROFILE Fall 1991: 1,909 undergraduates (322 freshmen) from 36 states and territories and 21 foreign countries; 7% part-time; 85% state residents; 15% transfers; 75% financial aid recipients; 57% women; 2% African Americans; 1% Native Americans; 6% Hispanics; 4% Asian Americans; 3% international students; 12% of undergraduates 25 years of age or older.

1991 FRESHMAN DATA 632 students applied for fall 1991 admission; 90% were accepted; 56% of those accepted enrolled. 28% of freshmen were in top 10% of secondary school class, 48% were in top 25%, 75% were in top half.

ENROLLMENT PATTERNS 59% of fall 1990 freshmen returned for fall 1991 term.

FRESHMAN ADMISSIONS Options: early entrance, deferred entrance. Required: high school transcript, 2 years of high school foreign language, 2 recommendations, SAT or ACT, TOEFL (for foreign students). Recommended: 3 years of high school math and science. Required for some: campus interview. Test scores used for counseling/placement. Application deadline: rolling. Notification date: continuous. College's own assessment of entrance difficulty level: moderately difficult.

TRANSFER ADMISSIONS Required: standardized test scores, 2 years of high school foreign language, 2 recommendations, college transcript, minimum 2.0 grade point average. Recommended: 3 years of high school math and science. Required for some: high school transcript, campus interview. Application deadline: rolling. Notification date: continuous. College's own assessment of entrance difficulty level: moderately difficult.

EXPENSES (1992–93) Comprehensive fee of $12,668 includes full-time tuition ($8704), mandatory fees ($134), and college room and board ($3830). College room only: $1730. Part-time tuition: $272 per unit.

FINANCIAL AID College-administered aid for all 1991–92 undergraduates: need-based scholarships; non-need scholarships; low-interest long-term loans from external sources (average $2000); SEOG; College Work-Study; 100 part-time jobs. Supporting data: FAF, institutional form, AFSA/SAR required. Priority application deadline: 4/10.

CAMPUS LIFE/STUDENT SERVICES Mandatory chapel; drama/theater group; student-run newspaper. Institution provides health clinic, personal/psychological counseling. Social organizations: national sorority, local fraternities, local sororities. 8% of eligible undergraduate men and 5% of eligible undergraduate women are members.

ATHLETICS Member NAIA. Intercollegiate sports: baseball M(s); basketball M(s), W(s); cross-country running M(s), W(s); golf M(s); soccer M(s); softball W; tennis M(s), W(s); track and field M(s), W(s); volleyball W(s). Intramural sports: badminton, baseball, basketball, bowling, cross-country running, football, golf, racquetball, sailing, soccer, softball, swimming and diving, table tennis (Ping Pong), tennis, track and field, volleyball, water polo, weight lifting.

MAJORS Accounting; art education; art/fine arts; athletic training; biblical studies; biochemistry; biology/biological sciences; business administration/commerce/management; business education; chemistry; child psychology/child development; communication; computer information systems; computer science; (pre)dentistry sequence; early childhood education; economics; engineering physics; English; graphic arts; history; home economics; home economics education; journalism; (pre)law sequence; liberal arts/general studies; literature; mathematics; (pre)medicine sequence; music; music business; music education; nursing; pastoral studies; philosophy; physical education; physics; piano/organ; political science/government; psychology; religious education; religious studies; sacred music; secretarial studies/office management; sociology; Spanish; speech therapy; stringed instruments; studio art; theater arts/drama; theology; (pre)veterinary medicine sequence; voice; wind and percussion instruments. Most popular majors of class of 1991: business administration/commerce/management, nursing, liberal arts/general studies.

SPECIAL NOTE FROM THE COLLEGE Point Loma Nazarene College is an 89-year-old Christian liberal arts college located in a semitropical, residential setting resting on the crest of historic Point Loma. Collegians enjoy a clear view westward overlooking the Pacific Ocean and eastward across downtown San Diego, where many cultural and employment advantages are available to them. Point Loma offers a wide variety of academic programs, continually modified to meet changing needs. The 17 academic programs offer 42 majors plus many subspecialties, credentials, and certificates. The 2,300 students come from 36 states and 40 countries. At Point Loma Nazarene, students strive for 3 lofty goals: spiritual development, academic excellence, and social and personal enhancement.

CONTACT Mr. Bill Young, Executive Director for Enrollment Services, Point Loma Nazarene College, 3900 Lomaland Drive, San Diego, CA 92106, 619-221-2225.

REDEEMER COLLEGE

Ancaster, Ontario, Canada

Total Enrollment: 503 (all UG)

Women: 60%

Application Deadline: rolling

Tuition & Fees: $5745 (Canadian $)

Room & Board: $3700 (Canadian $)

Entrance: moderately difficult

SAT ≥ 500: N/R

ACT ≥ 21: 90%

Denominational Affiliation: interdenominational

GENERAL INFORMATION Independent 4-year coed college. Founded 1980. Awards B. Primary accreditation: provincial charter. Small-town setting, with easy access to Toronto; 78-acre campus. Total enrollment: 503. Faculty: 63 (38 full-time, 25 part-time); 71% of full-time faculty have terminal degrees; graduate assistants teach a few undergraduate courses. Library holdings: 85,000 bound volumes, 275 periodical subscriptions, 1,000 records/tapes/CDs. Computer terminals/PCs available for student use: 20, located in computer center, dormitories.

UNDERGRADUATE PROFILE Fall 1991: 503 undergraduates (218 freshmen) from 7 provinces and territories and 7 foreign countries; 6% part-time; 97% province residents; 4% transfers; 93% financial aid recipients; 60% women; 1% African Americans; 0% Native Americans; 1% Hispanics; 1% Asian Americans; 2% international students; 7% of undergraduates 25 years of age or older.

1991 FRESHMAN DATA 326 students applied for fall 1991 admission; 96% were accepted; 70% of those accepted enrolled.

ENROLLMENT PATTERNS 89% of fall 1990 freshmen returned for fall 1991 term. 44% of students completing a degree program went on for further study.

FRESHMAN ADMISSIONS Preference given to Christians. Option: deferred entrance. Required: high school transcript, 2 recommendations, pastoral reference, TOEFL (for foreign students). Recommended: 4 years of high school math and science, 4 years of high school foreign language. Required for some: essay, interview, SAT or ACT, Achievement Tests, English Composition Test. Test scores used for counseling/placement.

Application deadline: rolling. College's own assessment of entrance difficulty level: moderately difficult.

TRANSFER ADMISSIONS Required: high school transcript, 2 recommendations college transcript, minimum 2.0 grade point average, pastoral reference. Recommended: 4 years of high school math and science, 4 years of high school foreign language. Required for some: essay, standardized test scores, interview, College's own assessment of entrance difficulty level: moderately difficult.

EXPENSES (1992–93) Comprehensive fee of $9445 includes full-time tuition ($5450), mandatory fees ($295), and college room and board ($3700). Part-time tuition: $525 per course.

FINANCIAL AID College-administered aid for all 1991–92 undergraduates: 138 need-based scholarships (average $2300); 121 non-need scholarships (average $1150); short-term loans (average $5380). Supporting data: government form required; institutional form required for some; FFS acceptable. Priority application deadline: 6/30.

CAMPUS LIFE/STUDENT SERVICES Drama/theater group; student-run newspaper. Institution provides personal/psychological counseling.

STUDY ABROAD SITES The Netherlands, France.

ATHLETICS Intercollegiate sports: badminton M, W; basketball M, W; cross-country running M, W; ice hockey M, W; soccer M, W; volleyball M, W. Intramural sports: archery, badminton, basketball, bowling, ice hockey, racquetball, skiing (cross-country), skiing (downhill), soccer, squash, swimming and diving, volleyball.

MAJORS Accounting; art/fine arts; behavioral sciences; biblical studies; biology/biological sciences; botany/plant sciences; business administration/commerce/management; classics; clinical psychology; computer science; (pre)dentistry sequence; education; elementary education; English; French; history; humanities; (pre)law sequence; liberal arts/general studies; literature; mathematics; (pre)medicine sequence; modern languages; music; natural sciences; philosophy; physical education; political science/government; psychology; religious studies; Romance languages; science; secondary education; sociology; theater arts/drama; theology; (pre)veterinary medicine sequence. Most popular majors of class of 1991: English, education, psychology.

SPECIAL NOTE FROM THE COLLEGE Redeemer College is a school that's big enough to offer a full range of majors and minors yet small enough for students to get to know their classmates and professors. It's a school where the dorms are fully equipped 4-bedroom town houses and the facilities are modern. The setting at Redeemer is suburban/rural, and the amenities of urban life are just minutes away. The College has the tradition of excellence of the British university system combined with the strengths of a Christian liberal arts program. An innovative financial aid program makes tuition surprisingly affordable.

CONTACT Mr. Mark Van Beveren, Admissions Director, Redeemer College, Ancaster, ON L9G 3N6, Canada, 416-648-2131 or toll-free 800-263-6467 (in Canada).

ROBERTS WESLEYAN COLLEGE

Rochester, New York

Total Enrollment: 988

UG Enrollment: 966 (60% W)

Application Deadline: rolling

Tuition & Fees: $9232

Room & Board: $3366

Entrance: moderately difficult

SAT ≥ 500: 64% V, 71% M

ACT ≥ 21: 65%

Denominational Affiliation: Free Methodist Church of North America

GENERAL INFORMATION Independent 4-year coed college. Founded 1866. Awards A (terminal), B, M. Primary accreditation: regional. Suburban setting; 75-acre campus. Total enrollment: 988. Faculty: 66 (47 full-time, 19 part-time); 62% of full-time faculty have terminal degrees; graduate assistants teach no undergraduate courses. Library holdings: 96,272 bound volumes, 510 titles on microform, 628 periodical subscriptions, 2,242 records/tapes/CDs. Computer terminals/PCs available for student use: 47, located in computer center, library.

UNDERGRADUATE PROFILE Fall 1991: 966 undergraduates (177 freshmen) from 24 states and territories and 6 foreign countries; 11% part-time; 80% state residents; 15% transfers; 93% financial aid recipients; 60% women; 6% African Americans; 1% Native Americans; 1% Hispanics; 1% Asian Americans; 8% international students; 22% of undergraduates 25 years of age or older.

1991 FRESHMAN DATA 333 students applied for fall 1991 admission; 91% were accepted; 58% of those accepted enrolled. 22% of freshmen were in top 10% of secondary school class, 49% were in top 25%, 73% were in top half.

ENROLLMENT PATTERNS 71% of fall 1990 freshmen returned for fall 1991 term.

FRESHMAN ADMISSIONS Options: early entrance, deferred entrance. Required: essay, high school transcript, 1 recommendation, SAT or ACT, TOEFL (for foreign students). Recommended: 3 years of high school math and science, 3 years of high school foreign language, campus interview. Test scores used for counseling/placement. Application deadline: rolling. College's own assessment of entrance difficulty level: moderately difficult.

TRANSFER ADMISSIONS Required: essay, high school transcript, 1 recommendation, college transcript, minimum 2.0 grade point average. Recommended: 3 years of high school math and science, 3 years of high school foreign language, campus interview. Application deadline: rolling. College's own assessment of entrance difficulty level: moderately difficult.

EXPENSES (1992–93) Comprehensive fee of $12,598 includes full-time tuition ($9022), mandatory fees ($210), and college room and board ($3366). College room only: $2210. Part-time tuition per semester hour ranges from $170 to $375.

FINANCIAL AID Fall 1991 college-administered aid for all 1991–92 undergraduates: 420 need-based scholarships; non-need scholarships; low-interest long-term loans from college funds (average $1000), from external sources (average $3029); SEOG; College Work-Study; 320 part-time jobs. Supporting data: FAF, institutional form required; IRS, state form required for some; FFS, AFSA/SAR acceptable. Priority application deadline: 6/15.

CAMPUS LIFE/STUDENT SERVICES Dress code; mandatory chapel; drama/theater group; student-run newspaper. Institution provides health clinic, personal/psychological counseling.

STUDY ABROAD SITES England, France, Commonwealth of Independent States (USSR), Dominican Republic.

ATHLETICS Intercollegiate sports: basketball M(s), W(s); cross-country running M(s), W(s); soccer M(s), W(s); track and field M(s), W(s). Intramural sports: basketball, racquetball, soccer, table tennis (Ping Pong), tennis, volleyball.

MAJORS Accounting; art education; art/fine arts; biochemistry; biology/biological sciences; business administration/commerce/management; chemistry; communication; computer science; criminal justice; (pre)dentistry sequence; education; elementary education; English; gerontology; graphic arts; history; humanities; human resources; mathematics; medical technology; ministries; music; music education; natural sciences; nursing; physical sciences; physics; piano/organ; psychology; religious studies; science; secondary education; social science; social work; sociology; studio art; voice. Most popular majors of class of 1991: education, business administration/commerce/management, human resourses.

SPECIAL NOTE FROM THE COLLEGE Roberts Wesleyan College provides the ideal setting for a contemporary liberal arts education in the Christian tradition. The modern, parklike campus, which is located just 10 miles from the center of Rochester, provides students with the advantages of a rural setting within a vibrant metropolitan area. Rochester offers numerous cultural, recreational, internship, and career opportunities for students and graduates. The College's broadly based curriculum of 40 majors and preprofessional programs includes 4 with national professional accreditation: art, music, nursing, and social work. Roberts is honoring its 125-year commitment to address society's ever-changing needs through high-quality, accredited educational programs in a climate where students are encouraged in their faith as well as in their intellectual and professional development.

CONTACT Miss Linda Kurtz, Director of Admissions, Roberts Wesleyan College, 2301 Westside Drive, Rochester, NY 14624, 716-594-9471 Ext. 410 or toll-free 800-777-4792.

SEATTLE PACIFIC UNIVERSITY

Seattle, Washington

Total Enrollment: 3,394

UG Enrollment: 2,224 (64% W)

Application Deadline: 9/1

Tuition & Fees: $11,301

Room & Board: $4278

Entrance: moderately difficult

SAT ≥ 500: 37% V, 48% M

ACT ≥ 21: N/R

Denominational Affiliation: Free Methodist

GENERAL INFORMATION Independent comprehensive coed institution. Founded 1891. Awards B, M. Primary accreditation: regional. Urban setting; 35-acre campus. Total enrollment: 3,394. Faculty: 241 (141 full-time, 100 part-time); 74% of full-time faculty have terminal degrees; graduate assistants teach no undergraduate courses. Library holdings: 180,000 bound volumes, 320,000 titles on microform, 1,400 periodical subscriptions, 3,000 records/tapes/CDs. Computer terminals/PCs available for student use: 102, located in 2 labs and the media center.

UNDERGRADUATE PROFILE Fall 1991: 2,224 undergraduates (381 freshmen) from 38 states and territories and 37 foreign countries; 17% part-time; 69% state residents; 37% transfers; 65% financial aid recipients; 64% women; 1% African Americans; 1% Native Americans; 1% Hispanics; 5% Asian Americans; 4% international students; 21% of undergraduates 25 years of age or older.

1991 FRESHMAN DATA 914 students applied for fall 1991 admission; 86% were accepted; 48% of those accepted enrolled.

ENROLLMENT PATTERNS 72% of fall 1990 freshmen returned for fall 1991 term. 39% of 1986 freshmen graduated within 5 years.

FRESHMAN ADMISSIONS Options: early entrance, deferred entrance. Required: essay, high school transcript, 2 recommendations, minimum 2.5 grade point average, SAT or ACT, TOEFL (for foreign students). Recommended: 3 years of high school math and science, some high school foreign language, interview. Test scores used for counseling/placement. Application deadlines: 9/1. Notification date: continuous. College's own assessment of entrance difficulty level: moderately difficult.

TRANSFER ADMISSIONS Required: essay, high school transcript, 2 recommendations, college transcript, minimum 2.0 grade point average. Recommended: 3 years of high school math and science, some high school foreign language, interview. Required for some: standardized test scores. Application deadline: 9/1. Notification date: continuous. College's own assessment of entrance difficulty level: moderately difficult.

EXPENSES (1992–93) Comprehensive fee of $15,579 includes full-time tuition ($11,301) and college room and board ($4278). Part-time tuition per credit: $180 for the first 8 credits, $315 for the next 3 credits.

FINANCIAL AID College-administered aid for all 1991–92 undergraduates: 1,303 need-based scholarships (average $4709); 1116 non-need scholarships (average $1682); short-term loans (average $350); low-interest long-term loans from college funds (average $3591), from external sources (average $3755); SEOG; College Work-Study; 331 part-time jobs. Supporting data: FAF required; IRS, AFSA/SAR required for some; FFS acceptable. Priority application deadline: 3/1.

CAMPUS LIFE/STUDENT SERVICES Mandatory chapel; drama/theater group; student-run newspaper. Institution provides health clinic, personal/psychological counseling.

STUDY ABROAD SITES Europe, Japan, Korea.

ATHLETICS Member NCAA (Division II). Intercollegiate sports: basketball M(s), W(s); crew M, W; cross-country running M(s), W(s); gymnastics W(s); soccer M(s); track and field M, W(s); volleyball W(s). Intramural sports: offers 65 men's, women's, and coed intramural sports.

MAJORS Accounting; art/fine arts; biblical studies; biology/biological sciences; business administration/commerce/management; chemistry; communication; computer science; economics; electrical engineering; elementary education; engineering sciences; English; European studies; exercise science; family and consumer studies; history; home economics education; interdisciplinary studies; language arts; liberal arts/general studies; mathematics; mathematics education; ministries; music; music education; nursing; nutrition; philosophy; physical education; physics; political science/government; psychology; reading education; recreation and leisure services; religious education; religious studies; science; secondary education; social science education; sociology; special education; textiles, clothing and interiors; theater arts/drama; theological studies. Most popular majors of class of 1991: nursing, psychology, computer science.

SPECIAL NOTE FROM THE COLLEGE Seattle Pacific University is a comprehensive university of liberal arts (arts and sciences) and professional programs (i.e., business, electrical engineering, nursing), with the premiere teacher-education program in the state of Washington. Regional accreditation is provided by the Northwest Association of Schools and Colleges, with national accreditation in dietetics, engineering, nursing, and teacher education. National accreditation is also in process for the School of Business and Economics. Seattle Pacific's urban setting is ideal for internship and service-learning opportunities. SPU provides students with numerous formal avenues for leadership development. SPU's location on the Pacific Rim provides a gateway to international study and learning experiences. Through internships, a diverse and innovative chapel program, leadership training, service opportunities, and mission and travel programs, SPU students are supported, encouraged, and educated for effective Christian living.

CONTACT Office of Admissions, Seattle Pacific University, 3307 Third Avenue West, Seattle, WA 98119, 206-281-2021 or toll-free 800-366-3344.

SIMPSON COLLEGE

Redding, California

Total Enrollment: 412

UG Enrollment: 316 (60% W)

Application Deadline: rolling

Tuition & Fees: $6738

Room & Board: $3570

Entrance: minimally difficult

SAT ≥ 500: 23% V, 30% M

ACT ≥ 21: 22%

Denominational Affiliation: The Christian and Missionary Alliance

GENERAL INFORMATION Independent comprehensive coed institution. Founded 1921. Awards A (terminal), B, M. Primary accreditation: regional. Suburban setting; 60-acre campus. Total enrollment: 412. Faculty: 34 (22 full-time, 12 part-time); 50% of full-time faculty have terminal degrees; graduate assistants teach no undergraduate courses. Library holdings: 53,373 bound volumes, 30 titles on microform, 332 periodical subscriptions, 1,848 records/tapes/CDs. Computer terminals/PCs available for student use: 8, located in computer center.

UNDERGRADUATE PROFILE Fall 1991: 316 undergraduates (47 freshmen) from 18 states and territories and 4 foreign countries; 2% part-time; 84% state residents; 65% transfers; 80% financial aid recipients; 60% women; 1% African Americans; 1% Native Americans; 1% Hispanics; 7% Asian Americans; 1% international students; 40% of undergraduates 25 years of age or older.

1991 FRESHMAN DATA 75 students applied for fall 1991 admission; 92% were accepted; 68% of those accepted enrolled. 33% of freshman were in top 10% of secondary school class, 45% were in top 25%, 78% were in top 50%.

ENROLLMENT PATTERNS 67% of fall 1990 freshmen returned for fall 1991 term.

FRESHMAN ADMISSIONS Options: early entrance, deferred entrance. Required: essay, high school transcript, 2 recommendations, interview, writing sample, SAT or ACT, TOEFL (for foreign students). Recommended: 3 years of high school math and science, some high school foreign language. Test scores used for admission. Application deadline: rolling. Notification date: continuous. College's own assessment of entrance difficulty level: minimally difficult.

TRANSFER ADMISSIONS Required: essay, 2 recommendations, college transcript, minimum 2.0 grade point average. Recommended: 3 years of high school math and science, some high school foreign language, minimum 3.0 grade point average. Required for some standardized test scores, high school transcript, interview. Application deadline: rolling. Notification date: continuous. College's own assessment of entrance difficulty level: minimally difficult.

EXPENSES (1992–93) Comprehensive fee of $10,308 includes full-time tuition ($6400), mandatory fees ($338), and college room and board ($3570). Part-time tuition and fees per credit: $320.

FINANCIAL AID College-administered aid for all 1991–92 undergraduates: 101 need-based scholarships (average $1428); 144 non-need scholarships (average $1182); low-interest long-term loans from college funds (average $1143), from external sources (average $2709); SEOG; College Work-Study; 35 part-time jobs. Supporting data: institutional form required; IRS, state form required for some; FFS, FAF, AFSA/SAR acceptable. Priority application deadline: 3/31.

CAMPUS LIFE/STUDENT SERVICES Dress code. Social organizations: men's and women's associations; 100% of eligible undergraduate men and 100% of eligible undergraduate women are members.

STUDY ABROAD SITE Israel.

ATHLETICS Intercollegiate sports: basketball M, W; soccer M; softball W; volleyball M, W. Intramural sports: basketball, football, softball, volleyball.

MAJORS Archaeology; biblical studies; business administration/commerce/management; education; elementary education; English; history; liberal arts/general studies; ministries; music; music education; pastoral studies; psychology; religious education; sacred music; secondary education; social science. Most popular majors of class of 1991: business administration/commerce/management, liberal arts/general studies, psychology.

SPECIAL NOTE FROM THE COLLEGE Simpson College is a Christian college offering baccalaureate and graduate programs. Its mission is to provide leadership education for the Church of Jesus Christ, preparing students for both lay and ministerial vocations. The undergraduate division is designed to build an educational foundation upon which professional majors can be based. This foundation integrates a biblical interpretation of knowledge with the broad liberal studies curriculum to develop a Christian world view. The major program offerings fall into 3 general tracts of professional ministry studies: lay professions, ministry, and liberal arts. The graduate program offers professional programs in Bible and theology and education.

CONTACT Mrs. Beth Spencer, Administrative Assistant for Recruitment, Simpson College, 2211 College View Drive, Redding, CA 96003-8606, 916-222-6360 Ext. 2060.

SIOUX FALLS COLLEGE

Sioux Falls, South Dakota

Total Enrollment: 949

UG Enrollment: 895 (60% W)

Application Deadline: rolling

Tuition & Fees: $7996

Room & Board: $2746

Entrance: moderately difficult

SAT ≥ 500: N/R

ACT ≥ 21: 54%

Denominational Affiliation: American Baptist

GENERAL INFORMATION Independent comprehensive coed institution. Founded 1883. Awards A (college transfer), B, M. Primary accreditation: regional. Suburban; 22-acre campus. Total enrollment: 949. Faculty: 75 (35 full-time, 40 part-time); 60% of full-time faculty have terminal degrees; graduate assistants teach no undergraduate courses. Library holdings: 75,000 bound volumes, 450 periodical subscriptions, 4,600 records/tapes/CDs. Computer terminals/PCs available for student use: 35, located in computer center, library.

UNDERGRADUATE PROFILE Fall 1991: 895 undergraduates (283 freshmen) from 19 states and territories and 5 foreign countries; 34% part-time; 72% state residents; 1% transfers; 94% financial aid recipients; 60% women; 1% African Americans; 1% Native Americans; 1% Hispanics; 0% Asian Americans; 1% international students; 46% of undergraduates 25 years of age or older.

1991 FRESHMAN DATA 437 students applied for fall 1991 admission; 87% were accepted; 74% of those accepted enrolled. 11% of freshmen were in top 10% of secondary school class, 28% were in top 25%, 51% were in top half.

ENROLLMENT PATTERNS 53% of fall 1990 freshmen returned for fall 1991 term. 15% of students completing a bachelor's program went on for further study.

FRESHMAN ADMISSIONS Options: early entrance, deferred entrance. Required: high school transcript, SAT, ACT, or TOEFL (for foreign students). Recommended: essay, 3 years of high school math and science, 1 year of high school foreign language. Required for some: 2 recommendations, interview. Test scores used for admission and counseling/placement. Application deadline: rolling. College's own assessment of entrance difficulty level: moderately difficult.

TRANSFER ADMISSIONS Required: high school transcript, college transcript, minimum 2.0 grade point average.

Recommended: essay, standardized test scores, 3 years of high school math and science, 1 year of high school foreign language. Required for some: 2 recommendations, interview. Application deadline: rolling.

EXPENSES (1992–93) Comprehensive fee of $10,742 includes full-time tuition ($7996) and college room and board ($2746). College room only: $1180. Part-time tuition per semester hour: ranges from $180 to $300.

FINANCIAL AID College-administered aid for all 1991–92 undergraduates: 70 need-based scholarships (average $400); 300 non-need scholarships (average $1500); low-interest long-term loans from external sources (average $3925); SEOG; College Work-Study; 45 part-time jobs. Supporting data: FFS, institutional form, AFSA/SAR required; IRS, state form required for some; FAF acceptable. Priority application deadline: 4/1.

CAMPUS LIFE/STUDENT SERVICES Drama/theater group; student-run newspaper and radio station. Institution provides health clinic, personal/psychological counseling, women's center.

STUDY ABROAD SITES Japan, China.

ATHLETICS Member NAIA. Intercollegiate sports: baseball M(s); basketball M(s), W(s); cross-country running M(s), W(s); football M(s); track and field M(s), W(s); volleyball W(s). Intramural sports: basketball, football, racquetball, table tennis (Ping Pong), tennis, volleyball.

MAJORS Accounting; applied art; applied mathematics; art education; biology/biological sciences; business administration/commerce/management; chemistry; child psychology/child development; commercial art; communication; computer information systems; computer science; (pre)dentistry sequence; early childhood education; economics; education; elementary education; (pre)engineering sequence; English; exercise science; health education; history; humanities; interdisciplinary studies; (pre)law sequence; liberal arts/general studies; management information systems; marketing/retailing/merchandising; mathematics; medical technology; (pre)medicine sequence; middle school education; music; music business; music education; pastoral studies; philosophy; physical education; physical fitness/human movement; piano/organ; political science/government; psychology; public relations; radio and television studies; radiological technology; religious studies; science education; secondary education; secretarial studies/office management; social science; social work; sociology; speech/rhetoric/public address/debate; theater arts/drama; (pre)veterinary medicine sequence; voice; wind and percussion instruments. Most popular majors of class of 1991: business administration/commerce/management, education, communications.

SPECIAL NOTE FROM THE COLLEGE Sioux Falls College is a 4-year Christian liberal arts college affiliated with the American Baptist Churches. In an environment that both challenges and supports, students are encouraged to develop knowledge and wisdom for discerning truth and meeting human needs, to build a value system in keeping with Christ's teachings, to achieve emotional maturity, to pursue physical fitness, and to gain interpersonal skills. Students develop close, caring relationships with professors in and out of the classroom. Beyond the classroom, there are numerous cocurricular activities important to a college education. Sioux Falls is large enough to provide many opportunities for involvement and small enough to encourage participation.

CONTACT Ms. Susan Reese, Director of Admissions, Sioux Falls College, 1501 South Prairie Avenue, Sioux Falls, SD 57105, 605-331-6600 or toll-free 800-888-1047 (out of state).

SOUTHERN CALIFORNIA COLLEGE

Costa Mesa, California

Total Enrollment: 873

UG Enrollment: 811 (52% W)

Application Deadline: 7/31

Tuition & Fees: $8164

Room & Board: $3640

Entrance: moderately difficult

SAT ≥ 500: 19% V, 43% M

ACT ≥ 21: 55%

Denominational Affiliation: Assemblies of God

GENERAL INFORMATION Independent comprehensive coed institution. Founded 1920. Awards B, M. Primary accreditation: regional. Suburban setting, with easy access to Los Angeles; 40-acre campus. Total enrollment: 873. Faculty: 81 (41 full-time, 40 part-time); 65% of full-time faculty have terminal degrees; graduate assistants teach no undergraduate courses. Library holdings: 91,800 bound volumes, 4,852 titles on microform, 680 periodical subscriptions, 3,238 records/tapes/CDs. Computer terminals/PCs available for student use: 50, located in computer center, library.

UNDERGRADUATE PROFILE Fall 1991: 811 undergraduates (184 freshmen) from 28 states and territories and 29 foreign countries; 14% part-time; 74% state residents; 30% transfers; 80% financial aid recipients; 52% women; 4% African Americans; 1% Native Americans; 9% Hispanics; 5% Asian Americans; 3% international students; 13% of undergraduates 25 years of age or older.

1991 FRESHMAN DATA 424 students applied for fall 1991 admission; 85% were accepted; 51% of those accepted enrolled. 15% of freshmen were in top 10% of secondary school class, 49% were in top 25%, 75% were in top half.

ENROLLMENT PATTERNS 70% of fall 1990 freshmen returned for fall 1991 term. 30% of 1986 freshmen graduated within 5 years.

FRESHMAN ADMISSIONS Preference given to Christians. Option: deferred entrance. Required: essay, high school transcript, 2 recommendations, SAT or ACT, TOEFL (for foreign students). Recommended: 3 years of high school math and science. Required for some: campus interview. Test scores used for counseling/placement. Application deadline: 7/31. Notification date: continuous until 8/31. College's own assessment of entrance difficulty level: moderately difficult.

TRANSFER ADMISSIONS Required: essay, 2 recommendations, college transcript, minimum 2.0 grade point average. Required for some: standardized test scores, high school transcript, campus interview. Application deadline: 7/31. Notification date: continuous until 8/31. College's own assessment of entrance difficulty level: moderately difficult.

EXPENSES (1992–93) Comprehensive fee of $11,804 includes full-time tuition ($7904), mandatory fees ($260), and college room and board ($3640). Part-time tuition: $308 per credit.

FINANCIAL AID College-administered aid for all 1991–92 undergraduates: need-based scholarships; non-need scholarships; short-term loans; low-interest long-term loans from college funds, from external sources; SEOG; College Work-Study; part-time jobs. Supporting data: FAF, state form, institutional form, AFSA/SAR required; IRS required for some. Priority application deadline: 3/2.

CAMPUS LIFE/STUDENT SERVICES Mandatory chapel; drama/theater group; student-run newspaper. Institution provides personal/psychological counseling.

STUDY ABROAD SITES Israel, Costa Rica.

ATHLETICS Member NAIA. Intercollegiate sports: baseball M(s); basketball M(s), W(s); cross-country running M(s), W(s); soccer M(s); softball W(s); tennis M; volleyball W(s). Intramural sports: badminton, basketball, football, golf, racquetball, table tennis (Ping Pong), tennis, volleyball, weight lifting.

MAJORS Accounting; anthropology; biblical studies; biology/biological sciences; broadcasting; business administration/commerce/management; chemistry; communication; education; elementary education; English; finance/banking; history; humanities; journalism; (pre)law sequence; marketing/retailing/merchandising; mathematics; (pre)medicine sequence; ministries; music; music education; pastoral studies; physical education; political science/government; psychology; radio and television studies; religious education; religious studies; science; secondary education; social science; sociology; speech/rhetoric/public address/debate; theater arts/drama; (pre)veterinary medicine sequence.

SPECIAL NOTE FROM THE COLLEGE Southern California College is located 5 miles from the Pacific Ocean in Costa Mesa, California. Founded in 1920 and affiliated with the Assemblies of God, SCC is the largest Christian college in the charismatic tradition west of the Rocky Mountains. SCC offers 29 academic majors and opportunities for off-campus study in archaeology during the summer in Israel or in missions and language at the College's study center in San José, Costa Rica. The campus is ideally located in Orange County, where business and recreational activities provide students with countless jobs, internships, and leisure opportunities.

CONTACT Mr. Rick Hardy, Assistant Dean for Enrollment Management, Southern California College, 55 Fair Drive, Costa Mesa, CA 92626, 714-556-3610 Ext. 223 or toll-free 800-722-6279.

SOUTHERN NAZARENE UNIVERSITY

Bethany, Oklahoma

Total Enrollment: 1,598

UG Enrollment: 1,425 (55% W)

Application Deadline: 8/15

Tuition & Fees: $5835

Room & Board: $3299

Entrance: noncompetitive

SAT ≥ 500: N/R

ACT ≥ 21: 42%

Denominational Affiliation: Church of the Nazarene

GENERAL INFORMATION Independent comprehensive coed institution. Founded 1899. Awards A (college transfer and terminal), B, M. Primary accreditation: regional. Suburban setting, with easy access to Oklahoma City; 40-acre campus. Total enrollment: 1,598. Faculty: 103 (66 full-time, 37 part-time); 53% of full-time faculty have terminal degrees; graduate assistants teach a few undergraduate courses. Library holdings: 108,200 bound volumes, 163,746 titles on microform, 610 periodical subscriptions, 2,927 records/tapes/CDs. Computer terminals/PCs available for student use: 55, located in computer center, library, academic classrooms.

UNDERGRADUATE PROFILE Fall 1991: 1,425 undergraduates (283 freshmen) from 31 states and territories and 22 foreign countries; 16% part-time; 65% state residents; 8% transfers; 72% financial aid recipients; 55% women; 5% African Americans; 1% Native Americans; 1% Hispanics; 1% Asian Americans; 5% international students; 21% of undergraduates 25 years of age or older.

1991 FRESHMAN DATA 411 students applied for fall 1991 admission; 100% were accepted; 69% of those accepted enrolled. 8% of freshmen were in top 10% of secondary school class, 25% were in top 25%, 40% were in top half.

ENROLLMENT PATTERNS 70% of fall 1990 freshmen returned for fall 1991 term. 22% of students completing a bachelor's program went on for further study.

FRESHMAN ADMISSIONS Open admissions. Option: deferred entrance. Required: high school transcript, SAT or ACT, TOEFL (for foreign students). Recommended: 3 years of high school math and science, 2 years of high school foreign language, recommendations, interview. Test scores used for counseling/placement. Application deadline: 8/15. Notification date: continuous. College's own assessment of entrance difficulty level: noncompetitive.

TRANSFER ADMISSIONS Required: high school transcript, college transcript. Recommended: 3 years of high school math and science, some high school foreign language, recommendations, interview, minimum 2.0 grade point average.

Application deadline: 8/15. Notification date: continuous. College's own assessment of entrance difficulty level: minimally difficult.

EXPENSES (1992–93) Comprehensive fee of $9134 includes full-time tuition ($5549), mandatory fees ($286), and college room and board ($3299). College room only: $1598. Part-time tuition: $196 per credit hour. Tuition prepayment plan available.

FINANCIAL AID College-administered aid for all 1991–92 undergraduates: 882 need-based scholarships (average $1250); 1,109 non-need scholarships (average $1824); low-interest long-term loans from college funds (average $1300), from external sources (average $3275); SEOG; College Work-Study; part-time jobs. Supporting data: FFS required; IRS required for some; FAF, state form, AFSA/SAR acceptable. Priority application deadline: 3/1.

CAMPUS LIFE/STUDENT SERVICES Dress code; mandatory chapel; drama/theater group; student-run newspaper. Institution provides health clinic, personal/psychological counseling.

STUDY ABROAD SITES Costa Rica, England.

ATHLETICS Member NAIA. Intercollegiate sports: basketball M(s), W(s); soccer M(s); volleyball W(s). Intramural sports: basketball, football, softball, swimming and diving, table tennis (Ping Pong), tennis, volleyball, weight lifting.

MAJORS Accounting; adult and continuing education; applied mathematics; art education; art/fine arts; aviation administration; behavioral sciences; biblical languages; biblical studies; biology/biological sciences; business administration/commerce/management; business economics; business education; chemistry; child care/child and family studies; child psychology/child development; commercial art; communication; computer information systems; computer programming; computer science; criminal justice; data processing; (pre)dentistry sequence; early childhood education; economics; education; elementary education; engineering (general); English; family and consumer studies; family services; fashion merchandising; German; gerontology; Greek; health education; health science; Hebrew; history; home economics; home economics education; human resources; information science; interior design; international studies; journalism; laboratory technologies; (pre)law sequence; liberal arts/general studies; literature; management information systems; marketing/retailing/merchandising; mathematics; medical laboratory technology; medical technology; (pre)medicine sequence; ministries; modern languages; music; music education; natural sciences; nursing; occupational therapy; opera; pastoral studies; pharmacy/pharmaceutical sciences; philosophy; physical education; physical therapy; physics; piano/organ; political science/government; psychology; public relations; reading education; recreation and leisure services; religious education; religious studies; sacred music; science; science education; secondary education; secretarial studies/office management; social science; sociology; Spanish; speech/rhetoric/public address/debate; theater arts/drama; theology; (pre)veterinary medicine sequence; voice; wind and percussion instruments; zoology.

SPECIAL NOTE FROM THE COLLEGE Southern Nazarene University has a reputation of excellence that spans a century. It includes a 90% acceptance rate of premedical students into medical colleges; a national championship in computer business assimilation competition (CASBEL); 2 national sports championships in a decade (it is the only NAIA school to ever achieve that); and alumni placed in leadership roles in business, the church, and various professions. Orientation involves students throughout the first semester in small contact groups. The University provides high-quality experience at a reasonable price.

CONTACT Mr. Jeff Williamson, Director of Admissions, Southern Nazarene University, 6729 Northwest 39th Expressway, Bethany, OK 73008, 405-491-6324 or toll-free 800-648-9899.

SPRING ARBOR COLLEGE

Spring Arbor, Michigan

Total Enrollment: 878 (all UG)

Women: 58%

Application Deadline: rolling

Tuition & Fees: $8006

Room & Board: $3400

Entrance: minimally difficult

SAT ≥ 500: N/R

ACT ≥ 21: 50%

Denominational Affiliation: Free Methodist

GENERAL INFORMATION Independent 4-year coed college. Founded 1873. Awards A (college transfer), B. Primary accreditation: regional. Rural setting; 70-acre campus. Total enrollment: 878. Faculty: 62 (52 full-time, 10 part-time); 44% of full-time faculty have terminal degrees; graduate assistants teach no undergraduate courses. Library holdings: 82,357 bound volumes, 44,307 titles on microform, 1,188 periodical subscriptions, 3,637 records/tapes/CDs. Computer terminals/PCs available for student use: 30, located in computer center, student center, learning center.

UNDERGRADUATE PROFILE Fall 1991: 878 undergraduates (151 freshmen) from 25 states and territories and 8 foreign countries; 21% part-time; 89% state residents; 10% transfers; 90% financial aid recipients; 58% women; 4% African Americans; 0% Native Americans; 0% Hispanics; 4% international students.

1991 FRESHMAN DATA 330 students applied for fall 1991 admission; 90% were accepted; 51% of those accepted enrolled. 24% of freshmen were in top 10% of secondary school class, 44% were in top 25%, 72% were in top half.

ENROLLMENT PATTERNS 73% of fall 1990 freshmen returned for fall 1991 term. 40% of 1986 freshmen graduated within 5 years; 12% of students completing a bachelor's program went on for further study.

FRESHMAN ADMISSIONS Options: early entrance, deferred entrance. Required: high school transcript, SAT or ACT, TOEFL (for foreign students). Recommended: essay, 2 years of high school foreign language, interview, guidance counselor's evaluation form. Test scores used for admission. Application deadline: rolling. Notification date: continuous. College's own assessment of entrance difficulty level: minimally difficult.

TRANSFER ADMISSIONS Required: high school transcript, college transcript, minimum 2.0 grade point average. Recommended: essay, interview. Required for some: standardized test scores. Application deadline: rolling. Notification date: continuous.

EXPENSES (1992–93) Comprehensive fee of $11,406 includes full-time tuition ($7900), mandatory fees ($106), and college room and board ($3400). Part-time tuition per credit: $160 for the first 8 credits, $250 for the next 3 credits.

FINANCIAL AID College-administered aid for all 1991–92 undergraduates: need-based scholarships; 1,004 non-need scholarships (average $900); short-term loans; low-interest long-term loans from external sources (average $3500); SEOG; College Work-Study; 153 part-time jobs. Supporting data: FAF required; IRS, institutional form required for some. Priority application deadline: 2/15.

CAMPUS LIFE/STUDENT SERVICES Mandatory chapel; student-run newspaper and radio station. Institution provides health clinic, personal/psychological counseling.

ATHLETICS Member NAIA. Intercollegiate sports: baseball M(s); basketball M(s), W(s); cross-country running M(s), W(s); golf M(s); soccer M(s); softball W(s); tennis M(s), W(s); track and field M(s), W(s); volleyball W(s). Intramural sports: basketball, football, soccer, softball, volleyball.

MAJORS Accounting; art/fine arts; biology/biological sciences; business administration/commerce/management; business economics; chemistry; communication; computer science; early childhood education; elementary education; English; French; history; liberal arts/general studies; mathematics; ministries; music; philosophy; physical education; physics; psychology; religious studies; secondary education; social science; social work; sociology; Spanish; speech/rhetoric/public address/debate. Most popular majors of class of 1991: elementary education, business administration/commerce/management, social science.

SPECIAL NOTE FROM THE COLLEGE At Spring Arbor College there is a community of learners with 3 essential commitments: the serious study of the liberal arts, Jesus Christ as the community's perspective for learning, and critical participation in the affairs of the contemporary world. Everything that is done at Spring Arbor is based on these ideas, from an interest in fostering lifelong learning and developing thinking skills with many different applications to chapel programming, ministry opportunities, and the recognition of the lordship of Christ over the environment and all of life to the College's cross-cultural study requirement and belief that students need to be informed world citizens with a global perspective.

CONTACT Mr. Steve Schippers, Director of Admissions, Spring Arbor College, 106 Main Street, Spring Arbor, MI 49283, 517-750-1200 Ext. 402 or toll-free 800-748-0011.

STERLING COLLEGE

Sterling, Kansas

Total Enrollment: 480 (all UG)

Women: 54%

Application Deadline: rolling

Tuition & Fees: $7330

Room & Board: $3100

Entrance: moderately difficult

SAT ≥ 500: 29% V, 39% M

ACT ≥ 21: 59%

Denominational Affiliation: Presbyterian

GENERAL INFORMATION Independent 4-year coed college. Founded 1887. Awards B. Primary accreditation: regional. Small-town setting; 46-acre campus. Total enrollment: 480. Faculty: 41 (29 full-time, 12 part-time); 29% of full-time faculty have terminal degrees; graduate assistants teach no undergraduate courses. Library holdings: 84,000 bound volumes, 1,200 titles on microform, 450 periodical subscriptions, 1,000 records/tapes/CDs. Computer terminals/PCs available for student use: 15, located in computer center.

UNDERGRADUATE PROFILE Fall 1991: 480 undergraduates (135 freshmen) from 26 states and territories and 7 foreign countries; 37% part-time; 66% state residents; 12% transfers; 90% financial aid recipients; 54% women; 3% African Americans; 1% Native Americans; 5% Hispanics; 1% Asian Americans; 2% international students; 15% of undergraduates 25 years of age or older.

1991 FRESHMAN DATA 334 students applied for fall 1991 admission; 94% were accepted; 43% of those accepted enrolled. 21% of freshmen were in top 10% of secondary school class, 45% were in top 25%, 70% were in top half.

ENROLLMENT PATTERNS 72% of fall 1990 freshmen returned for fall 1991 term.

FRESHMAN ADMISSIONS Options: early entrance, deferred entrance. Required: high school transcript, SAT or ACT, TOEFL (for foreign students). Recommended: 3 years of high school math and science, some high school foreign language. Test scores used for admission and counseling/placement. Application

deadline: rolling. Notification date: continuous. College's own assessment of entrance difficulty level: moderately difficult.

TRANSFER ADMISSIONS Required: college transcript, minimum 2.2 grade point average. Application deadline: rolling. Notification date: continuous. College's own assessment of entrance difficulty level: moderately difficult.

EXPENSES (1992–93) Comprehensive fee of $10,430 includes full-time tuition ($7230), mandatory fees ($100), and college room and board ($3100). Part-time tuition per credit hour: $165 for the first 6 credit hours, $225 for the next 5 credit hours.

FINANCIAL AID College-administered aid for all 1991–92 undergraduates: need-based scholarships; non-need scholarships (average $750); low-interest long-term loans from external sources (average $2000); SEOG; College Work-Study; part-time jobs. Supporting data: FFS, IRS, AFSA/SAR required; FAF acceptable. Priority application deadline: 4/21.

CAMPUS LIFE/STUDENT SERVICES Mandatory chapel; drama/theater group; student-run newspaper; personal/psychological counseling.

ATHLETICS Member NAIA. Intercollegiate sports: baseball M; basketball M(s), W(s); cross-country running M(s), W(s); football M(s); soccer M(s), W(s); softball W; tennis M(s), W(s); track and field M(s), W(s); volleyball W(s). Intramural sports: basketball, table tennis (Ping Pong), tennis, track and field, volleyball.

MAJORS Accounting; art education; art/fine arts; behavioral sciences; biology/biological sciences; business administration/commerce/management; business education; chemistry; child care/child and family studies; communication; computer science; criminal justice; (pre)dentistry sequence; education; elementary education; English; history; home economics; home economics education; (pre)law sequence; liberal arts/general studies; mathematics; (pre)medicine sequence; music; music business; music education; natural sciences; nutrition; philosophy; physical education; piano/organ; political science/government; psychology; religious education; religious studies; secondary education; sociology; special education; speech/rhetoric/public address/debate; theater arts/drama; (pre)veterinary medicine sequence; voice. Most popular majors of class of 1991: education, business administration/commerce/management, behavioral sciences.

SPECIAL NOTE FROM THE COLLEGE Sterling College is nationally recognized for developing creative and thoughtful leaders who understand a maturing Christian faith. The reason for this reputation is simple—Sterling cares about people. Sterling cares how its students are developing academically, socially, physically, and spiritually. Top-quality faculty members teach students how to think, not what to think. Strong theater, music, and art programs stretch students artistically and creatively. Dedicated staff provide active and enthusiastic student-life activities. Concerned coaches help students maintain a proper balance between athletics and academics. All this individual attention is directed toward one aim—helping each student to learn, to grow, and to excel.

CONTACT Mr. Dennis W. Dutton, Director of Admissions, Sterling College, Sterling, KS 67579, toll-free 800-346-1017.

TABOR COLLEGE

Hillsboro, Kansas

Total Enrollment: 460 (all UG)

Women: 44%

Application Deadline: rolling

Tuition & Fees: $7520

Room & Board: $3200

Entrance: moderately difficult

SAT ≥ 500: N/R

ACT ≥ 21: 54%

Denominational Affiliation: Mennonite Brethren

GENERAL INFORMATION Independent 4-year coed college. Founded 1908. Awards A (college transfer and terminal), B. Primary accreditation: regional. Small-town setting; 26-acre campus. Total enrollment: 460. Faculty: 50 (32 full-time, 18 part-time); 54% of full-time faculty have terminal degrees; graduate assistants teach no undergraduate courses. Library holdings: 70,000 bound volumes, 450 periodical subscriptions, 2,000 records/tapes/CDs. Computer terminals/PCs available for student use: 30, located in administration/business building.

UNDERGRADUATE PROFILE Fall 1991: 460 undergraduates (157 freshmen) from 23 states and territories and 8 foreign countries; 10% part-time; 57% state residents; 30% transfers; 100% financial aid recipients; 44% women; 4% African Americans; 1% Native Americans; 3% Hispanics; 0% Asian Americans; 4% international students; 11% of undergraduates 25 years of age or older.

1991 FRESHMAN DATA 293 students applied for fall 1991 admission; 64% were accepted; 84% of those accepted enrolled. 14% of freshmen were in top 10% of secondary school class, 38% were in top 25%, 77% were in top half.

ENROLLMENT PATTERNS 86% of fall 1990 freshmen returned for fall 1991 term. 46% of 1986 freshmen graduated within 5 years.

FRESHMAN ADMISSIONS Required: essay, high school transcript, 2 recommendations, SAT or ACT, TOEFL (for foreign students). Recommended: interview, test scores used for admission and counseling/placement. Application deadline: rolling. Notification date: continuous. College's own assessment of entrance difficulty level: moderately difficult.

TRANSFER ADMISSIONS Required: essay, standardized test scores, high school transcript, 2 recommendations, college transcript, minimum 2.0 grade point average. Recommended: interview, minimum 3.0 grade point average. Application deadline: rolling. Notification date: continuous.

EXPENSES (1992–93) Comprehensive fee of $10,720 includes full-time tuition ($7320), mandatory fees ($200), and college room and board ($3200). College room only: $1300. Part-time tuition and fees per semester (1 to 11 hours) range from $155 to $3355.

FINANCIAL AID College-administered aid for all 1991–92 undergraduates: 100 need-based scholarships (average $620); 420 non-need scholarships (average $1730); low-interest long-term loans from external sources (average $2000); SEOG; College Work-Study; 65 part-time jobs. Supporting data: FFS, IRS required; state form required for some; FAF, AFSA/SAR acceptable. Priority application deadline: 6/30.

CAMPUS LIFE/STUDENT SERVICES Mandatory chapel; drama/theater group; student-run newspaper. Institution provides personal/psychological counseling.

ATHLETICS Member NAIA. Intercollegiate sports: basketball M(s), W(s); cross-country running M, W; football M(s); soccer M(s); tennis M(s), W(s); track and field M(s), W(s); volleyball W(s). Intramural sports: basketball, football, racquetball, soccer, table tennis (Ping Pong), tennis, track and field, volleyball, weight lifting.

MAJORS Accounting; actuarial science; applied mathematics; biblical studies; biology/biological sciences; business administration/commerce/management; business education; chemistry; computer science; (pre)dentistry sequence; education; elementary education; (pre)engineering sequence; English; environmental biology; health education; history; humanities; international studies; journalism; (pre)law sequence; legal secretarial studies; mathematics; medical secretarial studies; medical technology; (pre)medicine sequence; ministries; music; music education; natural sciences; philosophy; physical education; piano/organ; psychology; religious studies; science; science education; secondary education; secretarial studies/office management; social science; social work; sociology; special education; voice. Most popular majors of class of 1991: business administration/commerce/management, social science, elementary education.

SPECIAL NOTE FROM THE COLLEGE Tabor's religious heritage places utmost importance on a voluntary, adult commitment to follow Christ. This includes a life of personal devotion and outer witness, serious corporate biblical study, and service to others, which is the foundation of Tabor's mission statement. The academic program, therefore, is designed to develop servants of Christ for all walks of life. This occurs in a Christian learning community, which emphasizes fellowship and mutual accountability. Themes of stewardship and service infuse the College's majors. The student development program stresses personal growth, self-discipline, acceptance of responsibility, and the development of decision-making skills. Tabor provides global travel/service experiences each Interterm and structured opportunities to serve others for Christ through a variety of local ministries.

CONTACT Mr. Glenn Lygrisse, Director of Enrollment Management, Tabor College, Hillsboro, KS 67063, 316-947-3121.

TAYLOR UNIVERSITY

Upland, Indiana

Total Enrollment: 1,790 (all UG)

Women: 54%

Application Deadline: rolling

Tuition & Fees: $10,000

Room & Board: $3650

Entrance: moderately difficult

Denominational Affiliation: interdenominational

GENERAL INFORMATION Independent 4-year coed college. Founded 1846. Awards A (terminal), B. Primary accreditation: regional. Rural setting, with easy access to Indianapolis; 250-acre campus. Total enrollment: 1,790. Faculty: 128 (96 full-time, 32 part-time); 66% of full-time faculty have terminal degrees; graduate assistants teach no undergraduate courses. Library holdings: 160,000 bound volumes, 8,120 titles on microform, 750 periodical subscriptions, 2,029 audiovisual holdings. Computer terminals/PCs available for student use: 182, located in computer center, library, dormitories, computer lab.

UNDERGRADUATE PROFILE Fall 1991: 1,790 undergraduates (468 freshmen) from 46 states and territories and 10 foreign countries; 3% part-time; 35% state residents; 6% transfers; 74% financial aid recipients; 54% women; 2% African Americans; 1% Hispanics; 1% Asian Americans; 2% international students.

1991 FRESHMAN DATA 1,396 students applied for fall 1991 admission; 76% were accepted; 44% of those accepted enrolled. 42% of freshmen were in top 10% of secondary school class, 70% were in top 25%, 99% were in top half.

ENROLLMENT PATTERNS 97% of fall 1990 freshmen returned for fall 1991 term. 85% of 1986 freshmen graduated within 5 years; 12% of students completing a bachelor's program went on for further study.

FRESHMAN ADMISSIONS Options: early admission. Required: essay, high school transcript, 3 years of high school math and science, recommendations, SAT or ACT, TOEFL (for foreign students). Recommended: some high school foreign language, interview required for early admission. Test scores used for admission. Application deadline: rolling. Notification date: continuous. College's own assessment of entrance difficulty level: moderately difficult.

TRANSFER ADMISSIONS Required: essay, high school transcript, recommendations, college transcript, minimum 2.5 grade point average. Recommended: standardized test scores, 3 years of high school math and science, some high school foreign language, interview. Application deadline: rolling. Notification date: continuous.

EXPENSES (1992–93) Comprehensive fee of $13,650 includes full-time tuition ($10,000) and college room and board ($3650). Part-time tuition per credit hour: $288 for the first 7 credit hours, $350 for the next 4 credit hours.

FINANCIAL AID College-administered aid for all 1991–92 undergraduates: 1,608 need-based scholarships (average $1731); 662 non-need scholarships (average $985); short-term loans; low-interest long-term loans from college funds (average $1350), from external sources; SEOG; College Work-Study; 600 part-time jobs. Supporting data: FAF, IRS required. Application deadline: 3/1.

CAMPUS LIFE/STUDENT SERVICES Dress code; mandatory chapel 3 times per week; drama/theater group; student-run newspaper and radio station. Institution provides health clinic, personal/psychological counseling.

STUDY ABROAD SITES France, Israel, Singapore, Spain, China, New Zealand, Australia, Central America, Commonwealth of Independent States (USSR) Kenya, England.

ATHLETICS Member NAIA. Intercollegiate sports: baseball M; basketball M, W; cross-country running M, W; football M; golf M; soccer M; softball W; tennis M, W; track and field M, W; volleyball W. Intramural sports: badminton, basketball, cross-country running, equestrian sports, football, golf, racquetball, soccer, softball, table tennis (Ping Pong), tennis, track and field, volleyball.

MAJORS Accounting; art education; art/fine arts; athletic training; biblical literature; biology/biological sciences; broadcasting; business administration/commerce/management; chemistry; Christian education; communication; computer information systems; computer programming; computer science; creative writing; (pre)dentistry sequence; early childhood education; economics; education; elementary education; English; environmental science; French; history; international studies; journalism; (pre)law sequence; liberal arts/general studies; literature; mathematics; medical technology; (pre)medicine sequence; middle school education; ministries; modern languages; music; music education; natural sciences; philosophy; physical education; physics; political science/government; psychology; public relations; recreation and leisure services; religious studies; robotics; sacred music; science education; secondary education; social science; social work; sociology; Spanish; speech/rhetoric/public address/debate; management information systems; theater arts/drama; theology; (pre)veterinary medicine sequence; voice. Most popular majors of class of 1991: business administration/commerce/management, elementary education, psychology.

SPECIAL NOTE FROM THE COLLEGE Taylor students define the uniqueness of the Taylor University program as "Opportunity for responsible decision making in the context of Christian freedom and a supportive campus community. . . ." Within the setting of a nationally recognized academic program, an emphasis on leadership development, a solid biblical foundation, and a supportive residential community students exercise their freedom to create and complete a personal "Taylor-made" program that best prepares them for life and for ministry. Now Taylor University announces a second campus option: students may choose between the country setting of Upland or the urban setting of the Taylor Fort Wayne campus. Taylor University also announces the opening of the new Randall Center for Environmental Studies that is prepared to equip students for emerging career opportunities. Dr. Jay Kesler, the president of Taylor University and a recognized authority on youth and higher education, sets an example of Christian leadership and guides the 147-year Taylor Tradition toward application in the next century.

CONTACT Mr. Herbert Frye, Dean of Admissions, Taylor University, 500 West Reade Avenue, Upland, IN 46989-1001, 317-998-5206 or toll-free 800-882-3456.

TREVECCA NAZARENE COLLEGE

Nashville, Tennessee

Total Enrollment: 1,591

UG Enrollment: 1,047 (57% W)

Application Deadline: rolling

Tuition & Fees: $6220

Room & Board: $3060

Entrance: noncompetitive

SAT ≥ 500: N/App

ACT ≥ 21: 33%

Denominational Affiliation: Nazarene

GENERAL INFORMATION Independent comprehensive coed institution. Founded 1901. Awards A (terminal), B, M. Primary accreditation: regional. Urban setting; 80-acre campus. Total enrollment: 1,591. Faculty: 131 (59 full-time, 72 part-time); 50% of full-time faculty have terminal degrees; graduate assistants teach no undergraduate courses. Library holdings: 85,500 bound volumes, 82,300 titles on microform, 482 periodical subscriptions, 1,908 records/tapes/CDs. Computer terminals/PCs available for student use: 30, located in computer center, library.

UNDERGRADUATE PROFILE Fall 1991: 1,047 undergraduates (196 freshmen) from 38 states and territories and 8 foreign countries; 18% part-time; 60% state residents; 20% transfers; 80% financial aid recipients; 57% women; 8% African Americans; 1% Native Americans; 1% Hispanics; 2% international students.

1991 FRESHMAN DATA 289 students applied for fall 1991 admission; 100% were accepted; 68% of those accepted enrolled.

ENROLLMENT PATTERNS 64% of fall 1990 freshmen returned for fall 1991 term.

FRESHMAN ADMISSIONS Open admissions. Options: early entrance, deferred entrance. Required: high school transcript, medical history, ACT, TOEFL (for foreign students). Required for some: recommendations. Test scores used for counseling/placement. Application deadline: rolling. College's own assessment of entrance difficulty level: noncompetitive.

TRANSFER ADMISSIONS Required: college transcript, medical history. Required for some: recommendations. Application deadline: rolling. College's own assessment of entrance difficulty level: noncompetitive.

EXPENSES (1992–93) Comprehensive fee of $9280 includes full-time tuition ($5920), mandatory fees ($300), and college room and board ($3060). College room only: $1190. Part-time tuition: $185 per semester hour, part-time fees: $75.

FINANCIAL AID College-administered aid for all 1991–92 undergraduates: need-based scholarships; 450 non-need scholarships (average $1329); short-term loans; low-interest long-term loans from external sources (average $2000); SEOG; College Work-Study; 221 part-time jobs. Supporting data: FFS required; FAF acceptable. Priority application deadline: 4/15.

CAMPUS LIFE/STUDENT SERVICES Dress code; mandatory chapel. Institution provides health clinic, personal/psychological counseling.

ATHLETICS Member NAIA. Intercollegiate sports: baseball M(s); basketball M(s); soccer M(s); tennis M(s), W(s); volleyball W(s). Intramural sports: badminton, basketball, bowling, football, gymnastics, racquetball, soccer, softball, swimming and diving, tennis, volleyball, weight lifting, wrestling.

MAJORS Accounting; allied health; behavioral sciences; biology/biological sciences; broadcasting; business administration/commerce/management; chemistry; child care/child and family studies; communication; computer information systems; computer science; early childhood education; education; elementary education; (pre)engineering sequence; English; fitness management; health; history; history/political science; humanities; intercultural communication; (pre)law sequence; liberal arts/general studies; mathematics; medical technology; (pre)medicine sequence; microcomputer technology; ministries; music; music business; music education; natural sciences; pastoral studies; philosophy; physical education; physical therapy; physician's assistant studies; psychology; radio and television studies; religious education; religious studies; sacred music; sales; science education; secondary education; social science; social work; speech/rhetoric/public address/debate; theater arts/drama; theology. Most popular majors of class of 1991: physician's assistant studies; business administration/commerce/management, education.

SPECIAL NOTE FROM THE COLLEGE Trevecca Nazarene's goal is to prepare students for Christian service in all areas of life by providing an education that integrates faith and learning. The College seeks to combine the best in liberal arts as "preparation for life" and the best in career education as "preparation to earn a living." It also provides many opportunities for spiritual growth through chapel services, student organizations, convocations and revivals, and visiting lecturers. In addition, students are actively involved with the Nashville community through local churches and service clubs, which reflects Trevecca's service-oriented philosophy.

CONTACT Mr. Jan R. Forman, Dean of Enrollment Services, Trevecca Nazarene College, 333 Murfreesboro Road, Nashville, TN 37210, 615-248-1782.

TRINITY CHRISTIAN COLLEGE

Palos Heights, Illinois

Total Enrollment: 565 (all UG)

Women: 64%

Application Deadline: 8/15

Tuition & Fees: $8910

Room & Board: $3620

Entrance: moderately difficult

SAT ≥ 500: N/App

ACT ≥ 21: 49%

Denominational Affiliation: interdenominational

GENERAL INFORMATION Independent 4-year coed college. Founded 1959. Awards B. Primary accreditation: regional. Suburban setting, with easy access to Chicago; 53-acre campus. Total enrollment: 565. Faculty: 67 (40 full-time, 27 part-time); 50% of full-time faculty have terminal degrees; graduate assistants teach no undergraduate courses. Library holdings: 55,000 bound volumes, 30,000 titles on microform, 325 periodical subscriptions, 600 records/tapes/CDs. Computer terminals/PCs available for student use: 40, located in computer center.

UNDERGRADUATE PROFILE Fall 1991: 565 undergraduates (117 freshmen) from 20 states and territories and 3 foreign countries; 11% part-time; 64% state residents; 25% transfers; 87% financial aid recipients; 64% women; 7% African Americans; 1% Native Americans; 1% Hispanics; 1% Asian Americans; 1% international students; 12% of undergraduates 25 years of age or older.

1991 FRESHMAN DATA 408 students applied for fall 1991 admission; 73% were accepted; 39% of those accepted enrolled. 10% of freshmen were in top 10% of secondary school class, 31% were in top 25%, 59% were in top half.

ENROLLMENT PATTERNS 60% of fall 1990 freshmen returned for fall 1991 term. 51% of 1986 freshmen graduated within 5 years; 15% of students completing a degree program went on for further study.

FRESHMAN ADMISSIONS Options: early entrance, deferred entrance. Required: high school transcript, ACT, TOEFL (for foreign students). Recommended: 3 years of high school math and science, some high school foreign language. Required for

some: essay, recommendations, interview. Test scores used for admission. Application deadline: 8/15. Notification date: continuous until 8/15. College's own assessment of entrance difficulty level: moderately difficult.

TRANSFER ADMISSIONS Required: college transcript. Recommended: standardized test scores, 3 years of high school math and science, some high school foreign language, minimum 2.0 grade point average. Required for some: essay, high school transcript, recommendations, interview. Application deadline: rolling. College's own assessment of entrance difficulty level: moderately difficult.

EXPENSES (1992–93) Comprehensive fee of $12,530 includes full-time tuition ($8910) and college room and board ($3620). College room only: $1860.

FINANCIAL AID College-administered aid for all 1991–92 undergraduates: 107 need-based scholarships (average $1405); 434 non-need scholarships (average $1283); low-interest long-term loans from external sources (average $2890); SEOG; College Work-Study; 175 part-time jobs. Supporting data: FAF required; IRS, state form required for some; FFS, AFSA/SAR acceptable. Priority application deadline: 2/15.

CAMPUS LIFE/STUDENT SERVICES Drama/theater group; student-run newspaper. Institution provides personal/psychological counseling.

STUDY ABROAD SITE Spain.

ATHLETICS Intercollegiate sports: baseball M; basketball M, W; golf M, W; soccer M; volleyball M, W. Intramural sports: badminton, basketball, cross-country running, field hockey, football, racquetball, soccer, table tennis (Ping Pong), tennis, track and field, volleyball, weight lifting.

MAJORS Accounting; art/fine arts; biology/biological sciences; business administration/commerce/management; business education; chemistry; communication; computer science; (pre)dentistry sequence; education; elementary education; English; history; mathematics; medical technology; (pre)medicine sequence; music; music education; nursing; painting/drawing; philosophy; physical education; piano/organ; psychology; religious education; religious studies; science education; secondary education; sociology; theology; (pre)veterinary medicine sequence; Western civilization and culture. Most popular majors of class of 1991: business administration/commerce/management, education, nursing.

SPECIAL NOTE FROM THE COLLEGE Trinity Christian College is located in Palos Heights, a suburb southwest of Chicago. Its proximity to the city offers students access to cultural, educational, and employment opportunities through the College-wide internship program and the Chicago Suburban Studies Program. Trinity offers majors in 21 areas of study; in addition, there are 25 minor programs available. The nursing program is fully accredited by the National League for Nursing. Trinity graduates enjoy the benefits of a solid, Christian, liberal arts education. They have an excellent acceptance rate into graduate programs in business, education, science, and medicine, as well as great success in career placement.

CONTACT Mr. Jon Bontekoe, Director of Admissions, Trinity Christian College, 6601 West College Drive, Palos Heights, IL 60463, 708-597-3000 Ext. 307 or toll-free 800-748-0085.

TRINITY COLLEGE

Deerfield, Illinois

Total Enrollment: 839 (all UG)

Women: 47%

Application Deadline: rolling

Tuition & Fees: $9200

Room & Board: $4030

Entrance: moderately difficult

SAT ≥ 500: N/R

ACT ≥ 21: 60%

Denominational Affiliation: Evangelical Free Church of America

GENERAL INFORMATION Independent 4-year coed college. Founded 1897. Awards B. Primary accreditation: regional. Small-town setting, with easy access to Chicago; 120-acre campus. Total enrollment: 839. Faculty: 70 (41 full-time, 29 part-time); 46% of full-time faculty have terminal degrees; graduate assistants teach no undergraduate courses. Library holdings: 115,000 bound volumes, 32,000 titles on microform, 508 periodical subscriptions, 929 records/tapes/CDs. Computer terminals/PCs available for student use: 25, located in computer center, library.

UNDERGRADUATE PROFILE Fall 1991: 839 undergraduates (279 freshmen) from 28 states and territories and 3 foreign countries; 6% part-time; 48% state residents; 13% transfers; 85% financial aid recipients; 47% women; 8% African Americans; 0% Native Americans; 2% Hispanics; 3% Asian Americans; 3% international students; 13% of undergraduates 25 years of age or older.

1991 FRESHMAN DATA 730 students applied for fall 1991 admission; 75% were accepted; 51% of those accepted enrolled. 1 freshman was a National Merit Scholarship Finalist. 17% of freshmen were in top 10% of secondary school class, 39% were in top 25%, 70% were in top half.

ENROLLMENT PATTERNS 78% of fall 1990 freshmen returned for fall 1991 term. 50% of 1986 freshmen graduated within 5 years.

FRESHMAN ADMISSIONS Required: essay, high school transcript, 1 recommendation, SAT or ACT, TOEFL (for foreign students). Recommended: 3 years of high school math and science. Test scores used for admission. Application deadline: rolling. College's own assessment of entrance difficulty level: moderately difficult.

TRANSFER ADMISSIONS Required: essay, high school transcript, 1 recommendation, college transcript, minimum 2.0 grade point average. Recommended: 3 years of high school math and science. Application deadline: rolling. College's own assessment of entrance difficulty level: moderately difficult.

EXPENSES (1992–93) Comprehensive fee of $13,230 includes full-time tuition ($9050), mandatory fees ($150), and college room and board ($4030). College room only: $2000. Part-time tuition: $380 per hour.

FINANCIAL AID College-administered aid for all 1991–92 undergraduates: need-based scholarships (average $300); non-need scholarships (average $750); low-interest long-term loans from college funds (average $900), from external sources (average $2000); SEOG; College Work-Study; part-time jobs. Supporting data: FAF, AFSA/SAR required; FFS acceptable. Priority application deadline: 5/1.

CAMPUS LIFE/STUDENT SERVICES Mandatory chapel; drama/theater group; student-run newspaper. Institution provides personal/psychological counseling.

ATHLETICS Member NAIA. Intercollegiate sports: basketball M(s), W(s); cross-country running M, W; football M(s); golf M(s); soccer M(s), W(s); tennis M(s), W(s); track and field M, W; volleyball M, W(s); wrestling M. Intramural sports: basketball, football, racquetball, soccer, table tennis (Ping Pong), tennis.

MAJORS Biblical studies; biology/biological sciences; business administration/commerce/management; chemistry; communication; computer information systems; computer science; economics; education; elementary education; English; history; humanities; liberal arts/general studies; mathematics; ministries; music; music education; philosophy; physical education; psychology; social science; sociology. Most popular majors of class of 1991: education, business administration/commerce/management, psychology.

SPECIAL NOTE FROM THE COLLEGE Trinity College, committed to a Christian liberal arts education, is located on Chicago's North Shore. Students are trained to make their profession of choice their mission field. They are challenged to honestly examine their faith and to discover personal answers to the "whys" and "hows" of believing and how their commitment to Christ relates to their academics, lifestyle, and professional goals. Students acquire book knowledge but also have opportunities to gain practical experience. Activities and internship programs provide chances for students to develop leadership, organizational, and communication skills, as well as gain valuable experience in their major. Trinity students discover challenging academics, an enlightening spiritual life, and lots of fun. They enjoy Chicago, a city with continuous energy, and, most important, build lifelong friendships with Christians from all over the country.

CONTACT Mr. Brian Medaglia, Director of Admissions, Trinity College, 2077 Half Day Road, Deerfield, IL 60015, 708-317-7075 or toll-free 800-822-3225 (out-of-state).

TRINITY WESTERN UNIVERSITY

Langley, British Columbia, Canada

Total Enrollment: 1,559

UG Enrollment: 1,495 (53% W)

Application Deadline: rolling

Tuition & Fees: $6258

Room & Board: $3990

Entrance: moderately difficult

SAT ≥ 500: 49% V, 61% M

ACT ≥ 21: 48%

Denominational Affiliation: Evangelical Free Church of America

---

GENERAL INFORMATION Independent comprehensive coed institution. Founded 1962. Awards B, M. Primary accreditation: provincial charter. Small-town setting, with easy access to Vancouver; 110-acre campus. Total enrollment: 1,559. Faculty: 86 (52 full-time, 34 part-time); 73% of full-time faculty have terminal degrees; graduate assistants teach no undergraduate courses. Library holdings: 87,167 bound volumes, 134,201 titles on microform, 598 periodical subscriptions, 221 records/tapes/CDs. Computer terminals/PCs available for student use: 36, located in computer center, library.

UNDERGRADUATE PROFILE Fall 1991: 1,495 undergraduates (543 freshmen) from 11 provinces and territories and 32 foreign countries; 22% part-time; 65% province residents; 10% transfers; 64% financial aid recipients; 53% women; 1% African Americans; 1% Native Americans; 7% international students; 20% of undergraduates 25 years of age or older.

1991 FRESHMAN DATA 1,210 students applied for fall 1991 admission; 78% were accepted; 58% of those accepted enrolled. 20% of freshmen were in top 10% of secondary school class, 20% were in top 25%, 60% were in top half.

ENROLLMENT PATTERNS 65% of fall 1990 freshmen returned for fall 1991 term.

FRESHMAN ADMISSIONS Options: early entrance, deferred entrance. Required: essay, high school transcript, 2 recommendations, TOEFL (for foreign students). Recommended: 3 years of high school math and science, some high school foreign language. Required for some: interview, SAT or ACT. Test scores used for admission. Standardized test score cutoffs for U.S. applicants: 970 on SAT (verbal and math combined), 22 on ACT (composite). Application deadline: rolling. Notification date: continuous. College's own assessment of entrance difficulty level: moderately difficult; very difficult for aviation technology program.

TRANSFER ADMISSIONS Required: essay, high school transcript, 2 recommendations, college transcript. Recommended: 3 years of high school math and science, some high school foreign language, minimum 2.0 grade point average. Required for some: standardized test scores, interview. Application deadline: rolling. Notification date: continuous. College's own assessment of entrance difficulty level: moderately difficult.

EXPENSES (1992–93) Comprehensive fee of $10,248 includes full-time tuition ($5990), mandatory fees ($268), and college room and board ($3990). Part-time tuition: $204 per semester hour. Part-time fees: $80. (All figures are in Canadian dollars.).

FINANCIAL AID College-administered aid for all 1991–92 undergraduates: 358 need-based scholarships (average $1101); 140 non-need scholarships (average $703); low-interest long-term loans from external sources (average $5054); 221 part-time jobs. Supporting data: institutional form required; government form required for some; FFS, FAF, IRS, AFSA/SAR acceptable. Priority application deadline: 4/1.

CAMPUS LIFE/STUDENT SERVICES Drama/theater group; student-run newspaper. Institution provides health clinic, personal/psychological counseling. Social organizations: social clubs.

ATHLETICS Intercollegiate sports: basketball M, W; rugby M; soccer M, W; volleyball M, W. Intramural sports: badminton, basketball, football, ice hockey, racquetball, soccer, table tennis (Ping Pong), tennis, volleyball.

MAJORS Applied mathematics; art/fine arts; biblical studies; biology/biological sciences; business administration/commerce/management; chemistry; communication; computer science; (pre)dentistry sequence; education; elementary education; English; flight training; geography; history; humanities; human services; (pre)law sequence; liberal arts/general studies; linguistics; mathematics; (pre)medicine sequence; music; natural sciences; philosophy; physical education; psychology; religious studies; science; secondary education; social science; theater arts/drama; (pre)veterinary medicine sequence.

SPECIAL NOTE FROM THE COLLEGE Trinity Western is set on a wooded 100-acre campus. Its students enjoy the solitude of a rural environment and have easy access to the beautiful urban center of Vancouver, just 20 miles away. Trinity is committed to the development of godly Christian leaders—men and women who will take their education and skills into the marketplace and work for the cause of Christ. The whole-student approach to education provides an environment that challenges students to develop intellectually, socially, physically, and spiritually.

CONTACT Mr. Kirk Kauffeldt, Director of Admissions, Trinity Western University, 7600 Glover Road, Langley, BC V3A 6H4, Canada, 604-888-7511 Ext. 2015.

WARNER PACIFIC COLLEGE

Portland, Oregon

Total Enrollment: 573
UG Enrollment: 557 (51% W)
Application Deadline: rolling
Tuition & Fees: $7511
Room & Board: $3800
Entrance: moderately difficult
SAT ≥ 500: 19% V, 34% M
ACT ≥ 21: 100%
Denominational Affiliation: Church of God

GENERAL INFORMATION Independent comprehensive coed institution. Founded 1937. Awards A (college transfer and terminal), B, M. Primary accreditation: regional. Urban setting; 15-acre campus. Total enrollment: 573. Faculty: 54 (40 full-time, 14 part-time); 60% of full-time faculty have terminal degrees; graduate assistants teach no undergraduate courses. Library holdings: 57,000 bound volumes, 125 titles on microform, 185 periodical subscriptions, 1,000 records/tapes/CDs. Computer terminals/PCs available for student use: 8, located in computer center, library.

UNDERGRADUATE PROFILE Fall 1991: 557 undergraduates (42 freshmen) from 20 states and territories and 19 foreign countries; 20% part-time; 69% state residents; 55% transfers; 78% financial aid recipients; 51% women; 4% African Americans; 1% Native Americans; 2% Hispanics; 3% Asian Americans; 12% international students; 40% of undergraduates 25 years of age or older.

1991 FRESHMAN DATA 82 students applied for fall 1991 admission; 65% were accepted; 79% of those accepted enrolled.

ENROLLMENT PATTERNS 60% of fall 1990 freshmen returned for fall 1991 term. 14% of students completing a bachelor's program went on for further study.

FRESHMAN ADMISSIONS Options: early entrance, deferred entrance, early action. Required: high school transcript, 2 recommendations, SAT or ACT, TOEFL (for foreign students). Required for some: interview. Test scores used for admission and counseling/placement. Application deadline: rolling, 12/15 for early action. Notification date: continuous, 1/30 for early action. College's own assessment of entrance difficulty level: moderately difficult.

TRANSFER ADMISSIONS Required: standardized test scores, 2 recommendations, college transcript, minimum 2.0 grade point average. Required for some: high school transcript, interview. Application deadline: rolling. Notification date: continuous.

EXPENSES (1992–93) Comprehensive fee of $11,311 includes full-time tuition ($7350), mandatory fees ($161), and college room and board ($3800). College room only: $1750. Part-time tuition per semester hour: $140 for the first 5 semester hours, $280 for the next 6 semester hours.

FINANCIAL AID College-administered aid for all 1991–92 undergraduates: 178 need-based scholarships (average $920); 240 non-need scholarships (average $1291); low-interest long-term loans from college funds (average $2428), from external sources (average $2748); SEOG; College Work-Study; 32 part-time jobs. Supporting data: IRS required for some; FFS, FAF, AFSA/SAR acceptable. Priority application deadline: 5/1.

CAMPUS LIFE/STUDENT SERVICES Mandatory chapel; drama/theater group; student-run newspaper. Institution provides legal services, health clinic, personal/psychological counseling.

STUDY ABROAD SITES Guatemala, Honduras, Commonwealth of Independent States (USSR).

ATHLETICS Intramural sports: badminton, basketball, bowling, cross-country running, field hockey, football, golf, racquetball, skiing (cross-country), skiing (downhill), soccer, softball, table tennis (Ping Pong), tennis, track and field, volleyball, weight lifting.

MAJORS American studies; biblical studies; biology/biological sciences; business administration/commerce/management; English; history; human development; liberal arts/general studies; mathematics; ministries; music; music education; pastoral studies; physical education; psychology; religious education; religious studies; science; science education; secondary education; social science; social work; sociology; theology. Majors with the highest enrollment: business administration/commerce/management, social science, human development.

SPECIAL NOTE FROM THE COLLEGE Warner Pacific College is shaped by an assumption that there must be a strong and reinforcing relationship between faith, learning, and life. Faculty members are selected for their ability to teach; for evidence of thoughtful personal, spiritual, and professional growth; and for being expert in their subject area. There is a conviction that students are expected to develop servant leadership and a global perspective by staffing and managing the Bethlehem Inn, an overnight shelter for homeless families, and through international experiences such as the exchange program with Kiev Pedagogical Language Institute in the former Soviet Union. Well-trained residence and counseling staffs help students resolve normal difficulties. All students benefit from the Academic Support Center. Warner Pacific is located 15 minutes from downtown Portland, Oregon, and less than 2 hours by car from Mt. Hood ski slopes and Pacific Ocean beaches.

CONTACT Mr. Kenneth S. T. Thomas, Director of Admissions, Warner Pacific College, 2219 Southeast 68th Avenue, Portland, OR 97215, 503-775-4366 Ext. 510.

WARNER SOUTHERN COLLEGE

Lake Wales, Florida

Total Enrollment: 484 (all UG)

Women: 56%

Application Deadline: rolling

Tuition & Fees: $5930

Room & Board: $3265

Entrance: minimally difficult

SAT ≥ 500: 13% V, 29% M

ACT ≥ 21: 16%

Denominational Affiliation: Church of God

GENERAL INFORMATION Independent 4-year coed college. Founded 1968. Awards A (college transfer and terminal), B. Primary accreditation: regional. Rural setting, with easy access to Orlando and Tampa; 350-acre campus. Total enrollment: 484. Faculty: 47 (22 full-time, 25 part-time); 45% of full-time faculty have terminal degrees; graduate assistants teach no undergraduate courses. Library holdings: 66,000 bound volumes, 6,200 titles on microform, 5,500 periodical subscriptions, 3,320 records/tapes/CDs. Computer terminals/PCs available for student use: 21, located in computer center.

UNDERGRADUATE PROFILE Fall 1991: 484 undergraduates (90 freshmen) from 28 states and territories and 6 foreign countries; 8% part-time; 76% state residents; 49% transfers; 83% financial aid recipients; 56% women; 8% African Americans; 0% Native Americans; 1% Hispanics; 1% Asian Americans; 3% international students; 54% of undergraduates 25 years of age or older.

1991 FRESHMAN DATA 268 students applied for fall 1991 admission; 82% were accepted; 41% of those accepted enrolled. 12% of freshmen were in top 10% of secondary school class, 41% were in top 25%, 86% were in top half.

ENROLLMENT PATTERNS 61% of fall 1990 freshmen returned for fall 1991 term. 34% of 1986 freshmen graduated within 5 years; 20% of students completing a bachelor's program went on for further study.

FRESHMAN ADMISSIONS Preference given to Christians. Options: early entrance, deferred entrance. Required: essay, high school transcript, 1 recommendation, SAT or ACT. Required for some: interview. Test scores used for admission and counseling/placement. Application deadline: rolling. Notification date: continuous. College's own assessment of entrance difficulty level: minimally difficult.

TRANSFER ADMISSIONS Required: essay, standardized test scores, 1 recommendation, college transcript, minimum 2.0 grade point average. Required for some: interview. Application deadline: rolling. Notification date: continuous. College's own assessment of entrance difficulty level: minimally difficult.

EXPENSES (1992–93) Comprehensive fee of $9195 includes full-time tuition ($5550), mandatory fees ($380), and college room and board ($3265). College room only: $1400. Part-time tuition per semester hour: ranges from $140 to $180.

FINANCIAL AID College-administered aid for all 1991–92 undergraduates: 72 need-based scholarships (average $618); 204 non-need scholarships (average $904); low-interest long-term loans from external sources (average $3154); SEOG; College Work-Study; 60 part-time jobs. Supporting data: FFS, AFSA/SAR required for some; FAF acceptable. Priority application deadline: 4/1.

CAMPUS LIFE/STUDENT SERVICES Dress code; mandatory chapel; student-run newspaper and radio station. Institution provides health clinic, personal/psychological counseling.

ATHLETICS Member NAIA. Intercollegiate sports: baseball M(s); basketball M(s), W(s); soccer M(s); volleyball W(s). Intramural sports: basketball, football, racquetball, table tennis (Ping Pong), tennis, volleyball.

MAJORS Adult and continuing education; biblical studies; biology/biological sciences; business administration/management; communication; elementary education; English; international studies; liberal arts/general studies; ministries; music; music education; pastoral studies; physical education; psychology; religious education; religious studies; science education; secondary education; social science; sociology; theology. Most popular majors of class of 1991: elementary education, business administration/management.

SPECIAL NOTE FROM THE COLLEGE Warner Southern College is located in beautiful central Florida just a few miles south of Walt Disney World on Lake Caloosa. Warner Southern offers a rich atmosphere of concern for each student and is committed to serving students in every area of their lives. It is an accredited 4-year Christian college in the liberal arts tradition, offering a broad scope of majors in which students are able to excel. Students develop a close bond with their professors because of the low student-faculty ratio and with fellow students because of the friendly atmosphere. Students often remark that they enjoy the size of the classes and the spiritual atmosphere that exists on campus.

CONTACT Mrs. Valerie Rutland, Director of Admissions, Warner Southern College, U.S. Highway 27 South, Lake Wales, FL 33853, 813-638-1426 Ext. 208 or toll-free 800-949-7248.

WESTERN BAPTIST COLLEGE

Salem, Oregon

Total Enrollment: 406 (all UG)

Women: 52%

Application Deadline: rolling

Tuition & Fees: $7900

Room & Board: $3500

Entrance: minimally difficult

SAT ≥ 500: 21% V, 24% M

ACT ≥ 21: N/R

Denominational Affiliation: Baptist

GENERAL INFORMATION Independent 4-year coed college. Founded 1935. Awards A (college transfer), B. Primary accreditation: regional. Urban setting, with easy access to Portland; 107-acre campus. Total enrollment: 406. Faculty: 56 (37 full-time, 19 part-time); 19% of full-time faculty have terminal degrees; graduate assistants teach no undergraduate courses. Library holdings: 58,378 bound volumes, 1,205 titles on microform, 385 periodical subscriptions, 2,223 records/tapes/CDs. Computer terminals/PCs available for student use: 12, located in computer center.

UNDERGRADUATE PROFILE Fall 1991: 406 undergraduates (92 freshmen) from 15 states and territories and 1 foreign country; 9% part-time; 51% state residents; 9% transfers; 95% financial aid recipients; 52% women; 0% African Americans; 1% Native Americans; 1% Hispanics; 1% Asian Americans; 12% of undergraduates 25 years of age or older.

1991 FRESHMAN DATA 176 students applied for fall 1991 admission; 88% were accepted; 60% of those accepted enrolled.

ENROLLMENT PATTERNS 85% of fall 1990 freshmen returned for fall 1991 term.

FRESHMAN ADMISSIONS Required: essay, high school transcript, 3 recommendations, SAT or ACT, TOEFL (for foreign students). Test scores used for admission. Application deadline: rolling. College's own assessment of entrance difficulty level: minimally difficult.

TRANSFER ADMISSIONS Required: essay, standardized test scores, high school transcript, 3 recommendations, college transcript, minimum 2.0 grade point average.

EXPENSES (1992–93) Comprehensive fee of $11,400 includes full-time tuition ($7700), mandatory fees ($200), and college room and board ($3500). Part-time tuition: $325 per semester hour.

FINANCIAL AID College-administered aid for all 1991–92 undergraduates: 96 need-based scholarships (average $377); 251 non-need scholarships (average $2238); short-term loans; low-interest long-term loans from college funds (average $765), from external sources (average $3074); SEOG; College Work-Study; 140 part-time jobs. Supporting data: FAF, AFSA/SAR required; IRS required for some; FFS acceptable. Priority application deadline: 3/1.

CAMPUS LIFE/STUDENT SERVICES Dress code; mandatory chapel; drama/theater group. Institution provides health clinic.

ATHLETICS Member NAIA and NCCAA. Intercollegiate sports: basketball M(s), W(s); soccer M(s); volleyball W(s). Intramural sports: basketball, football, soccer, volleyball.

MAJORS Accounting; biblical studies; business administration/commerce/management; community services; education; elementary education; English; finance/banking; humanities; intercultural studies; interdisciplinary studies; international studies; (pre)law sequence; liberal arts/general studies; mathematics; ministries; missions; music education; pastoral studies; psychology; recreation and leisure services; religious education; religious studies; sacred music; secondary education; social science; theology; youth work. Most popular majors of class of 1991: business administration/commerce/management, education.

SPECIAL NOTE FROM THE COLLEGE A Christian college with a difference! As soon as students step onto the beautiful 100-acre campus in Salem, Oregon, they discover the family atmosphere and caring community that make Western Baptist College so special. They also discover a high-quality Bible-centered education coupled with a strong liberal arts program. Each freshman joins a core group of students from the same geographical area, and transfer students join together to bond in a "new student experience." This initial experience is enhanced by Western Baptist's fellowship system—permanent groups designed to integrate all students both spiritually and socially. Yes, Western is a college with a difference.

CONTACT Mr. Sheldon Nord, Vice-President for Student Life, Western Baptist College, 5000 Deer Park Drive, SE, Salem, OR 97301-9392, 503-581-8600 Ext. 2510.

WESTMONT COLLEGE
Santa Barbara, California

Total Enrollment: 1,189 (all UG)

Women: 59%

Application Deadline: 3/1

Tuition & Fees: $13,546

Room & Board: $4850

Entrance: moderately difficult

SAT ≥ 500: 39% V, 60% M

ACT ≥ 21: 95%

Denominational Affiliation: nondenominational

GENERAL INFORMATION Independent-religious 4-year coed college. Founded 1940. Awards B. Primary accreditation: regional. Suburban setting; 133-acre campus. Total enrollment: 1,189. Faculty: 103 (71 full-time, 32 part-time); 77% of full-time faculty have terminal degrees; graduate assistants teach no undergraduate courses. Library holdings: 147,000 bound volumes, 20,000 titles on microform, 800 periodical subscriptions, 4,900 records/tapes/CDs. Computer terminals/PCs available for student use: 35, located in library.

UNDERGRADUATE PROFILE Fall 1991: 1,189 undergraduates (278 freshmen) from 39 states and territories and 17 foreign countries; 1% part-time; 67% state residents; 20% transfers; 76% financial aid recipients; 59% women; 1% African Americans; 2% Native Americans; 3% Hispanics; 2% Asian Americans; 2% international students; 0% of undergraduates 25 years of age or older.

1991 FRESHMAN DATA 802 students applied for fall 1991 admission; 82% were accepted; 42% of those accepted enrolled. 2 freshmen were National Merit Scholarship Finalists; both received a National Merit Scholarship. 40% of freshmen were in top 10% of secondary school class, 73% were in top 25%, 95% were in top half.

ENROLLMENT PATTERNS 85% of fall 1990 freshmen returned for fall 1991 term. 60% of 1986 freshmen graduated within 5 years.

FRESHMAN ADMISSIONS Options: deferred entrance. Required: essay, high school transcript, SAT or ACT, TOEFL (for foreign students). Recommended: 3 years of high school math and science, 2 years of high school foreign language, recommendations, interview, English Composition Test (with essay). Test scores used for admission. Application deadline: 3/1.

Notification date: continuous until 6/1. College's own assessment of entrance difficulty level: moderately difficult.

TRANSFER ADMISSIONS Required: essay, high school transcript, college transcript, minimum 2.0 grade point average, minimum 2.5 grade point average for transfers from 2-year colleges. Recommended: 3 years of high school math and science, some high school foreign language, recommendations, interview. Required for some: standardized test scores. Application deadline: 3/1. Notification date: continuous until 6/1. College's own assessment of entrance difficulty level: moderately difficult.

EXPENSES (1992–93) Comprehensive fee of $18,396 includes full-time tuition ($12,766), mandatory fees ($780), and college room and board ($4850). College room only: $2796. Part-time tuition: $600 per unit.

FINANCIAL AID College-administered aid for all 1991–92 undergraduates: 574 need-based scholarships (average $4000); 280 non-need scholarships (average $3000); short-term loans (average $100); low-interest long-term loans from college funds (average $3000), from external sources (average $2500); SEOG; College Work-Study; 250 part-time jobs. Supporting data: IRS, institutional form, AFSA/SAR required; state form required for some; FFS, FAF acceptable. Priority application deadline: 3/1.

CAMPUS LIFE/STUDENT SERVICES Mandatory chapel; drama/theater group; student-run newspaper; radio station; Mexico ministry program (Potters Clay); dorm ministries; off-campus and world ministries. Institution provides legal services, health clinic, personal/psychological counseling.

STUDY ABROAD SITES Africa, England, Costa Rica, Europe, Israel, East Asia.

ATHLETICS Member NAIA. Intercollegiate sports: basketball M(s); cross-country running M(s), W(s); soccer M(s), W(s); tennis M(s), W(s); track and field M(s), W(s); volleyball W(s). Intramural sports: badminton, basketball, cross-country running, football, golf, racquetball, soccer, swimming and diving, table tennis (Ping Pong), tennis, volleyball, water polo.

MAJORS Art/fine arts; behavioral sciences; biology/biological sciences; business economics; chemistry; communication; computer science; (pre)dentistry sequence; economics; education; elementary education; engineering (general); engineering physics; English; French; history; (pre)law sequence; liberal arts/general studies; literature; mathematics; (pre)medicine sequence; ministries; modern languages; music; natural sciences; philosophy; physical education; physical sciences; physics; political science/government; psychology; religious studies; secondary education; social science; sociology; Spanish; theater arts/drama; (pre)veterinary medicine sequence.

SPECIAL NOTE FROM THE COLLEGE Westmont's mission is to provide a program uncompromised in its commitment to a high-quality liberal arts education and integrated with enthusiastic, evangelical Christian faith. Close interaction between students and faculty is a Westmont hallmark. Opportunities beyond the classroom include cross-cultural studies in Western and Eastern Europe, Africa, Costa Rica, and the Holy Lands. Semester study programs are available in San Francisco and Washington, DC, as well as at 1 of the 12 other member colleges of the Christian College Consortium.

CONTACT Mr. David Morley, Director of Admissions, Westmont College, 955 La Paz Road, Santa Barbara, CA 93108, 805-565-6200.

WHEATON COLLEGE

Wheaton, Illinois

Total Enrollment: 2,520

UG Enrollment: 2,214 (52% W)

Application Deadline: 2/15

Tuition & Fees: $10,280

Room & Board: $3970

Entrance: very difficult

SAT ≥ 500: 77% V, 91% M

ACT ≥ 21: 95%

Denominational Affiliation: interdenominational

GENERAL INFORMATION Independent comprehensive coed institution. Founded 1860. Awards B, M. Primary accreditation: regional. Suburban setting, with easy access to Chicago; 80-acre campus. Total enrollment: 2,520. Faculty: 254 (146 full-time, 108 part-time); 83% of full-time faculty have terminal degrees; graduate assistants teach no undergraduate courses. Library holdings: 356,289 bound volumes, 127,119 titles on microform, 2,164 periodical subscriptions, 11,809 records/tapes/CDs. Computer terminals/PCs available for student use: 40, located in computer center, computer labs.

UNDERGRADUATE PROFILE Fall 1991: 2,214 undergraduates (545 freshmen) from 50 states and territories and 10 foreign countries; 2% part-time; 22% state residents; 12% transfers; 55% financial aid recipients; 52% women; 1% African Americans; 1% Hispanics; 5% Asian Americans; 1% international students; 2% of undergraduates 25 years of age or older.

1991 FRESHMAN DATA 1,311 students applied for fall 1991 admission; 71% were accepted; 59% of those accepted enrolled. 40 freshmen were National Merit Scholarship Finalists; all received a National Merit Scholarship. 50% of freshmen were in top 10% of secondary school class, 85% were in top 25%, 98% were in top half.

ENROLLMENT PATTERNS 92% of fall 1990 freshmen returned for fall 1991 term. 81% of 1987 freshmen graduated within 5 years.

FRESHMAN ADMISSIONS Preference given to Christians. Options: early action, deferred entrance. Required: essay, high school transcript, 2 recommendations, interview, SAT or ACT, TOEFL (for foreign students). Recommended: 3 years of high school math and science, 2 years of high school foreign language, Achievement Tests, English Composition Test. Test scores used for admission. Application deadlines: 2/15, 12/1 for early action.

Notification dates: 4/10, 2/10 for early action. College's own assessment of entrance difficulty level: very difficult.

TRANSFER ADMISSIONS Required: essay, high school transcript, 2 recommendations, interview, college transcript. Recommended: 3 years of high school math and science, 2 years of high school foreign language. Application deadline: 3/1. Notification date: 4/15. College's own assessment of entrance difficulty level: moderately difficult.

EXPENSES (1992–93) Comprehensive fee of $14,250 includes full-time tuition ($10,280) and college room and board ($3970). College room only: $2300. Part-time tuition: $430 per hour.

FINANCIAL AID College-administered aid for all 1991–92 undergraduates: 1,191 need-based scholarships (average $3369); 155 non-need scholarships (average $747); low-interest long-term loans from college funds (average $1001), from external sources (average $2347); SEOG; College Work-Study; part-time jobs. Supporting data: FAF required; IRS required for some. Priority application deadline: 3/15.

CAMPUS LIFE/STUDENT SERVICES Mandatory chapel; drama/theater group; student-run newspaper and radio station. Institution provides health clinic, personal/psychological counseling.

STUDY ABROAD SITES England, France, Germany, Israel, Spain, the Netherlands, Asia.

ATHLETICS Member NCAA (Division III). Intercollegiate sports: basketball M, W; cross-country running M, W; football M; golf M; soccer M, W; softball W; swimming and diving M, W; tennis M, W; track and field M, W; volleyball W; wrestling M. Intramural sports: badminton, baseball, basketball, football, racquetball, soccer, softball, tennis, ultimate frisbee, volleyball, weight lifting.

MAJORS Archaeology; art education; art/fine arts; art history; biblical languages; biblical studies; biology/biological sciences; broadcasting; business economics; chemistry; classics; communication; computer science; (pre)dentistry sequence; economics; elementary education; environmental sciences; French; geology; German; history; interdisciplinary studies; journalism; (pre)law sequence; literature; mathematics; (pre)medicine sequence; modern languages; music; music business; music education; music history; philosophy; physical education; physics; piano/organ; political science/government; psychology; religious education; religious studies; science education; secondary education; sociology; Spanish; speech/rhetoric/public address/debate; stringed instruments; studio art; theater arts/drama; voice; wind and percussion instruments. Most popular majors of class of 1991: business economics, literature, psychology.

SPECIAL NOTE FROM THE COLLEGE Convinced that "all truth is God's truth," Wheaton College actively pursues the integration of biblical Christianity with rigorous academic study in the liberal arts, with the goal of serving Christ in this world. Wheaton has a national reputation built upon a distinguished and dedicated faculty known for its outstanding teaching and scholarship and a student body that is committed to academic achievement, leadership, and Christian service. Extensive athletic and other student activities add to the friendly and supportive community on campus.

CONTACT Mr. Dan Crabtree, Director of Admissions, Wheaton College, 501 East College Avenue, Wheaton, IL 60187, 708-752-5005 or toll-free 800-222-2419 (out-of-state).

WHITWORTH COLLEGE

Spokane, Washington

Total Enrollment: 1,706

UG Enrollment: 1,400 (62% W)

Application Deadline: 3/1

Tuition & Fees: $11,095

Room & Board: $4075

Entrance: moderately difficult

SAT ≥ 500: 37% V, 52% M

ACT ≥ 21: 75%

Denominational Affiliation: Presbyterian

GENERAL INFORMATION Independent comprehensive coed institution. Founded 1890. Awards B, M. Primary accreditation: regional. Suburban setting; 200-acre campus. Total enrollment: 1,706. Faculty: 95 (80 full-time, 15 part-time); 80% of full-time faculty have terminal degrees; graduate assistants teach no undergraduate courses. Library holdings: 170,000 bound volumes, 55,209 titles on microform, 729 periodical subscriptions, 1,977 records/tapes/CDs. Computer terminals/PCs available for student use: 90, located in computer center, labs.

UNDERGRADUATE PROFILE Fall 1991: 1,400 undergraduates (246 freshmen) from 27 states and territories and 21 foreign countries; 19% part-time; 60% state residents; 31% transfers; 86% financial aid recipients; 62% women; 1% African Americans; 1% Native Americans; 2% Hispanics; 3% Asian Americans; 4% international students; 17% of undergraduates 25 years of age or older.

1991 FRESHMAN DATA 787 students applied for fall 1991 admission; 89% were accepted; 35% of those accepted enrolled. 25% of freshmen were in top 10% of secondary school class, 60% were in top 25%, 92% were in top half.

ENROLLMENT PATTERNS 70% of fall 1990 freshmen returned for fall 1991 term.

FRESHMAN ADMISSIONS Options: early decision, deferred entrance. Required: essay, high school transcript, recommendations, SAT or ACT, TOEFL (for foreign students). Recommended: 3 years of high school math and science, some high school foreign language. Required for some: interview. Test scores used for admission. Application deadlines: 3/1, 11/30 for early decision. Notification date: 12/15 for early decision. College's own assessment of entrance difficulty level: moderately difficult.

TRANSFER ADMISSIONS Required: essay, recommendations, college transcript, minimum 2.3 grade point average.

Recommended: 3 years of high school math and science, some high school foreign language. Required for some: standardized test scores, high school transcript, interview. Application deadline: 7/1. College's own assessment of entrance difficulty level: moderately difficult.

EXPENSES (1992–93 estimated) Comprehensive fee of $15,170 includes full-time tuition ($10,970), mandatory fees ($125), and college room and board ($4075). Part-time tuition and fees per semester (1 to 3 courses) ranges from $228 per credit for the first four credits to $456 for the next seven credits.

FINANCIAL AID College-administered aid for all 1991–92 undergraduates: 843 need-based scholarships (average $4396); 98 non-need scholarships (average $1966); low-interest long-term loans from college funds (average $1443), from external sources (average $2408); SEOG; College Work-Study; 340 part-time jobs. Supporting data: FAF required; IRS required for some; FFS, AFSA/SAR acceptable. Priority application deadline: 3/1.

CAMPUS LIFE/STUDENT SERVICES Drama/theater group; student-run newspaper and radio station. Institution provides health clinic, personal/psychological counseling.

STUDY ABROAD SITES China, Mexico, England, Korea, Costa Rica, Guatemala, Nicaragua, France, Israel, Honduras, Hong Kong, Germany.

ATHLETICS Member NAIA. Intercollegiate sports: baseball M; basketball M(s), W(s); cross-country running M(s), W(s); football M(s); soccer M(s), W(s); swimming and diving M(s), W(s); tennis M(s), W(s); track and field M(s), W(s); volleyball W(s). Intramural sports: baseball, basketball, football, rugby, skiing (cross-country), skiing (downhill), softball, table tennis (Ping Pong), volleyball, water polo.

MAJORS Accounting; American studies; art education; art/fine arts; art history; arts administration; biology/biological sciences; business administration/commerce/management; chemistry; communication; computer science; (pre)dentistry sequence; economics; elementary education; English; French; history; international business; international political economy; international studies; journalism; (pre)law sequence; mathematics; (pre)medicine sequence; music; music education; nursing; peace studies; philosophy; physical education; physics; piano/organ; political science/government; psychology; religious studies; secondary education; sociology; Spanish; special education; speech/rhetoric/public address/debate; sports medicine; studio art; theater arts/drama; (pre)veterinary medicine sequence; voice. Most popular majors of class of 1991: business administration/commerce/management, elementary education, English.

SPECIAL NOTE FROM THE COLLEGE For a century, Whitworth has dedicated itself to a blend of educational components: rigorous academics, teaching by Christian scholars, deep Christian roots, active residential life, and a commitment to fostering an understanding of other cultures within the nation and the world. Study tours and exchanges provide opportunities for students to visit such countries as France, Germany, Spain, and Thailand. Internships to allow students to gain experience and build contacts in the professional community are encouraged. Whitworth has a clear mission to prepare students for a career and for a life that will be lived to honor God.

CONTACT Mr. Ken Moyer, Director of Admissions, Whitworth College, Spokane, WA 99251, 509-466-3212 or toll-free 800-533-4668.

WILLIAM JENNINGS BRYAN COLLEGE

Dayton, Tennessee

Total Enrollment: 478 (all UG)

Women: 48%

Application Deadline: rolling

Tuition & Fees: $7050

Room & Board: $3730

Entrance: moderately difficult

SAT ≥ 500: 34% V, 50% M

ACT ≥ 21: 68%

Denominational Affiliation: interdenominational

GENERAL INFORMATION Independent 4-year coed college. Founded 1930. Awards A (terminal), B. Primary accreditation: regional. Small-town setting; 100-acre campus. Total enrollment: 478. Faculty: 52 (28 full-time, 24 part-time); 67% of full-time faculty have terminal degrees; graduate assistants teach no undergraduate courses. Library holdings: 66,627 bound volumes, 318 titles on microform, 300 periodical subscriptions. Computer terminals/PCs available for student use: 100, located in computer center, library, dormitories.

UNDERGRADUATE PROFILE Fall 1991: 478 undergraduates (116 freshmen) from 29 states and territories and 6 foreign countries; 17% part-time; 31% state residents; 6% transfers; 85% financial aid recipients; 48% women; 5% African Americans; 0% Native Americans; 1% Hispanics; 1% Asian Americans; 1% international students; 18% of undergraduates 25 years of age or older.

1991 FRESHMAN DATA 315 students applied for fall 1991 admission; 77% were accepted; 48% of those accepted enrolled.

ENROLLMENT PATTERNS 68% of fall 1990 freshmen returned for fall 1991 term. 48% of 1986 freshmen graduated within 5 years.

FRESHMAN ADMISSIONS Options: early entrance, deferred entrance. Required: high school transcript, 3 recommendations, SAT or ACT, TOEFL (for foreign students). Required for some: interview. Test scores used for counseling/placement. Application deadline: rolling. College's own assessment of entrance difficulty level: moderately difficult.

TRANSFER ADMISSIONS Required: high school transcript, 3 recommendations, college transcript, minimum 2.0 grade point average. Required for some: interview. Application deadline: rolling. College's own assessment of entrance difficulty level: moderately difficult.

EXPENSES (1992–93) Comprehensive fee of $10,780 includes full-time tuition ($6770), mandatory fees ($280), and college room and board ($3730). College room only: $1650. Part-time tuition: $285 per semester hour.

FINANCIAL AID College-administered aid for all 1991–92 undergraduates: 113 need-based scholarships; 215 non-need scholarships; short-term loans (average $2000); low-interest long-term loans from external sources (average $2400); SEOG; College Work-Study; 40 part-time jobs. Supporting data: FFS, IRS, institutional form required; state form required for some; FAF, AFSA/SAR acceptable. Priority application deadline: 5/1.

CAMPUS LIFE/STUDENT SERVICES Dress code; mandatory chapel; drama/theater group; student-run newspaper. Institution provides personal/psychological counseling.

ATHLETICS Member NAIA. Intercollegiate sports: basketball M(s), W(s); cross-country running M(s), W(s); soccer M(s); volleyball W(s). Intramural sports: basketball, football, soccer, tennis, track and field, volleyball.

MAJORS Accounting; biblical studies; biology/biological sciences; business administration/commerce/management; chemistry; communication; elementary education; English; history; liberal arts/general studies; mathematics; music; music education; psychology; religious education; secondary education.

SPECIAL NOTE FROM THE COLLEGE William Jennings Bryan College's mission is to educate servants of Christ for today's world. The College offers the Residence Hall of Tomorrow, an innovative computer network that allows students to access a variety of software programs from computers in their dormitories. A major in communication arts was initiated in 1990. More than two thirds of all students at Bryan participate in voluntary Practical Christian Involvement programs. Bryan emphasizes a firm biblical basis within a high-quality academic program.

CONTACT Mr. Thomas A. Shaw, Director of Admissions, William Jennings Bryan College, Box 7000, Dayton, TN 37321, 615-775-2041 or toll-free 800-277-9522.

Christian College Coalition Programs

In addition to study-abroad opportunities administered by the individual colleges, the Christian College Coalition makes five independent study programs available to the students of its member schools. These programs, which are described in detail on the following pages, provide for off-campus study in Washington, D.C.; at the Au Sable Institute of Environmental Studies in Michigan; in San Jose, Costa Rica; in Los Angeles; and at Oxford University in England.

American Studies Program

Students at each of the colleges listed in this guide are eligible and invited to apply for participation in the Christian College Coalition's American Studies Program (ASP), which serves as a Washington campus for the Coalition member colleges.

The American Studies Program, which began in September 1976, provides a variety of work-study opportunities for approximately 40 students from Coalition institutions each semester. Based on the principle of integrating faith, learning, and living, students spend time in Washington, D.C., earning academic credit by serving as interns and participating in a contemporary issue-oriented seminar program. There they analyze current topics in American domestic, economic, and international policy through three non-traditional, interdisciplinary, issue-oriented public policy units. In addition, each term begins and ends with a two-week unit on the foundations of Christian public involvement.

The American Studies Program is designed for juniors and seniors with a wide range of academic majors and vocational interests. Because of its unique location in the nation's capital, the ASP is a special way of challenging students to consider the meaning of proclaiming the Lordship of Jesus Christ in all areas of life, including career choices, public policy issues, and personal relationships. ASP students live and study in the Coalition's Dellenback Center on Capitol Hill, which includes 8 student apartments, a library, dining facilities, and a classroom.

During the fall and spring terms, students participating in the American Studies Program are engaged in two principal activities: they spend about 25 hours a week working as unpaid interns in their intended vocational fields as well as studying public policy issues in seminar classes. Over 1,300 students have been placed in internships in Congressional offices, executive agencies, legal offices, lobbying and research groups, Christian ministries, social service agencies, cultural institutions, and other businesses throughout Washington.

The Program has had a life-changing impact on its participants, as related by alumni:

> I loved the Program because it challenged me to look deeper into beliefs I already had and to explore beliefs I'd never considered, substantiating them through Scripture and faith. Additionally, the responsibilities expected of me on the Program, combined with the job skills I learned in the internship, provided a smoother transition from college to the workplace. (ASP alumna Sharlene Case)

The Program has been enlightening in a variety of ways. Through the internship, I've learned how to be a Christian in a professional setting. In the seminars, I've learned how to apply my Christian faith to the urgent public policy issues of our times. (ASP alumnus Keith Williams)

Additional information on the American Studies Program is available from the academic dean's office at any of the colleges listed in this guide or by writing to:

American Studies Program
Christian College Coalition
327 Eighth Street, NE
Washington, D.C. 20002
202-546-3086

Au Sable Institute of Environmental Studies

Students from the colleges listed in this guide are eligible for participation in the programs at Au Sable Institute of Environmental Studies. This institution is located in the beautiful northwoods country of Michigan's Lower Peninsula.

Activities at the Institute fall into three main categories: the environmental education center, where over 4,000 kindergarten to twelfth grade students experience and learn about the natural world; retreats and conferences for college, church, and organizational groups; and the college program, in which Coalition college students participate.

Au Sable's college program focuses on enabling students to be knowledgeable caretakers of the environment. Courses cover different aspects of environmental studies, ecology, and stewardship and provide ecological information and experience in both field and laboratory techniques. Vocational certificates for water resources analyst, land resources analyst, environmental analyst, and naturalist are available to those who have completed the required courses and demonstrated proficiency in specific techniques. Students receive their certificate after they complete their bachelor's degree.

The college program was designed to support and serve Christian liberal arts colleges. It provides course work that normally is not available at the student's home campus. Classes are small and individualized, and teaching excellence is emphasized.

The campus includes an earth-sheltered classroom and laboratory building, a dining hall, a lodge, an environmental learning center, various recreational facilities, and living accommodations ranging from rustic to modern. With ready access to diverse land and water resources, the Institute is particularly suited to its goals.

Students who seek certification, as well as those who simply wish to take a course at the Institute, enroll through their home college in one or more of the four sessions. January and May terms are 3 weeks long and coincide with periods when many colleges are not meeting for regular classes. Two 5-week summer sessions begin in early June and end by mid-August.

Au Sable financial aid is available to students recommended by their home college. For students at thirty Coalition colleges directly affiliated with the Institute, financial aid recommendations go through a designated faculty representative. At other Coalition schools, financial assistance is administered by the Christian College Coalition and the Institute.

For those students interested in teaching or natural history interpretation, Au Sable offers paid internships as part of its environmental education center program. Internships provide students with direct teaching experience in diverse situations.

Additional information on opportunities at Au Sable is available from the academic dean's office at any of the colleges listed in this guide, from the Christian College Coalition, or by contacting:

Au Sable Institute
7526 Sunset Trail, NE
Mancelona, Michigan 49659
616-587-8686

Latin American Studies Program

An opportunity to live and learn in Latin America is available to students in their junior or senior year from Coalition member colleges through the Latin American Studies Program (LASP). Located in San José, Costa Rica, the Program is committed to helping students examine and live out the Lordship of Jesus Christ in an international context.

Each semester, a group of approximately 25 to 30 students is selected to participate in this seminar/ service experience in Latin America. The academic program, credit for which is awarded by the student's home institution, involves a combination of learning, serving, and observing.

The learning component includes intensive language study at the Spanish Language Institute in San José, where class assignments are based on previous ability in Spanish. In this program, students study for a period of six weeks and practice their language skills with local Costa Ricans, including the host families that provide a home away from home for each LASP student. These families are chosen for their Christian commitment and their willingness to share their culture and their friendship. At the same time, students take part in seminars that deal with such issues as third world development, Latin American history and culture, and the role of the church. Conducted in English by the LASP staff, seminar sessions enable students to interact with outside speakers who bring varying perspectives on current issues.

The serving component involves hands-on experience working in a "servant role" in the third world through participation in a service project or internship. In order to get a better understanding of the complexities of Latin society, students are placed in a variety of service activities in such fields as agriculture, economic development, education, environmental stewardship, and health.

In addition to living with Costa Rican families, the observing component of the program gives students the opportunity to take part in a 3-week travel experience, following the language training and seminar sessions. By visiting Latin American countries outside Costa Rica, including Guatemala, Honduras, and Nicaragua, students enjoy the rich diversity of cultures in the cities, villages, and countryside of those areas.

After participating in the Coalition's Latin American Studies Program, one student had this to say of his experience:

> I feel this semester has been one of the hardest, most fun, most worthwhile experiences of my whole life, and I know that what I have learned will affect me always.

Students should have the equivalent of one year of college-level Spanish to apply. Additional information on the Latin American Studies Program is available from the academic dean's office at any of the colleges listed in this guide or by writing to:

Latin American Studies Program
Christian College Coalition
329 Eighth Street, NE
Washington, D.C. 20002
202-546-8713

Los Angeles Film Studies Center

In January 1991, the Christian College Coalition inaugurated the Los Angeles Film Studies Center (LAFSC). This Center, which serves as an extension campus for Coalition institutions, offers study programs and internship experiences in the Hollywood area to students from member colleges and universities. Its purpose is to enable its graduates to serve in various aspects of the film industry with professional skill and Christian integrity.

The LAFSC is a unique educational opportunity open to juniors and seniors and is geared to multidisciplinary exposure to the complex film industry and to ethical and critical considerations of its workings and products. It is a place where students from Coalition colleges can learn about how film affects our culture (and vice versa), how the industry itself works, and how to respond to the many ethical challenges working in Hollywood provides.

Each student is placed in an unpaid internship with a business in the Hollywood area. Such placements vary from semester to semester and can include development companies, production offices, agencies, and personal-management companies. Academic course offerings include:

- Inside Hollywood: The Work and Workings of the Film Industry, providing exposure to the creative and operational aspects of the film business and incorporating a filmmaking lab where students make short Super-8 films,
- Keeping Conscience: Ethical Challenges in the Entertainment Industry, an examination of common social and professional ethical problems that arise within the film industry, with special emphasis on the central moral themes of the Christian tradition, and

- Film in Culture: Exploring a Christian Perspective on the Nature and Influence of Film, a survey of major theoretical approaches to film supplemented by a broad understanding of entertainment and culture. Academic credit is recommended by the Coalition and is granted by the student's home institution.

At present, students live and study in an exceptional apartment complex in Burbank, within walking distance of major production studios such as Warner Brothers Studios and NBC. The program's location also gives students ready access to film screenings, studio tours, and visits to location filmings.

Students interested in the Los Angeles Film Studies Center are invited to request additional information from the academic dean's office at any of the colleges listed in this guide or by writing to:

Los Angeles Film Studies Center
Christian College Coalition
915 North Cordova St.
Burbank, CA 91505
213-878-6104

Oxford
Summer School Program

Students at the colleges and universities listed in this guide are eligible to apply for admission to the Oxford Summer School Program, a multidisciplinary study of the events of the Renaissance and Reformation. Located in Oxford, England, the program is cosponsored by the Christian College Coalition and the Centre for Medieval and Renaissance Studies, which is affiliated with Oxford's Keble College.

Inaugurated in 1991, the six-week program explores the Renaissance and Reformation through the study of the philosophy, art, literature, science, music, politics, and religion of this era. Many classes are conducted by Oxford dons, who also meet with students in seminars and in one-on-one tutorials that are typical of the Oxford method of education.

Lectures, classes, meals, and social activities are held in Wycliffe Hall, a theological college of the Church of England. The Hall also houses up to 40 students in single or shared rooms.

Weekly field trips to places of importance outside Oxford introduce students to the great cathedrals, castles, and historic towns nearby. The resources of Oxford, such as the world-famous Bodleian Library, Canterbury Cathedral, and Shakespeare's Stratford-upon-Avon, are also available to students.

The Program has positively influenced the students who have participated, as shown in their remarks:

I would definitely suggest this program for all students, regardless of one's major.

The Oxford summer program is an excellent opportunity for students to grow intellectually, but more importantly to grow in ther personal faith.

Further information is available from the academic dean's office at any of the colleges listed in this guide or by contacting:

Oxford Summer School Program
Christian College Coalition
329 Eighth Street, NE
Washington, D.C. 20002
202-546-8713

Majors Index

A—associate degree; B—bachelor's degree

Accounting

Anderson University, IN	B
Asbury College, KY	B
Azusa Pacific University, CA	B
Bartlesville Wesleyan College, OK	A,B
Belhaven College, MS	B
Bethel College, IN	A,B
Bethel College, KS	B
Bethel College, MN	B
Biola University, CA	B
Bluffton College, OH	B
Calvin College, MI	B
Campbell University, NC	B
Cedarville College, OH	B
Central Wesleyan College, SC	B
Colorado Christian University, CO	B
Dallas Baptist University, TX	B
Dordt College, IA	B
Eastern College, PA	B
Eastern Mennonite College, VA	B
Erskine College, SC	B
Evangel College, MO	A,B
Fresno Pacific College, CA	B
Geneva College, PA	B
Gordon College, MA	B
Goshen College, IN	B
Grace College, IN	B
Grand Canyon University, AZ	B
Grand Rapids Baptist College and Seminary, MI	B
Greenville College, IL	B
Houghton College, NY	B
Huntington College, IN	A,B
Indiana Wesleyan University, IN	A,B
John Brown University, AR	B
Judson College, IL	B
King College, TN	B
King's College, NY	B
Lee College, TN	B
LeTourneau University, TX	B
Malone College, OH	B
Master's College, CA	B
Messiah College, PA	B
MidAmerica Nazarene College, KS	B
Milligan College, TN	B
Mississippi College, MS	B
Mount Vernon Nazarene College, OH	B
North Park College, IL	B
Northwestern College, IA	B
Northwestern College, MN	A,B
Northwest Nazarene College, ID	B
Olivet Nazarene University, IL	B
Palm Beach Atlantic College, FL	B
Point Loma Nazarene College, CA	B
Redeemer College, ON	B
Roberts Wesleyan College, NY	B
Seattle Pacific University, WA	B
Sioux Falls College, SD	B
Southern California College, CA	B
Southern Nazarene University, OK	B
Spring Arbor College, MI	B
Sterling College, KS	B
Tabor College, KS	B
Taylor University, IN	B
Trevecca Nazarene College, TN	B
Trinity Christian College, IL	B
Western Baptist College, OR	B
Whitworth College, WA	B
William Jennings Bryan College, TN	B

Actuarial Science

Tabor College, KS	B

Adult and Continuing Education

Bethel College, MN	B
Biola University, CA	B
Colorado Christian University, CO	B
Northwestern College, MN	B
Nyack College, NY	B
Olivet Nazarene University, IL	B
Southern Nazarene University, OK	B
Warner Southern College, FL	B

Advertising

Campbell University, NC	B

Aerospace Engineering

Eastern Nazarene College, MA	B

Agricultural Business

Dordt College, IA	A,B
MidAmerica Nazarene College, KS	A,B
Northwestern College, MN	A

Agricultural Sciences

Dordt College, IA	B
Eastern Mennonite College, VA	B

Aircraft and Missile Maintenance

LeTourneau University, TX	A

American Studies

Anderson University, IN	B
Cedarville College, OH	B
Warner Pacific College, OR	B
Whitworth College, WA	B

Anesthesiology

Malone College, OH	B

Animal Sciences

Dordt College, IA	

Anthropology

Bethel College, MN	B
Biola University, CA	B
Goshen College, IN	B
Judson College, IL	B
North Park College, IL	B
Southern California College, CA	B

Applied Art

Azusa Pacific University, CA	B
Mississippi College, MS	B
Mount Vernon Nazarene College, OH	B
Sioux Falls College, SD	B

Applied Mathematics

Asbury College, KY	B
Campbell University, NC	B
Geneva College, PA	B
Sioux Falls College, SD	B
Southern Nazarene University, OK	B
Tabor College, KS	B
Trinity Western University, BC	B

Archaeology

Simpson College, CA	B
Wheaton College, IL	B

Art Education

Anderson University, IN	B
Asbury College, KY	B
Bethel College, MN	B
Biola University, CA	B
Bluffton College, OH	B
Calvin College, MI	B
Evangel College, MO	B
Goshen College, IN	B
Grace College, IN	B
Grand Canyon University, AZ	B
Greenville College, IL	B
Houghton College, NY	B

Art Education (continued)

Art Education (continued)

Indiana Wesleyan University, IN	B
Mississippi College, MS	B
Mount Vernon Nazarene College, OH	B
North Park College, IL	B
Northwestern College, IA	B
Northwestern College, MN	B
Olivet Nazarene University, IL	B
Palm Beach Atlantic College, FL	B
Point Loma Nazarene College, CA	B
Roberts Wesleyan College, NY	B
Sioux Falls College, SD	B
Southern Nazarene University, OK	B
Sterling College, KS	B
Taylor University, IN	B
Wheaton College, IL	B
Whitworth College, WA	B

Art/Fine Arts

Anderson University, IN	B
Asbury College, KY	B
Azusa Pacific University, CA	B
Belhaven College, MS	B
Bethel College, IN	A,B
Bethel College, KS	B
Bethel College, MN	B
Biola University, CA	B
Bluffton College, OH	B
California Baptist College, CA	B
Calvin College, MI	B
Campbell University, NC	B
Dallas Baptist University, TX	B
Dordt College, IA	B
Eastern Mennonite College, VA	B
Evangel College, MO	B
Goshen College, IN	B
Grace College, IN	B
Grand Canyon University, AZ	B
Greenville College, IL	B
Houghton College, NY	B
Huntington College, IN	B
Indiana Wesleyan University, IN	A,B
John Brown University, AR	A
Judson College, IL	B
King College, TN	B
Malone College, OH	B
Messiah College, PA	B
Mississippi College, MS	B
Mount Vernon Nazarene College, OH	B
North Park College, IL	B
Northwestern College, MN	B
Northwest Nazarene College, ID	A,B
Olivet Nazarene University, IL	B
Palm Beach Atlantic College, FL	B
Point Loma Nazarene College, CA	B
Redeemer College, ON	B
Roberts Wesleyan College, NY	B
Seattle Pacific University, WA	B
Southern Nazarene University, OK	B
Spring Arbor College, MI	B
Sterling College, KS	B
Taylor University, IN	B
Trinity Christian College, IL	B
Trinity Western University, BC	B
Westmont College, CA	B
Wheaton College, IL	B
Whitworth College, WA	B

Art History

Bethel College, MN	B
Calvin College, MI	B
Eastern College, PA	B
Messiah College, PA	B
Wheaton College, IL	B
Whitworth College, WA	B

Arts Administration

Whitworth College, WA	B

Art Therapy

Biola University, CA	B
Goshen College, IN	B

Astronomy

Eastern College, PA	B

Athletic Training

Anderson University, IN	B
John Brown University, AR	B
MidAmerica Nazarene College, KS	B
Northwest Nazarene College, ID	B
Olivet Nazarene University, IL	B
Point Loma Nazarene College, CA	B
Taylor University, IN	B

Automotive Technologies

LeTourneau University, TX	A

Aviation Administration

Dallas Baptist University, TX	B
Geneva College, PA	B
Southern Nazarene University, OK	B

Aviation Technology

LeTourneau University, TX	A,B

Behavioral Sciences

Bartlesville Wesleyan College, OK	A,B
California Baptist College, CA	B
Cedarville College, OH	B
Erskine College, SC	B
Evangel College, MO	B
Grace College, IN	B
Messiah College, PA	B
Northwest College of the Assemblies of God, WA	B
Redeemer College, ON	B
Southern Nazarene University, OK	B
Sterling College, KS	B
Trevecca Nazarene College, TN	B
Westmont College, CA	B

Biblical Languages

Asbury College, KY	B
Azusa Pacific University, CA	B
Bethel College, IN	A
Grace College, IN	B
Grand Rapids Baptist College and Seminary, MI	B
Master's College, CA	B
Southern Nazarene University, OK	B
Wheaton College, IL	B

Biblical Studies

Anderson University, IN	B
Asbury College, KY	B

Azusa Pacific University, CA	B
Belhaven College, MS	B
Bethel College, IN	A,B
Bethel College, KS	B
Bethel College, MN	B
Biola University, CA	B
Calvin College, MI	B
Campbell University, NC	B
Cedarville College, OH	B
Colorado Christian University, CO	B
Covenant College, GA	A,B
Dallas Baptist University, TX	B
Eastern College, PA	B
Eastern Mennonite College, VA	A,B
Eastern Nazarene College, MA	A
Erskine College, SC	B
Evangel College, MO	B
Fresno Pacific College, CA	A,B
Geneva College, PA	B
George Fox College, OR	B
Gordon College, MA	B
Goshen College, IN	B
Grace College, IN	B
Grand Canyon University, AZ	B
Grand Rapids Baptist College and Seminary, MI	B
Greenville College, IL	B
Houghton College, NY	A,B
Huntington College, IN	B
Indiana Wesleyan University, IN	A,B
John Brown University, AR	A,B
Judson College, IL	B
King College, TN	B
King's College, NY	B
Lee College, TN	B
LeTourneau University, TX	B
Malone College, OH	B
Master's College, CA	B
Messiah College, PA	B
Milligan College, TN	B
Mississippi College, MS	B
Mount Vernon Nazarene College, OH	B
North Park College, IL	B
Northwest Christian College, OR	A,B
Northwest College of the Assemblies of God, WA	B
Northwestern College, MN	A,B
Nyack College, NY	B
Olivet Nazarene University, IL	B
Point Loma Nazarene College, CA	B
Redeemer College, ON	B
Seattle Pacific University, WA	B
Simpson College, CA	A,B
Southern California College, CA	B
Southern Nazarene University, OK	B
Tabor College, KS	A,B
Trinity College, IL	B
Trinity Western University, BC	B
Warner Pacific College, OR	A,B
Warner Southern College, FL	A,B
Western Baptist College, OR	A,B
Wheaton College, IL	B
William Jennings Bryan College, TN	B

Bilingual/Bicultural Education

Goshen College, IN	B

Biochemistry

Azusa Pacific University, CA	B
Biola University, CA	B
Calvin College, MI	B
Mount Vernon Nazarene College, OH	B
Point Loma Nazarene College, CA	B
Roberts Wesleyan College, NY	B

Biology/Biological Sciences

Anderson University, IN	B
Asbury College, KY	B
Azusa Pacific University, CA	B
Bartlesville Wesleyan College, OK	A,B
Belhaven College, MS	B
Bethel College, IN	A,B
Bethel College, KS	B
Bethel College, MN	B
Biola University, CA	B
Bluffton College, OH	B
California Baptist College, CA	B
Calvin College, MI	B
Campbellsville College, KY	B
Campbell University, NC	B
Cedarville College, OH	B
Central Wesleyan College, SC	B
Colorado Christian University, CO	B
Covenant College, GA	B
Dallas Baptist University, TX	B
Dordt College, IA	B
Eastern College, PA	B
Eastern Mennonite College, VA	B
Eastern Nazarene College, MA	B
Erskine College, SC	B
Evangel College, MO	B
Fresno Pacific College, CA	A,B
Geneva College, PA	B
George Fox College, OR	B
Gordon College, MA	B
Goshen College, IN	B
Grace College, IN	B
Grand Canyon University, AZ	B
Grand Rapids Baptist College and Seminary, MI	B
Greenville College, IL	B
Houghton College, NY	B
Huntington College, IN	B
Indiana Wesleyan University, IN	B
John Brown University, AR	B
Judson College, IL	B
King College, TN	B
King's College, NY	B
The King's College, AB	B
Lee College, TN	B
LeTourneau University, TX	B
Malone College, OH	B
Master's College, CA	B
MidAmerica Nazarene College, KS	B
Milligan College, TN	B
Mississippi College, MS	B
Mount Vernon Nazarene College, OH	B
North Park College, IL	B
Northwestern College, IA	B
Northwest Nazarene College, ID	B
Olivet Nazarene University, IL	B
Palm Beach Atlantic College, FL	B
Point Loma Nazarene College, CA	B
Redeemer College, ON	B
Roberts Wesleyan College, NY	B
Seattle Pacific University, WA	B
Sioux Falls College, SD	B
Southern California College, CA	B
Southern Nazarene University, OK	B
Spring Arbor College, MI	B
Sterling College, KS	B
Tabor College, KS	B
Taylor University, IN	B
Trevecca Nazarene College, TN	B
Trinity Christian College, IL	B
Trinity College, IL	B
Trinity Western University, BC	B
Warner Pacific College, OR	B
Warner Southern College, FL	B
Westmont College, CA	B
Wheaton College, IL	B
Whitworth College, WA	B
William Jennings Bryan College, TN	B

Biomedical Engineering

Eastern Nazarene College, MA	B

Biomedical Technologies

Campbell University, NC	B

Botany/Plant Sciences

Dordt College, IA	
Redeemer College, ON	B

Broadcasting

Anderson University, IN	B
Asbury College, KY	B
Biola University, CA	B
Campbell University, NC	B
Cedarville College, OH	B
Evangel College, MO	A,B
Geneva College, PA	B
George Fox College, OR	B
Goshen College, IN	B
Grand Rapids Baptist College and Seminary, MI	A
John Brown University, AR	A,B
Malone College, OH	B
Mount Vernon Nazarene College, OH	B
Northwestern College, MN	A,B
Olivet Nazarene University, IL	B
Southern California College, CA	B
Taylor University, IN	B
Trevecca Nazarene College, TN	A,B
Wheaton College, IL	B

Business Administration/ Commerce/Management

Anderson University, IN	B
Asbury College, KY	B
Azusa Pacific University, CA	B
Bartlesville Wesleyan College, OK	A,B
Belhaven College, MS	B
Bethel College, IN	A,B
Bethel College, KS	B
Bethel College, MN	B
Biola University, CA	B
Bluffton College, OH	B
California Baptist College, CA	B
Calvin College, MI	B
Campbellsville College, KY	A,B
Campbell University, NC	B
Cedarville College, OH	B
Central Wesleyan College, SC	B
Colorado Christian University, CO	B
Covenant College, GA	A,B
Dallas Baptist University, TX	B
Dordt College, IA	B
Eastern College, PA	B
Eastern Mennonite College, VA	B
Eastern Nazarene College, MA	B
Erskine College, SC	B
Evangel College, MO	B
Fresno Pacific College, CA	A,B
Geneva College, PA	A,B
George Fox College, OR	B
Gordon College, MA	B
Goshen College, IN	B
Grace College, IN	B
Grand Canyon University, AZ	B
Grand Rapids Baptist College and Seminary, MI	B
Greenville College, IL	B
Houghton College, NY	B
Huntington College, IN	A,B
Indiana Wesleyan University, IN	A,B
John Brown University, AR	B
Judson College, IL	B
King College, TN	B
King's College, NY	B
Lee College, TN	B
LeTourneau University, TX	B
Malone College, OH	B
Master's College, CA	B
Messiah College, PA	B
MidAmerica Nazarene College, KS	A,B
Milligan College, TN	B
Mississippi College, MS	B
Montreat-Anderson College, NC	B
Mount Vernon Nazarene College, OH	A,B
North Park College, IL	B
Northwest Christian College, OR	B
Northwest College of the Assemblies of God, WA	A,B
Northwestern College, IA	B
Northwestern College, MN	A,B
Northwest Nazarene College, ID	A,B
Nyack College, NY	B
Olivet Nazarene University, IL	B
Palm Beach Atlantic College, FL	B
Point Loma Nazarene College, CA	B
Redeemer College, ON	B
Roberts Wesleyan College, NY	B
Seattle Pacific University, WA	B
Simpson College, CA	B
Sioux Falls College, SD	A,B
Southern California College, CA	B
Southern Nazarene University, OK	A,B
Spring Arbor College, MI	B
Sterling College, KS	B
Tabor College, KS	B
Taylor University, IN	A,B
Trevecca Nazarene College, TN	B
Trinity Christian College, IL	B
Trinity College, IL	B
Trinity Western University, BC	B
Warner Pacific College, OR	B
Warner Southern College, FL	A,B
Western Baptist College, OR	A,B

Business Administration/Commerce/Management (continued)

Whitworth College, WA	B
William Jennings Bryan College, TN	A,B

Business Economics

Biola University, CA	B
Calvin College, MI	B
Campbell University, NC	B
Cedarville College, OH	B
George Fox College, OR	B
Grand Canyon University, AZ	B
Huntington College, IN	B
King College, TN	B
Olivet Nazarene University, IL	B
Southern Nazarene University, OK	B
Spring Arbor College, MI	B
Westmont College, CA	B
Wheaton College, IL	B

Business Education

Anderson University, IN	B
Bartlesville Wesleyan College, OK	B
Bethel College, IN	B
Biola University, CA	B
Bluffton College, OH	B
Cedarville College, OH	B
Dordt College, IA	B
Evangel College, MO	B
Fresno Pacific College, CA	B
Geneva College, PA	B
Goshen College, IN	B
Grand Canyon University, AZ	B
Grand Rapids Baptist College and Seminary, MI	B
Greenville College, IL	B
Huntington College, IN	B
John Brown University, AR	B
Lee College, TN	B
Malone College, OH	B
MidAmerica Nazarene College, KS	B
Mount Vernon Nazarene College, OH	B
Northwestern College, IA	B
Point Loma Nazarene College, CA	B
Southern Nazarene University, OK	B
Sterling College, KS	B
Tabor College, KS	B
Trinity Christian College, IL	B

Business Machine Technologies

Biola University, CA	B
Northwest College of the Assemblies of God, WA	A

Chemical Engineering

Geneva College, PA	B

Chemistry

Anderson University, IN	B
Asbury College, KY	B
Azusa Pacific University, CA	B
Bartlesville Wesleyan College, OK	A,B
Belhaven College, MS	B
Bethel College, IN	A,B
Bethel College, KS	B
Bethel College, MN	B
Biola University, CA	B

Bluffton College, OH	B
Calvin College, MI	B
Campbellsville College, KY	B
Campbell University, NC	B
Cedarville College, OH	B
Central Wesleyan College, SC	B
Covenant College, GA	B
Dordt College, IA	B
Eastern College, PA	B
Eastern Mennonite College, VA	B
Eastern Nazarene College, MA	B
Erskine College, SC	B
Evangel College, MO	B
Geneva College, PA	B
George Fox College, OR	B
Gordon College, MA	B
Goshen College, IN	B
Grand Canyon University, AZ	B
Greenville College, IL	B
Houghton College, NY	B
Huntington College, IN	B
Indiana Wesleyan University, IN	B
John Brown University, AR	B
Judson College, IL	B
King College, TN	B
King's College, NY	B
The King's College, AB	B
Lee College, TN	B
LeTourneau University, TX	B
Malone College, OH	B
Messiah College, PA	B
MidAmerica Nazarene College, KS	B
Milligan College, TN	B
Mississippi College, MS	B
Mount Vernon Nazarene College, OH	B
North Park College, IL	B
Northwestern College, IA	B
Northwest Nazarene College, ID	A,B
Olivet Nazarene University, IL	B
Point Loma Nazarene College, CA	B
Roberts Wesleyan College, NY	B
Seattle Pacific University, WA	B
Sioux Falls College, SD	B
Southern California College, CA	B
Southern Nazarene University, OK	B
Spring Arbor College, MI	B
Sterling College, KS	B
Tabor College, KS	B
Taylor University, IN	B
Trevecca Nazarene College, TN	B
Trinity Christian College, IL	B
Trinity College, IL	B
Trinity Western University, BC	B
Westmont College, CA	B
Wheaton College, IL	B
Whitworth College, WA	B
William Jennings Bryan College, TN	B

Child Care/Child and Family Studies

Anderson University, IN	B
Bethel College, MN	B
Bluffton College, OH	B
Campbell University, NC	B
Evangel College, MO	A
Goshen College, IN	B
Montreat-Anderson College, NC	B

Northwest Nazarene College, ID	B
Olivet Nazarene University, IL	B
Southern Nazarene University, OK	A,B
Sterling College, KS	B
Trevecca Nazarene College, TN	A

Child Psychology/Child Development

Bethel College, MN	B
Fresno Pacific College, CA	A,B
Olivet Nazarene University, IL	B
Point Loma Nazarene College, CA	B
Sioux Falls College, SD	A
Southern Nazarene University, OK	B

Civil Engineering

Calvin College, MI	B
Geneva College, PA	B
George Fox College, OR	B

Civil Engineering Technology

Messiah College, PA	B

Classics

Calvin College, MI	B
Redeemer College, ON	B
Wheaton College, IL	B

Clinical Psychology

Messiah College, PA	B
Redeemer College, ON	B

Commercial Art

Bethel College, IN	A,B
Campbell University, NC	B
Grace College, IN	B
John Brown University, AR	B
Sioux Falls College, SD	B
Southern Nazarene University, OK	A

Communication

Anderson University, IN	B
Azusa Pacific University, CA	B
Bartlesville Wesleyan College, OK	B
Bethel College, IN	A,B
Bethel College, KS	B
Bethel College, MN	B
Biola University, CA	B
Bluffton College, OH	B
California Baptist College, CA	B
Calvin College, MI	B
Campbell University, NC	B
Cedarville College, OH	B
Colorado Christian University, CO	B
Dordt College, IA	B
Eastern College, PA	B
Eastern Nazarene College, MA	B
Evangel College, MO	A,B
Fresno Pacific College, CA	A,B
Geneva College, PA	B
George Fox College, OR	B
Goshen College, IN	B
Grace College, IN	B
Grand Canyon University, AZ	B
Grand Rapids Baptist College and Seminary, MI	B
Greenville College, IL	B

Houghton College, NY — B
Huntington College, IN — B
Indiana Wesleyan University, IN — B
John Brown University, AR — B
Judson College, IL — B
King's College, NY — B
Lee College, TN — B
Malone College, OH — B
Master's College, CA — B
Messiah College, PA — B
MidAmerica Nazarene College, KS — B
Milligan College, TN — B
Mississippi College, MS — B
Mount Vernon Nazarene College, OH — B
North Park College, IL — B
Northwest Christian College, OR — B
Northwestern College, IA — B
Northwestern College, MN — B
Nyack College, NY — B
Olivet Nazarene University, IL — B
Point Loma Nazarene College, CA — B
Roberts Wesleyan College, NY — B
Seattle Pacific University, WA — B
Sioux Falls College, SD — B
Southern California College, CA — B
Southern Nazarene University, OK — B
Spring Arbor College, MI — B
Sterling College, KS — B
Taylor University, IN — B
Trevecca Nazarene College, TN — B
Trinity Christian College, IL — B
Trinity College, IL — B
Trinity Western University, BC — B
Warner Southern College, FL — B
Westmont College, CA — B
Wheaton College, IL — B
Whitworth College, WA — B
William Jennings Bryan College, TN — B

Community Services

Eastern Mennonite College, VA — B
Western Baptist College, OR — B

Computer Engineering

Eastern Nazarene College, MA — B
George Fox College, OR — B
LeTourneau University, TX — B

Computer Information Systems

Bartlesville Wesleyan College, OK — A,B
Biola University, CA — B
Campbellsville College, KY — A,B
Campbell University, NC — B
Cedarville College, OH — B
Colorado Christian University, CO — A,B
Eastern Mennonite College, VA — B
Eastern Nazarene College, MA — B
George Fox College, OR — B
Goshen College, IN — B
Grand Rapids Baptist College and Seminary, MI — B
Indiana Wesleyan University, IN — A,B
Judson College, IL — B
Lee College, TN — B
Messiah College, PA — B
Northwestern College, MN — A,B

Northwest Nazarene College, ID — B
Olivet Nazarene University, IL — B
Palm Beach Atlantic College, FL — B
Point Loma Nazarene College, CA — B
Sioux Falls College, SD — B
Southern Nazarene University, OK — B
Taylor University, IN — B
Trevecca Nazarene College, TN — A,B
Trinity College, IL — B

Computer Management

Dallas Baptist University, TX — B

Computer Programming

Biola University, CA — B
Eastern Mennonite College, VA — A
Southern Nazarene University, OK — B
Taylor University, IN — B

Computer Science

Anderson University, IN — B
Asbury College, KY — B
Azusa Pacific University, CA — B
Belhaven College, MS — B
Bethel College, IN — A
Bethel College, KS — B
Bethel College, MN — B
Biola University, CA — B
Bluffton College, OH — B
Calvin College, MI — B
Campbell University, NC — B
Covenant College, GA — B
Dallas Baptist University, TX — B
Dordt College, IA — B
Eastern Mennonite College, VA — B
Eastern Nazarene College, MA — B
Evangel College, MO — B
Fresno Pacific College, CA — B
Geneva College, PA — B
George Fox College, OR — B
Gordon College, MA — B
Goshen College, IN — B
Grand Canyon University, AZ — B
Greenville College, IL — B
Huntington College, IN — A,B
Judson College, IL — B
King's College, NY — B
LeTourneau University, TX — B
Malone College, OH — B
Messiah College, PA — B
MidAmerica Nazarene College, KS — B
Milligan College, TN — B
Mississippi College, MS — B
Mount Vernon Nazarene College, OH — B
Northwestern College, IA — B
Northwest Nazarene College, ID — B
Olivet Nazarene University, IL — B
Point Loma Nazarene College, CA — B
Redeemer College, ON — B
Roberts Wesleyan College, NY — B
Seattle Pacific University, WA — B
Sioux Falls College, SD — B
Southern Nazarene University, OK — A,B
Spring Arbor College, MI — B
Sterling College, KS — B
Tabor College, KS — A,B
Taylor University, IN — B

Trevecca Nazarene College, TN — A,B
Trinity Christian College, IL — B
Trinity College, IL — B
Trinity Western Univevsity, BC — B
Westmont College, CA — B
Wheaton College, IL — B
Whitworth College, WA — B

Computer Technologies

LeTourneau University, TX — B
Mount Vernon Nazarene College, OH — A
Trevecca Nazarene College, TN — B

Construction Engineering

John Brown University, AR — B

Construction Management

John Brown University, AR — A,B

Creative Writing

Bethel College, MN — B
Eastern College, PA — B
Houghton College, NY — B
Indiana Wesleyan University, IN — B
Taylor University, IN — B

Criminal Justice

Anderson University, IN — A,B
Bluffton College, OH — B
Calvin College, MI — B
Cedarville College, OH — B
Dallas Baptist University, TX — B
Grace College, IN — B
Grand Canyon University, AZ — B
Indiana Wesleyan University, IN — A,B
Mississippi College, MS — B
Mount Vernon Nazarene College, OH — B
Northwestern College, IA — B
Olivet Nazarene University, IL — B
Roberts Wesleyan College, NY — B
Southern Nazarene University, OK — B
Sterling College, KS — B

Data Processing

Campbell University, NC — B
Eastern Mennonite College, VA — A
Mississippi College, MS — B
Mount Vernon Nazarene College, OH — A,B
Northwest Nazarene College, ID — A
Southern Nazarene University, OK — B

(Pre)Dentistry Sequence

Anderson University, IN — B
Azusa Pacific University, CA — B
Belhaven College, MS — B
Bethel College, IN — B
Bethel College, KS — B
Bethel College, MN — B
Calvin College, MI — B
Campbellsville College, KY — B
Campbell University, NC — B
Cedarville College, OH — B
Dordt College, IA — B
Eastern Mennonite College, VA — B
Eastern Nazarene College, MA — B
Evangel College, MO — B

George Fox College, OR	B
Goshen College, IN	B
Grand Canyon University, AZ	B
Greenville College, IL	B
Houghton College, NY	B
Huntington College, IN	B
Indiana Wesleyan University, IN	B
King College, TN	B
LeTourneau University, TX	B
Malone College, OH	B
Milligan College, TN	B
Mississippi College, MS	B
Mount Vernon Nazarene College, OH	B
North Park College, IL	B
Northwestern College, IA	B
Northwest Nazarene College, ID	B
Olivet Nazarene University, IL	B
Palm Beach Atlantic College, FL	B
Point Loma Nazarene College, CA	B
Redeemer College, ON	B
Roberts Wesleyan College, NY	B
Sioux Falls College, SD	B
Southern Nazarene University, OK	B
Sterling College, KS	B
Tabor College, KS	B
Taylor University, IN	B
Trinity Christian College, IL	B
Trinity Western University, BC	B
Westmont College, CA	B
Wheaton College, IL	B
Whitworth College, WA	B

Dietetics

Bluffton College, OH	B
Eastern Mennonite College, VA	B
Goshen College, IN	B
Messiah College, PA	B
Northwest Nazarene College, ID	B
Olivet Nazarene University, IL	A,B

Drafting and Design

LeTourneau University, TX	A

Early Childhood Education

Anderson University, IN	A
Bethel College, IN	A
Bethel College, KS	B
Bethel College, MN	B
Bluffton College, OH	B
Campbell University, NC	B
Cedarville College, OH	B
Eastern Mennonite College, VA	B
Eastern Nazarene College, MA	A,B
Erskine College, SC	B
Evangel College, MO	B
Gordon College, MA	B
Goshen College, IN	B
Greenville College, IL	B
Houghton College, NY	B
John Brown University, AR	B
King's College, NY	B
Malone College, OH	A
Messiah College, PA	B
MidAmerica Nazarene College, KS	A,B
Milligan College, TN	B
Mississippi College, MS	B

Mount Vernon Nazarene College, OH	A,B
North Park College, IL	B
Northwestern College, IA	B
Nyack College, NY	A
Olivet Nazarene University, IL	B
Palm Beach Atlantic College, FL	B
Point Loma Nazarene College, CA	B
Sioux Falls College, SD	A
Southern Nazarene University, OK	B
Spring Arbor College, MI	B
Taylor University, IN	A
Trevecca Nazarene College, TN	B

Earth Science

Campbell University, NC	B
Olivet Nazarene University, IL	B

Ecology/Environmental Studies

Anderson University, IN	B
Seattle Pacific University, WA	B

Economics

Anderson University, IN	B
Bethel College, IN	A
Bethel College, KS	B
Bethel College, MN	B
Biola University, CA	B
Bluffton College, OH	B
Calvin College, MI	B
Campbellsville College, KY	B
Campbell Unmversity, NC	B
Cedarville College, OH	B
Dallas Baptist University, TX	B
Eastern College, PA	B
Geneva College, PA	B
George Fox College, OR	B
Gordon College, MA	B
Goshen College, IN	B
Grand Canyon University, AZ	B
Greenville College, IL	B
Huntington College, IN	B
Indiana Wesleyan University, IN	B
King College, TN	B
Mississippi College, MS	B
North Park College, IL	B
Northwestern College, IA	B
Olivet Nazarene University, IL	B
Palm Beach Atlantic College, FL	B
Point Loma Nazarene College, CA	B
Seattle Pacific University, WA	B
Sioux Falls College, SD	A,B
Southern Nazarene University, OK	B
Taylor University, IN	B
Trinity College, IL	B
Westmont College, CA	B
Wheaton College, IL	B
Whitworth College, WA	B

Education

Anderson University, IN	B
Asbury College, KY	B
Azusa Pacific University, CA	B
Bethel College, IN	B
Bethel College, KS	B
Bethel College, MN	B

Biola University, CA	B
Bluffton College, OH	B
California Baptist College, CA	B
Calvin College, MI	B
Campbell University, NC	B
Cedarville College, OH	B
Dordt College, IA	B
Eastern Mennonite College, VA	A,B
Eastern Nazarene College, MA	B
Evangel College, MO	A,B
Fresno Pacific College, CA	B
Geneva College, PA	B
George Fox College, OR	B
Gordon College, MA	B
Goshen College, IN	B
Grand Rapids Baptist College and Seminary, MI	B
Greenville College, IL	B
Houghton College, NY	B
Huntington College, IN	B
Indiana Wesleyan University, IN	B
John Brown University, AR	B
Judson College, IL	B
King College, TN	B
King's College, NY	B
Lee College, TN	B
Malone College, OH	B
Master's College, CA	B
Messiah College, PA	B
Mississippi College, MS	B
Mount Vernon Nazarene College, OH	B
North Park College, IL	B
Northwestern College, IA	B
Northwestern College, MN	B
Northwest Nazarene College, ID	B
Nyack College, NY	A
Olivet Nazarene University, IL	B
Palm Beach Atlantic College, FL	B
Redeemer College, ON	B
Roberts Wesleyan College, NY	B
Simpson College, CA	B
Sioux Falls College, SD	B
Southern California College, CA	B
Southern Nazarene University, OK	B
Sterling College, KS	B
Tabor College, KS	B
Taylor University, IN	B
Trevecca Nazarene College, TN	B
Trinity Christian College, IL	B
Trinity College, IL	B
Trinity Western University, BC	B
Western Baptist College, OR	B
Westmont College, CA	B

Educational Administration

Campbell University, NC	B

Electrical Engineering

Calvin College, MI	B
Cedarville College, OH	B
Eastern Nazarene College, MA	B
Geneva College, PA	B
George Fox College, OR	B
John Brown University, AR	B
LeTourneau University, TX	B
Seattle Pacific University, WA	B

Electrical Engineering Technology

LeTourneau University, TX   B

Elementary Education

Anderson University, IN   B
Asbury College, KY   B
Azusa Pacific University, CA   B
Bartlesville Wesleyan College, OK   B
Belhaven College, MS   B
Bethel College, IN   B
Bethel College, KS   B
Bethel College, MN   B
Biola University, CA   B
Bluffton College, OH   B
California Baptist College, CA   B
Calvin College, MI   B
Campbell University, NC   B
Cedarville College, OH   B
Central Wesleyan College, SC   B
Colorado Christian University, CO   B
Covenant College, GA   B
Dordt College, IA   B
Eastern College, PA   B
Eastern Mennonite College, VA   B
Eastern Nazarene College, MA   B
Erskine College, SC   B
Evangel College, MO   B
Fresno Pacific College, CA   B
Geneva College, PA   B
George Fox College, OR   B
Gordon College, MA   B
Goshen College, IN   B
Grace College, IN   B
Grand Canyon University, AZ   B
Grand Rapids Baptist College and Seminary, MI   B
Greenville College, IL   B
Houghton College, NY   B
Huntington College, IN   B
Indiana Wesleyan University, IN   B
John Brown University, AR   B
Judson College, IL   B
King College, TN   B
King's College, NY   B
Lee College, TN   B
Malone College, OH   B
Master's College, CA   B
Messiah College, PA   B
MidAmerica Nazarene College, KS   B
Milligan College, TN   B
Mississippi College, MS   B
Mount Vernon Nazarene College, OH   B
North Park College, IL   B
Northwest College of the Assemblies of God, WA   B
Northwestern College, IA   B
Northwestern College, MN   B
Northwest Nazarene College, ID   B
Nyack College, NY   B
Olivet Nazarene University, IL   B
Palm Beach Atlantic College, FL   B
Redeemer College, ON   B
Roberts Wesleyan College, NY   B
Seattle Pacific University, WA   B
Simpson College, CA   B
Sioux Falls College, SD   B

Southern California College, CA   B
Southern Nazarene University, OK   B
Spring Arbor College, MI   B
Sterling College, KS   B
Tabor College, KS   B
Taylor University, IN   B
Trevecca Nazarene College, TN   B
Trinity Christian College, IL   B
Trinity College, IL   B
Trinity Western University, BC   B
Warner Southern College, FL   B
Western Baptist College, OR   B
Westmont College, CA   B
Wheaton College, IL   B
Whitworth College, WA   B
William Jennings Bryan College, TN   B

Engineering (General)

Calvin College, MI   B
Dordt College, IA   B
Geneva College, PA   A,B
George Fox College, OR   B
John Brown University, AR   B
LeTourneau University, TX   B
Olivet Nazarene University, IL   B
Southern Nazarene University, OK   B
Westmont College, CA   B

Engineering Management

John Brown University, AR   B

Engineering Physics

Eastern Nazarene College, MA   B
Northwest Nazarene College, ID   B
Point Loma Nazarene College, CA   B
Westmont College, CA   B

Engineering Sciences

Belhaven College, MS   B
Dordt College, IA
George Fox College, OR   B
Olivet Nazarene University, IL   B
Seattle Pacific University, WA   B

(Pre)Engineering Sequence

Anderson University, IN   A
Bethel College, MN   A
Campbell University, NC   A
Cedarville College, OH   A
Covenant College, GA   A
Eastern Mennonite College, VA   A
Houghton College, NY   A
Huntington College, IN   A
Indiana Wesleyan University, IN   A
Malone College, OH   A
Mount Vernon Nazarene College, OH   A
Northwestern College, MN   A
Northwest Nazarene College, ID   A
Sioux Falls College, SD   A
Tabor College, KS   A
Trevecca Nazarene College, TN   A

Engineering Technology

John Brown University, AR   A
LeTourneau University, TX   B

English

Anderson University, IN   B
Asbury College, KY   B
Azusa Pacific University, CA   B
Bartlesville Wesleyan College, OK   B
Belhaven College, MS   B
Bethel College, IN   A,B
Bethel College, KS   B
Bethel College, MN   B
Biola University, CA   B
Bluffton College, OH   B
California Baptist College, CA   B
Calvin College, MI   B
Campbellsville College, KY   B
Campbell University, NC   B
Cedarville College, OH   B
Central Wesleyan College, SC   B
Colorado Christian University, CO   B
Covenant College, GA   B
Dallas Baptist University, TX   B
Dordt College, IA   B
Eastern Mennonite College, VA   B
Eastern Nazarene College, MA   B
Erskine College, SC   B
Evangel College, MO   B
Fresno Pacific College, CA   A,B
Geneva College, PA   B
George Fox College, OR   B
Gordon College, MA   B
Goshen College, IN   B
Grace College, IN   B
Grand Canyon University, AZ   B
Grand Rapids Baptist College and Seminary, MI   B
Greenville College, IL   B
Houghton College, NY   B
Huntington College, IN   B
Indiana Wesleyan University, IN   A,B
John Brown University, AR   B
Judson College, IL   B
King College, TN   B
King's College, NY   B
The King's College, AB   B
Lee College, TN   B
LeTourneau University, TX   B
Malone College, OH   B
Master's College, CA   B
Messiah College, PA   B
MidAmerica Nazarene College, KS   B
Milligan College, TN   B
Mississippi College, MS   B
Montreat-Anderson College, NC   B
Mount Vernon Nazarene College, OH   B
North Park College, IL   B
Northwestern College, IA   B
Northwestern College, MN   B
Northwest Nazarene College, ID   B
Nyack College, NY   B
Olivet Nazarene University, IL   B
Palm Beach Atlantic College, FL   B
Point Loma Nazarene College, CA   B
Redeemer College, ON   B
Roberts Wesleyan College, NY   B
Seattle Pacific University, WA   B
Simpson College, CA   B
Sioux Falls College, SD   B
Southern California College, CA   B

Southern Nazarene University, OK   B
Spring Arbor College, MI   B
Sterling College, KS   B
Tabor College, KS   B
Taylor University, IN   B
Trevecca Nazarene College, TN   B
Trinity Christian College, IL   B
Trinity College, IL   B
Trinity Western University, BC   B
Warner Pacific College, OR   B
Warner Southern College, FL   B
Western Baptist College, OR   B
Westmont College, CA   B
Whitworth College, WA   B
William Jennings Bryan College, TN   B

Environmental Biology
Cedarville College, OH   B
Grand Canyon University, AZ   B
Tabor College, KS   B

Environmental Sciences
Anderson University, IN   B
Bethel College, KS   B
Dordt College, IA   B
Olivet Nazarene University, IL   B
Taylor University, IN   B
Wheaton College, IL   B

European Studies
Biola University, CA   B
Calvin College, MI   B
Seattle Pacific University, WA   B

Experimental Psychology
Messiah College, PA   B

Family and Consumer Studies
Seattle Pacific University, WA   B
Southern Nazarene University, OK   B

Family Services
Goshen College, IN   B
Messiah College, PA   B
Olivet Nazarene University, IL   B
Southern Nazarene University, OK   B

Fashion Design and Technology
Campbell University, NC   B

Fashion Merchandising
Bluffton College, OH   B
Campbell University, NC   B
Northwest Nazarene College, ID   B
Olivet Nazarene University, IL   B
Southern Nazarene University, OK   A,B

Film Studies
Biola University, CA   B
Olivet Nazarene University, IL   B

Finance/Banking
Bethel College, MN   B
Campbell University, NC   B
Cedarville College, OH   B
Dallas Baptist University, TX   B

Grand Canyon University, AZ   B
Indiana Wesleyan University, IN   A,B
North Park College, IL   B
Northwestern College, MN   B
Northwest Nazarene College, ID   B
Olivet Nazarene University, IL   B
Palm Beach Atlantic College, FL   B
Southern California College, CA   B
Western Baptist College, OR   B

Flight Training
LeTourneau University, TX   B
Trinity Western University, BC   B

Food Services Management
Campbell University, NC   B
Eastern Mennonite College, VA   B
Olivet Nazarene University, IL   B

French
Anderson University, IN   B
Asbury College, KY   B
Bethel College, IN   A
Calvin College, MI   B
Campbell University, NC   B
Eastern College, PA   B
Eastern Mennonite College, VA   B
Eastern Nazarene College, MA   B
Erskine College, SC   B
Gordon College, MA   B
Grace College, IN   B
Greenville College, IL   B
Houghton College, NY   B
King College, TN   B
King's College, NY   B
Messiah College, PA   B
North Park College, IL   B
Northwestern College, IA   B
Redeemer College, ON   B
Spring Arbor College, MI   B
Taylor University, IN   B
Westmont College, CA   B
Wheaton College, IL   B
Whitworth College, WA   B

Geography
Calvin College, MI   B
Messiah College, PA   B
Trinity Western University, BC   B

Geology
Calvin College, MI   B
Olivet Nazarene University, IL   B
Wheaton College, IL   B

German
Anderson University, IN   B
Bethel College, KS   B
Calvin College, MI   B
Dordt College, IA   B
Eastern Mennonite College, VA   B
Goshen College, IN   B
Grace College, IN   B
Messiah College, PA   B
North Park College, IL   B
Southern Nazarene University, OK   B
Wheaton College, IL   B

Germanic Languages and Literature
Calvin College, MI   B

Gerontology
Bethel College, IN   A
Greenville College, IL   B
Roberts Wesleyan College, NY   B
Southern Nazarene University, OK   B

Graphic Arts
Anderson University, IN   B
Bethel College, KS,   B
Grace College, IN   B
Grand Canyon University, AZ   B
Huntington College, IN   B
John Brown University, AR   B
Northwestern College, MN   A,B
Olivet Nazarene University, IL   B
Point Loma Nazarene College, CA   B
Roberts Wesleyan College, NY   B

Greek
Biola University, CA   B
Calvin College, MI   B
Grace College, IN   B
Southern Nazarene University, OK   B

Guidance and Counseling
Geneva College, PA   B

Health Education
Anderson University, IN   B
Bethel College, IN   A
Bethel College, KS   B
Bethel College, MN   B
Bluffton College, OH   B
Campbell University, NC   B
Cedarville College, OH   B
Eastern College, PA   B
John Brown University, AR   B
Lee College, TN   B
Malone College, OH   B
MidAmerica Nazarene College, KS   B
Milligan College, TN   B
Northwest Nazarene College, ID   B
Sioux Falls College, SD   B
Southern Nazarene University, OK   B
Tabor College, KS   B
Trevecca Nazarene College, TN   B

Health Science
Campbell University, NC   B
Covenant College, GA   A
Mount Vernon Nazarene College, OH   A
Northwest College of the Assemblies of God, WA   A
Northwestern College, IA   B
Northwest Nazarene College, ID   B
Southern Nazarene University, OK   A

Health Services Administration
Eastern College, PA   B
John Brown University, AR   B
Milligan College, TN   B

Hebrew

Southern Nazarene University, OK   B

Hispanic Studies

Goshen College, IN   B

History

Anderson University, IN   B
Asbury College, KY   B
Azusa Pacific University, CA   B
Bartlesville Wesleyan College, OK   A
Belhaven College, MS   B
Bethel College, IN   A
Bethel College, KS   B
Bethel College, MN   B
Biola University, CA   B
Bluffton College, OH   B
California Baptist College, CA   B
Calvin College, MI   B
Campbellsville College, KY   B
Campbell University, NC   B
Cedarville College, OH   B
Central Wesleyan College, SC   B
Colorado Christian University, CO   B
Covenant College, GA   B
Dallas Baptist University, TX   B
Dordt College, IA   B
Eastern College, PA   B
Eastern Mennonite College, VA   B
Eastern Nazarene College, MA   B
Erskine College, SC   B
Evangel College, MO   B
Fresno Pacific College, CA   A,B
Geneva College, PA   B
George Fox College, OR   B
Gordon College, MA   B
Goshen College, IN   B
Grand Canyon University, AZ   B
Grand Rapids Baptist College and
     Seminary, MI   B
Greenville College, IL   B
Houghton College, NY   B
Huntington College, IN   B
Indiana Wesleyan University, IN   B
John Brown University, AR   B
Judson College, IL   B
King College, TN   B
King's College, NY   B
The King's College, AB   B
Lee College, TN   B
LeTourneau University, TX   B
Malone College, OH   B
Master's College, CA   B
Messiah College, PA   B
MidAmerica Nazarene College, KS   B
Milligan College, TN   B
Mississippi College, MS   B
Montreat-Anderson College, NC   B
Mount Vernon Nazarene College,
     OH   B
North Park College, IL   B
Northwestern College, IA   B
Northwest Nazarene College, ID   B
Nyack College, NY   B
Olivet Nazarene University, IL   B
Palm Beach Atlantic College, FL   B
Point Loma Nazarene College, CA   B
Redeemer College, ON   B

Roberts Wesleyan College, NY   B
Seattle Pacific University, WA   B
Simpson College, CA   B
Sioux Falls College, SD   B
Southern California College, CA   B
Southern Nazarene University, OK   B
Spring Arbor College, MI   B
Sterling College, KS   B
Tabor College, KS   B
Taylor University, IN   B
Trevecca Nazarene College, TN   B
Trinity Christian College, IL   B
Trinity College, IL   B
Trinity Western University, BC   B
Warner Pacific College, OR   B
Westmont College, CA   B
Wheaton College, IL   B
Whitworth College, WA   B
William Jennings Bryan College, TN   B

Home Economics

Bluffton College, OH   B
Campbell University, NC   B
George Fox College, OR   B
Master's College, CA   B
Messiah College, PA   B
Mississippi College, MS   B
Mount Vernon Nazarene College,
     OH   A,B
Northwest Nazarene College, ID   B
Olivet Nazarene University, IL   B
Point Loma Nazarene College, CA   B
Southern Nazarene University, OK   B
Sterling College, KS   B

Home Economics Education

Bethel College, KS   B
Bluffton College, OH   B
Campbell University, NC   B
George Fox College, OR   B
Mississippi College, MS   B
Mount Vernon Nazarene College,
     OH   B
Northwest Nazarene College, ID   B
Olivet Nazarene University, IL   B
Point Loma Nazarene College, CA   B
Seattle Pacific University, WA   B
Southern Nazarene University, OK   B
Sterling College, KS   B

Human Development

Warner Pacific College, OR   B

Humanities

Belhaven College, MS   B
Biola University, CA   B
Bluffton College, OH   B
Calvin College, MI   B
Colorado Christian University, CO   B
Fresno Pacific College, CA   B
Houghton College, NY   B
Messiah College, PA   B
Milligan College, TN   B
Northwestern College, IA   B
Redeemer College, ON   B
Roberts Wesleyan College, NY   B
Sioux Falls College, SD   A
Southern California College, CA   B
Tabor College, KS   B

Trevecca Nazarene College, TN   B
Trinity College, IL   B
Trinity Western University, BC   B
Western Baptist College, OR   B

Human Resources

Bethel College, IN   B
George Fox College, OR   B
Grand Canyon University, AZ   B
Messiah College, PA   B
MidAmerica Nazarene College, KS   B
Northwestern College, MN   B
Olivet Nazarene University, IL   B
Roberts Wesleyan College, NY   B
Southern Nazarene University, OK   B

Human Services

Asbury College, KY   B
Bethel College, KS   B
Milligan College, TN   B
Montreat-Anderson College, NC   B
Mount Vernon Nazarene College,
     OH   A
Northwest Nazarene College, ID   B
Trinity Western University, BC   B

Industrial Administration

LeTourneau University, TX   B

Industrial Engineering

Geneva College, PA   B

Information Science

Dallas Baptist University, TX   B
Southern Nazarene University, OK   B

Interdisciplinary Studies

Bethel College, KS   B
Calvin College, MI   B
Covenant College, GA   B
Dallas Baptist University, TX   B
George Fox College, OR   B
Grand Rapids Baptist College and
     Seminary, MI   B
John Brown University, AR   B
Northwest Christian College, OR   B
Northwest College of the Assemblies
     of God, WA   A,B
Nyack College, NY   B
Olivet Nazarene University, IL   B
Seattle Pacific University, WA   B
Sioux Falls College, SD   A,B
Western Baptist College, OR   B
Wheaton College, IL   B

Interior Design

Campbell University, NC   B
Mississippi College, MS   B
Southern Nazarene University, OK   A,B

International Business

Campbell University, NC   B
Cedarville College, OH   B
Grand Canyon University, AZ   B
King College, TN   B
MidAmerica Nazarene College, KS   B
North Park College, IL   B
Northwestern College, MN   B
Palm Beach Atlantic College, FL   B

International Business (continued)
Whitworth College, WA — B

International Economics
Cedarville College, OH — B

International Studies
Azusa Pacific University, CA — B
Bethel College, KS — B
Bethel College, MN — B
Biola University, CA — B
Cedarville College, OH — B
George Fox College, OR — B
Gordon College, MA — B
Houghton College, NY — B
North Park College, IL — B
Northwest Nazarene College, ID — B
Southern Nazarene Univevsity, OK — B
Tabor College, KS — B
Taylor University, IN — B
Warner Southern College, FL — B
Western Baptist College, OR — A,B
Whitworth College, WA — B

Journalism
Anderson University, IN — B
Asbury College, KY — B
Bethel College, IN — A
Biola University, CA — B
Campbell University, NC — B
Dordt College, IA — B
Evangel College, MO — A,B
Geneva College, PA — B
Goshen College, IN — B
John Brown University, AR — A,B
Malone College, OH — B
Messiah College, PA — B
Mississippi College, MS — B
Northwestern College, MN — B
Olivet Nazarene University, IL — B
Point Loma Nazarene College, CA — B
Southern California College, CA — B
Southern Nazarene University, OK — B
Tabor College, KS — B
Taylor University, IN — B
Wheaton College, IL — B
Whitworth College, WA — B

Laboratory Technologies
Evangel College, MO — A
Southern Nazarene University, OK — A

Latin
Calvin College, MI — B

Latin American Studies
Geneva College, PA — B

Law Enforcement/Police Sciences
Indiana Wesleyan University, IN — A
Mississippi College, MS — B

(Pre)Law Sequence
Anderson University, IN — B
Azusa Pacific University, CA — B
Belhaven College, MS — B
Bethel College, KS — B

Bethel College, MN — B
Bluffton College, OH — B
Calvin College, MI — B
Campbellsville College, KY — B
Campbell University, NC — B
Cedarville College, OH — B
Covenant College, GA — B
Eastern Mennonite College, VA — B
Eastern Nazarene College, MA — B
Evangel College, MO — B
Fresno Pacific College, CA — B
Geneva College, PA — B
George Fox College, OR — B
Goshen College, IN — B
Grace College, IN — B
Grand Canyon University, AZ — B
Grand Rapids Baptist College and
  Seminary, MI — B
Greenville College, IL — B
Houghton College, NY — B
Huntington College, IN — B
Indiana Wesleyan University, IN — B
Judson College, IL — B
King College, TN — B
LeTourneau University, TX — B
Malone College, OH — B
Messiah College, PA — B
Mississippi College, MS — B
Mount Vernon Nazarene College,
  OH — B
North Park College, IL — B
Northwestern College, IA — B
Northwest Nazarene College, ID — B
Olivet Nazarene University, IL — B
Palm Beach Atlantic College, FL — B
Point Loma Nazarene College, CA — B
Redeemer College, ON — B
Sioux Falls College, SD — B
Southern California College, CA — B
Southern Nazarene University, OK — B
Sterling College, KS — B
Tabor College, KS — B
Taylor University, IN — B
Trevecca Nazarene College, TN — B
Trinity Western University, BC — B
Western Baptist College, OR — B
Westmont College, CA — B
Wheaton College, IL — B
Whitworth College, WA — B

Legal Secretarial Studies
Northwestern College, MN — A
Tabor College, KS — B

Liberal Arts/General Studies
Azusa Pacific University, CA — B
Bartlesville Wesleyan College, OK — A
Bethel College, IN — A,B
Bethel College, KS — B
Bethel College, MN — A
Biola University, CA — B
Bluffton College, OH — B
California Baptist College, CA — B
Calvin College, MI — B
Campbell University, NC — A
Colorado Christian University, CO — A,B
Dallas Baptist University, TX — B
Eastern Mennonite College, VA — A,B

Eastern Nazarene College, MA — A
Fresno Pacific College, CA — A,B
George Fox College, OR — B
Goshen College, IN — B
Grand Canyon University, AZ — B
Greenville College, IL — B
Indiana Wesleyan University, IN — A,B
John Brown University, AR — A
Malone College, OH — B
Master's College, CA — B
Messiah College, PA — B
MidAmerica Nazarene College, KS — A
Montreat-Anderson College, NC — A,B
Mount Vernon Nazarene College,
  OH — A
Northwest Christian College, OR — A
Northwest College of the Assemblies
  of God, WA — A,B
Northwestern College, MN — A
Northwest Nazarene College, ID — B
Nyack College, NY — A
Olivet Nazarene University, IL — B
Point Loma Nazarene College, CA — B
Redeemer College, ON — B
Seattle Pacific University, WA — B
Simpson College, CA — B
Sioux Falls College, SD — B
Southern Nazarene University, OK — B
Spring Arbor College, MI — A
Sterling College, KS — B
Taylor University, IN — B
Trevecca Nazarene College, TN — A
Trinity College, IL — B
Trinity Western University, BC — B
Warner Pacific College, OR — B
Warner Southern College, FL — A
Western Baptist College, OR — B
Westmont College, CA — B
William Jennings Bryan College, TN — A,B

Linguistics
Gordon College, MA — B
Judson College, IL — B
Trinity Western University, BC — B

Literature
Asbury College, KY — B
Bethel College, MN — B
Biola University, CA — B
Calvin College, MI — B
Eastern College, PA — B
Fresno Pacific College, CA — B
George Fox College, OR — B
Grand Canyon University, AZ — B
Houghton College, NY — B
Judson College, IL — B
Mount Vernon Nazarene College,
  OH — B
North Park College, IL — B
Northwestern College, IA — B
Northwestern College, MN — B
Olivet Nazarene University, IL — B
Point Loma Nazarene College, CA — B
Redeemer College, ON — B
Southern Nazarene University, OK — B
Taylor University, IN — B
Westmont College, CA — B
Wheaton College, IL — B

Management Information Systems

Azusa Pacific University, CA	B
Bethel College, MN	B
Dordt College, IA	B
Fresno Pacific College, CA	B
Geneva College, PA	B
Greenville College, IL	B
Sioux Falls College, SD	B
Southern Nazarene University, OK	B
Taylor University, IN	A

Manufacturing Engineering

Eastern Nazarene College, MA	B

Marketing/Retailing/Merchandising

Anderson University, IN	B
Azusa Pacific University, CA	B
Biola University, CA	B
Cedarville College, OH	B
Dallas Baptist University, TX	B
Evangel College, MO	B
Grand Canyon University, AZ	B
Grand Rapids Baptist College and Seminary, MI	B
Greenville College, IL	B
LeTourneau University, TX	B
Messiah College, PA	B
Mississippi College, MS	B
Mount Vernon Nazarene College, OH	B
North Park College, IL	B
Northwestern College, MN	B
Northwest Nazarene College, ID	B
Olivet Nazarene University, IL	B
Sioux Falls College, SD	A,B
Southern California College, CA	B
Southern Nazarene University, OK	A,B

Marriage and Family Counseling

Anderson University, IN	B

Mathematics

Anderson University, IN	B
Asbury College, KY	B
Azusa Pacific University, CA	B
Bartlesville Wesleyan College, OK	A,B
Belhaven College, MS	B
Bethel College, IN	A,B
Bethel College, KS	B
Bethel College, MN	B
Biola University, CA	B
Bluffton College, OH	B
Calvin College, MI	B
Campbell University, NC	B
Cedarville College, OH	B
Central Wesleyan College, SC	B
Colorado Christian University, CO	B
Dallas Baptist University, TX	B
Dordt College, IA	B
Eastern College, PA	B
Eastern Mennonite College, VA	B
Eastern Nazarene College, MA	B
Erskine College, SC	B
Evangel College, MO	B

Fresno Pacific College, CA	A,B
Geneva College, PA	B
George Fox College, OR	B
Gordon College, MA	B
Goshen College, IN	B
Grace College, IN	B
Grand Canyon University, AZ	B
Greenville College, IL	B
Houghton College, NY	B
Huntington College, IN	B
Indiana Wesleyan University, IN	B
John Brown University, AR	B
Judson College, IL	B
King College, TN	B
King's College, NY	B
Lee College, TN	B
LeTourneau University, TX	B
Malone College, OH	B
Master's College, CA	B
Messiah College, PA	B
MidAmerica Nazarene College, KS	B
Milligan College, TN	B
Mississippi College, MS	B
Mount Vernon Nazarene College, OH	B
North Park College, IL	B
Northwestern College, IA	B
Northwestern College, MN	B
Northwest Nazarene College, ID	B
Olivet Nazarene University, IL	B
Palm Beach Atlantic College, FL	B
Point Loma Nazarene College, CA	B
Redeemer College, ON	B
Roberts Wesleyan College, NY	B
Seattle Pacific University, WA	B
Sioux Falls College, SD	B
Southern California College, CA	B
Southern Nazarene University, OK	B
Spring Arbor College, MI	B
Sterling College, KS	B
Tabor College, KS	B
Taylor University, IN	B
Trevecca Nazarene College, TN	B
Trinity Christian College, IL	B
Trinity College, IL	B
Trinity Western University, BC	B
Warner Pacific College, OR	A,B
Western Baptist College, OR	B
Westmont College, CA	B
Wheaton College, IL	B
Whitworth College, WA	B
William Jennings Bryan College, TN	B

Mechanical Engineering

Calvin College, MI	B
Cedarville College, OH	B
Eastern Nazarene College, MA	B
Geneva College, PA	B
John Brown University, AR	B
LeTourneau University, TX	B

Mechanical Engineering Technology

LeTourneau University, TX	B

Medical Laboratory Technology

Houghton College, NY	B

Indiana Wesleyan University, IN	A
Southern Nazarene University, OK	A

Medical Secretarial Studies

Tabor College, KS	B

Medical Technology

Anderson University, IN	B
Asbury College, KY	B
Calvin College, MI	B
Campbellsville College, KY	B
Campbell University, NC	B
Cedarville College, OH	B
Central Wesleyan College, SC	B
Dordt College, IA	B
Eastern College, PA	B
Eastern Mennonite College, VA	B
Evangel College, MO	B
Geneva College, PA	B
Greenville College, IL	B
Houghton College, NY	B
Huntington College, IN	B
Indiana Wesleyan University, IN	B
John Brown University, AR	B
King College, TN	B
King's College, NY	B
Lee College, TN	B
LeTourneau University, TX	B
Malone College, OH	B
Messiah College, PA	B
Mississippi College, MS	B
Mount Vernon Nazarene College, OH	B
North Park College, IL	B
Northwestern College, IA	B
Olivet Nazarene University, IL	B
Roberts Wesleyan College, NY	B
Sioux Falls College, SD	B
Southern Nazarene University, OK	B
Tabor College, KS	B
Taylor University, IN	B
Trevecca Nazarene College, TN	B
Trinity Christian College, IL	B

(Pre)Medicine Sequence

Anderson University, IN	B
Asbury College, KY	B
Azusa Pacific University, CA	B
Belhaven College, MS	B
Bethel College, IN	B
Bethel College, KS	B
Bethel College, MN	B
Biola University, CA	B
Bluffton College, OH	B
Calvin College, MI	B
Campbellsville College, KY	B
Campbell University, NC	B
Cedarville College, OH	B
Covenant College, GA	B
Dordt College, IA	B
Eastern Mennonite College, VA	B
Eastern Nazarene College, MA	B
Evangel College, MO	B
Fresno Pacific College, CA	B
Geneva College, PA	B
George Fox College, OR	B
Goshen College, IN	B
Grace College, IN	B
Grand Canyon University, AZ	B

(Pre)Medicine Sequence (continued)

Greenville College, IL	B
Houghton College, NY	B
Huntington College, IN	B
Indiana Wesleyan University, IN	B
John Brown University, AR	B
Judson College, IL	B
King College, TN	B
LeTourneau University, TX	B
Malone College, OH	B
Messiah College, PA	B
Milligan College, TN	B
Mississippi College, MS	B
Mount Vernon Nazarene College, OH	B
North Park College, IL	B
Northwestern College, IA	B
Northwest Nazarene College, ID	B
Olivet Nazarene University, IL	B
Palm Beach Atlantic College, FL	B
Point Loma Nazarene College, CA	B
Redeemer College, ON	B
Sioux Falls College, SD	B
Southern California College, CA	B
Southern Nazarene University, OK	B
Sterling College, KS	B
Tabor College, KS	B
Taylor University, IN	B
Trevecca Nazarene College, TN	B
Trinity Christian College, IL	B
Trinity Western University, BC	B
Westmont College, CA	B
Wheaton College, IL	B
Whitworth College, WA	B

Mental Health/ Rehabilitation Counseling

Evangel College, MO	A,B
Indiana Wesleyan University, IN	A,B

Middle School Education

John Brown University, AR	B
Sioux Falls College, SD	B
Taylor University, IN	B

Military Science

Campbell University, NC	B

Ministries

Asbury College, KY	B
Azusa Pacific University, CA	B
Bartlesville Wesleyan College, OK	B
Belhaven College, MS	B
Bethel College, IN	B
Bethel College, MN	B
Biola University, CA	B
Bluffton College, OH	B
Central Wesleyan College, SC	B
Colorado Christian University, CO	B
Dallas Baptist University, TX	B
Eastern College, PA	B
Eastern Mennonite College, VA	B
Eastern Nazarene College, MA	B
Fresno Pacific College, CA	B
Geneva College, PA	B
George Fox College, OR	B
Gordon College, MA	B

Grand Canyon University, AZ	B
Greenville College, IL	B
Houghton College, NY	B
Huntington College, IN	B
Indiana Wesleyan University, IN	A,B
John Brown University, AR	B
King's College, NY	B
Malone College, OH	B
Master's College, CA	B
MidAmerica Nazarene College, KS	A
Milligan College, TN	B
Montreat-Anderson College, NC	B
Northwest Christian College, OR	B
Northwest College of the Assemblies of God, WA	B
Northwestern College, MN	B
Northwest Nazarene College, ID	B
Nyack College, NY	B
Olivet Nazarene University, IL	A,B
Roberts Wesleyan College, NY	B
Seattle Pacific University, WA	B
Simpson College, CA	B
Southern California College, CA	B
Southern Nazarene University, OK	B
Spring Arbor College, MI	B
Tabor College, KS	B
Taylor University, IN	B
Trevecca Nazarene College, TN	A,B
Trinity College, IL	B
Warner Pacific College, OR	A,B
Warner Southern College, FL	A,B
Western Baptist College, OR	B
Westmont College, CA	B

Modern Languages

Biola University, CA	B
Eastern Mennonite College, VA	B
Greenville College, IL	B
King's College, NY	B
Lee College, TN	B
Messiah College, PA	B
MidAmerica Nazarene College, KS	B
Mississippi College, MS	B
Mount Vernon Nazarene College, OH	B
Olivet Nazarene University, IL	B
Redeemer College, ON	B
Southern Nazarene University, OK	B
Taylor University, IN	B
Westmont College, CA	B
Wheauon College, IL	B

Molecular Biology

Bethel College, MN	B

Museum Studies

Anderson University, IN	B

Music

Anderson University, IN	B
Asbury College, KY	B
Azusa Pacific University, CA	B
Belhaven College, MS	B
Bethel College, IN	A,B
Bethel College, KS	B
Bethel College, MN	B
Biola University, CA	B
Bluffton College, OH	B
California Baptist College, CA	B

Calvin College, MI	B
Campbellsville College, KY	B
Campbell University, NC	B
Cedarville College, OH	B
Central Wesleyan College, SC	B
Colorado Christian University, CO	B
Covenant College, GA	B
Dallas Baptist University, TX	B
Dordt College, IA	B
Eastern Mennonite College, VA	B
Eastern Nazarene College, MA	B
Erskine College, SC	B
Evangel College, MO	B
Fresno Pacifmc College, CA	A,B
Geneva College, PA	B
George Fox College, OR	B
Gordon College, MA	B
Goshen College, IN	B
Grace College, IN	B
Grand Canyon University, AZ	B
Grand Rapids Baptist College and Seminary, MI	B
Greenville College, IL	B
Houghton College, NY	B
Huntington College, IN	B
Indiana Wesleyan University, IN	A,B
John Brown University, AR	A,B
Judson College, IL	B
King College, TN	B
King's College, NY	B
The King's College, AB	B
Lee College, TN	B
Malone College, OH	B
Master's College, CA	B
Messiah College, PA	B
MidAmerica Nazarene College, KS	B
Milligan College, TN	B
Mississippi College, MS	B
Mount Vernon Nazarene College, OH	B
North Park College, IL	B
Northwestern College, IA	B
Northwestern College, MN	A,B
Northwest Nazarene College, ID	B
Nyack College, NY	B
Olivet Nazarene University, IL	B
Palm Beach Atlantic College, FL	B
Point Loma Nazarene College, CA	B
Redeemer College, ON	B
Roberts Wesleyan College, NY	A,B
Seattle Pacific University, WA	B
Simpson College, CA	B
Sioux Falls College, SD	B
Southern California College, CA	B
Southern Nazarene University, OK	B
Spring Arbor College, MI	B
Sterling College, KS	B
Tabor College, KS	B
Taylor University, IN	B
Trevecca Nazarene College, TN	B
Trinity Christian College, IL	B
Trinity College, IL	B
Trinity Western University, BC	B
Warner Pacific College, OR	B
Warner Southern College, FL	A,B
Westmont College, CA	B
Wheaton College, IL	B
Whitworth College, WA	B
William Jennings Bryan College, TN	B

Music Business

Anderson University, IN	B
Geneva College, PA	B
Grand Canyon University, AZ	B
Indiana Wesleyan University, IN	B
Point Loma Nazarene College, CA	B
Sioux Falls College, SD	B
Sterling College, KS	B
Trevecca Nazarene College, TN	B
Wheaton College, IL	B

Music Education

Anderson University, IN	B
Asbury College, KY	B
Azusa Pacific University, CA	B
Bethel College, IN	A,B
Bethel College, MN	B
Biola University, CA	B
Bluffton College, OH	B
Calvin College, MI	B
Campbellsville College, KY	B
Campbell University, NC	B
Cedarville College, OH	B
Central Wesleyan College, SC	B
Colorado Christian University, CO	B
Covenant College, GA	B
Dordt College, IA	B
Eastern Mennonite College, VA	B
Eastern Nazarene College, MA	B
Erskine College, SC	B
Evangel College, MO	B
Geneva College, PA	B
George Fox College, OR	B
Gordon College, MA	B
Goshen College, IN	B
Grace College, IN	B
Grand Canyon University, AZ	B
Grand Rapids Baptist College and Seminary, MI	B
Greenville College, IL	B
Houghton College, NY	B
Huntington College, IN	B
Indiana Wesleyan University, IN	B
John Brown University, AR	B
King's College, NY	B
Lee College, TN	B
Malone College, OH	B
Master's College, CA	B
Messiah College, PA	B
MidAmerica Nazarene College, KS	B
Milligan College, TN	B
Mississippi College, MS	B
Mount Vernon Nazarene College, OH	B
North Park College, IL	B
Northwestern College, IA	B
Northwestern College, MN	B
Nyack College, NY	B
Olivet Nazarene University, IL	B
Palm Beach Atlantic College, FL	B
Point Loma Nazarene College, CA	B
Roberts Wesleyan College, NY	B
Seattle Pacific University, WA	B
Simpson College, CA	B
Sioux Falls College, SD	B
Southern California College, CA	B
Southern Nazarene University, OK	B
Sterling College, KS	B

Tabor College, KS	B
Taylor University, IN	B
Trevecca Nazarene College, TN	B
Trinity Christian College, IL	B
Trinity College, IL	B
Warner Pacific College, OR	B
Warner Southern College, FL	B
Western Baptist College, OR	B
Wheaton College, IL	B
Whitworth College, WA	B
William Jennings Bryan College, TN	B

Music History

Cedarville College, OH	B
Wheaton College, IL	B

Natural Resource Management

Huntington College, IN	B
Mount Vernon Nazarene College, OH	A

Natural Sciences

Bethel College, KS	B
Bethel College, MN	B
Campbell University, NC	B
Covenant College, GA	B
Dordt College, IA	B
Erskine College, SC	B
Fresno Pacific College, CA	A,B
Goshen College, IN	B
Houghton College, NY	B
Lee College, TN	B
LeTourneau University, TX	B
Master's College, CA	B
Messiah College, PA	B
North Park College, IL	B
Northwestern College, IA	B
Northwest Nazarene College, ID	B
Olivet Nazarene University, IL	B
Redeemer College, ON	B
Roberts Wesleyan College, NY	A
Southern Nazarene University, OK	B
Sterling College, KS	B
Tabor College, KS	B
Taylor University, IN	B
Trevecca Nazarene College, TN	B
Trinity Western University, BC	B
Westmont College, CA	B

Nursing

Anderson University, IN	A,B
Azusa Pacific University, CA	B
Belhaven College, MS	B
Bethel College, IN	A,B
Bethel College, KS	B
Bethel College, MN	B
Biola University, CA	B
Calvin College, MI	B
Cedarville College, OH	B
Central Wesleyan College, SC	B
Covenant College, GA	A
Eastern College, PA	B
Eastern Mennonite College, VA	B
Goshen College, IN	B
Grand Canyon University, AZ	B
Indiana Wesleyan University, IN	B
Judson College, IL	B

King's College, NY	B
Malone College, OH	B
Messiah College, PA	B
MidAmerica Nazarene College, KS	B
Mississippi College, MS	B
North Park College, IL	B
Northwest Nazarene College, ID	B
Nyack College, NY	A
Olivet Nazarene University, IL	B
Point Loma Nazarene College, CA	B
Roberts Wesleyan College, NY	B
Seattle Pacific University, WA	B
Southern Nazarene University, OK	B
Trinity Christian College, IL	B
Whitworth College, WA	B

Nutrition

Bluffton College, OH	B
Eastern Mennonite College, VA	B
Goshen College, IN	B
Mississippi College, MS	B
Seattle Pacific University, WA	B
Sterling College, KS	B

Occupational Therapy

Mississippi College, MS	B
Southern Nazarene University, OK	A

Opera

Southern Nazarene University, OK	B

Optometry

Northwest Nazarene College, ID	B

Painting/Drawing

Biola University, CA	B
Judson College, IL	B
Trinity Christian College, IL	B

Paralegal Studies

Eastern Mennonite College, VA	A
Milligan College, TN	B
Mississippi College, MS	B

Pastoral Studies

Anderson University, IN	B
Azusa Pacific University, CA	B
Bethel College, IN	B
Biola University, CA	B
Campbell University, NC	B
Cedarville College, OH	B
Colorado Christian University, CO	B
Eastern Mennonite College, VA	B
Eastern Nazarene College, MA	B
Geneva College, PA	B
Grand Rapids Baptist College and Seminary, MI	B
Greenville College, IL	B
Houghton College, NY	B
Indiana Wesleyan University, IN	A,B
John Brown University, AR	B
Lee College, TN	B
Messiah College, PA	B
Northwest Christian College, OR	B
Northwest College of the Assemblies of God, WA	B
Northwestern College, MN	B
Nyack College, NY	B

Pastoral Studies (continued)

Olivet Nazarene University, IL — B
Point Loma Nazarene College, CA — B
Simpson College, CA — B
Sioux Falls College, SD — B
Southern California College, CA — B
Southern Nazarene University, OK — B
Trevecca Nazarene College, TN — B
Warner Pacific College, OR — B
Warner Southern College, FL — B
Western Baptist College, OR — B

Peace Studies

Bethel College, KS — B
Bluffton College, OH — B
Eastern Mennonite College, VA — B
Whitworth College, WA — B

Pharmacy/Pharmaceutical Sciences

Southern Nazarene University, OK — A

Philosophy

Anderson University, IN — B
Asbury College, KY — B
Azusa Pacific University, CA — B
Belhaven College, MS — B
Bethel College, IN — A
Bethel College, KS — B
Bethel College, MN — B
Biola University, CA — B
Bluffton College, OH — B
Calvin College, MI — B
Dordt College, IA — B
Eastern College, PA — B
Eastern Mennonite College, VA — B
Geneva College, PA — B
Gordon College, MA — B
Greenville College, IL — B
Houghton College, NY — B
Huntington College, IN — B
Indiana Wesleyan University, IN — B
Judson College, IL — B
The King's College, AB — B
Mount Vernon Nazarene College, OH — B
North Park College, IL — B
Northwest College of the Assemblies of God, WA — B
Northwestern College, IA — B
Northwest Nazarene College, ID — B
Nyack College, NY — B
Point Loma Nazarene College, CA — B
Redeemer College, ON — B
Seattle Pacific University, WA — B
Sioux Falls College, SD — B
Southern Nazarene University, OK — B
Spring Arbor College, MI — B
Sterling College, KS — B
Tabor College, KS — B
Taylor University, IN — B
Trevecca Nazarene College, TN — B
Trinity Christian College, IL — B
Trinity College, IL — B
Trinity Western University, BC — B
Westmont College, CA — B
Wheaton College, IL — B
Whitworth College, WA — B

Physical Education

Anderson University, IN — B
Asbury College, KY — B
Azusa Pacific University, CA — B
Bartlesville Wesleyan College, OK — B
Bethel College, IN — A,B
Bethel College, MN — B
Biola University, CA — B
Bluffton College, OH — B
California Baptist College, CA — B
Calvin College, MI — B
Campbellsville College, KY — B
Campbell University, NC — B
Cedarville College, OH — B
Central Wesleyan College, SC — B
Dallas Baptist University, TX — B
Dordt College, IA — B
Eastern College, PA — B
Eastern Mennonite College, VA — B
Eastern Nazarene College, MA — B
Erskine College, SC — B
Evangel College, MO — B
Fresno Pacific College, CA — A,B
George Fox College, OR — B
Goshen College, IN — B
Grace College, IN — B
Grand Canyon University, AZ — B
Grand Rapids Baptist College and Seminary, MI — B
Greenville College, IL — B
Houghton College, NY — B
Huntington College, IN — B
Indiana Wesleyan University, IN — B
John Brown University, AR — B
Judson College, IL — B
King's College, NY — B
Lee College, TN — B
LeTourneau University, TX — B
Malone College, OH — B
Master's College, CA — B
Messiah College, PA — B
MidAmerica Nazarene College, KS — B
Milligan College, TN — B
Mount Vernon Nazarene College, OH — B
North Park College, IL — B
Northwestern College, IA — B
Northwestern College, MN — B
Northwest Nazarene College, ID — B
Olivet Nazarene University, IL — B
Palm Beach Atlantic College, FL — B
Point Loma Nazarene College, CA — B
Redeemer College, ON — B
Seattle Pacific University, WA — B
Sioux Falls College, SD — B
Southern California College, CA — B
Southern Nazarene University, OK — B
Spring Arbor College, MI — B
Sterling College, KS — B
Tabor College, KS — B
Taylor University, IN — B
Trevecca Nazarene College, TN — B
Trinity Christian College, IL — B
Trinity College, IL — B
Trinity Western University, BC — B
Warner Pacific College, OR — B
Warner Southern College, FL — B
Westmont College, CA — B
Wheaton College, IL — B
Whitworth College, WA — B

Physical Fitness/Human Movement

Bluffton College, OH — B
Campbell University, NC — B
Cedarville College, OH — B
Gordon College, MA — B
John Brown University, AR — B
Sioux Falls College, SD — B

Physical Sciences

Biola University, CA — B
California Baptist College, CA — B
Calvin College, MI — B
Goshen College, IN — B
Houghton College, NY — B
Indiana Wesleyan University, IN — B
Judson College, IL — B
Northwest Nazarene College, ID — B
Olivet Nazarene University, IL — A,B
Roberts Wesleyan College, NY — A
Westmont College, CA — B

Physical Therapy

Campbell University, NC — B
Northwest Nazarene College, ID — B
Southern Nazarene University, OK — A
Trevecca Nazarene College, TN — A

Physician's Assistant Studies

Campbell University, NC — B
Trevecca Nazarene College, TN — B

Physics

Anderson University, IN — B
Azusa Pacific University, CA — B
Bethel College, KS — B
Bethel College, MN — B
Biola University, CA — B
Bluffton College, OH — B
Calvin College, MI — B
Dordt College, IA — B
Eastern Nazarene College, MA — B
Erskine College, SC — B
Geneva College, PA — B
Gordon College, MA — B
Goshen College, IN — B
Greenville College, IL — B
Houghton College, NY — B
King College, TN — B
Messiah College, PA — B
MidAmerica Nazarene College, KS — B
Mississippi College, MS — B
North Park College, IL — B
Northwestern College, IA — B
Northwest Nazarene College, ID — B
Point Loma Nazarene College, CA — B
Roberts Wesleyan College, NY — B
Seattle Pacific University, WA — B
Southern Nazarene University, OK — B
Spring Arbor College, MI — B
Taylor University, IN — B
Westmont College, CA — B
Wheaton College, IL — B
Whitworth College, WA — B

Piano/Organ

Anderson University, IN	B
Belhaven College, MS	B
Bethel College, IN	A,B
Biola University, CA	B
Campbellsville College, KY	B
Campbell University, NC	B
Covenant College, GA	B
Dallas Baptist University, TX	B
Erskine College, SC	B
Grace College, IN	B
Grand Canyon University, AZ	B
Houghton College, NY	B
Huntington College, IN	B
Indiana Wesleyan University, IN	B
John Brown University, AR	A
Lee College, TN	B
Mississippi College, MS	B
Mount Vernon Nazarene College, OH	B
Nyack College, NY	B
Olivet Nazarene University, IL	B
Point Loma Nazarene College, CA	B
Roberts Wesleyan College, NY	A,B
Sioux Falls College, SD	B
Southevn Nazarene University, OK	B
Sterling College, KS	B
Tabor College, KS	B
Trinity Christian College, IL	B
Wheaton College, IL	B
Whitworth College, WA	B

Political Science/ Government

Anderson University, IN	B
Azusa Pacific University, CA	B
Bethel College, KS	B
Bethel College, MN	B
Bluffton College, OH	B
California Baptist College, CA	B
Calvin College, MI	B
Campbellsville College, KY	B
Campbell University, NC	B
Cedarville College, OH	B
Colorado Christian University, CO	B
Dallas Baptist University, TX	B
Dordt College, IA	B
Eastern College, PA	B
Evangel College, MO	B
Fresno Pacific College, CA	A,B
Geneva College, PA	B
Gordon College, MA	B
Goshen College, IN	B
Greenville College, IL	B
Houghton College, NY	B
Indiana Wesleyan University, IN	B
King College, TN	B
Master's College, CA	B
Mississippi College, MS	B
North Park College, IL	B
Northwestern College, IA	B
Northwest Nazarene College, ID	B
Palm Beach Atlantic College, FL	B
Point Loma Nazarene College, CA	B
Redeemer College, ON	B
Seattle Pacific University, WA	B
Sioux Falls College, SD	B
Southern California College, CA	B

Southern Nazarene University, OK	
Sterling College, KS	B
Taylor University, IN	B
Trevecca Nazarene College, TN	B
Westmont College, CA	B
Wheaton College, IL	B
Whitworth College, WA	B

Psychology

Anderson University, IN	B
Asbury College, KY	B
Azusa Pacific University, CA	B
Belhaven College, MS	B
Bethel College, IN	A,B
Bethel College, KS	B
Bethel College, MN	B
Biola University, CA	B
Bluffton College, OH	B
California Baptist College, CA	B
Calvin College, MI	B
Campbellsville College, KY	B
Campbell University, NC	B
Cedarville College, OH	B
Central Wesleyan College, SC	B
Colorado Christian University, CO	B
Covenant College, GA	B
Dallas Baptist University, TX	B
Dordt College, IA	B
Eastern College, PA	B
Eastern Mennonite College, VA	B
Eastern Nazarene College, MA	B
Erskine College, SC	B
Evangel College, MO	B
Fresno Pacific College, CA	A,B
Geneva College, PA	B
George Fox College, OR	B
Gordon College, MA	B
Goshen College, IN	B
Grace College, IN	B
Grand Canyon University, AZ	B
Grand Rapids Baptist College and Seminary, MI	B
Greenville College, IL	B
Houghton College, NY	B
Huntington College, IN	B
Indiana Wesleyan University, IN	B
John Brown University, AR	B
Judson College, IL	B
King College, TN	B
King's College, NY	B
The King's College, AB	B
Lee College, TN	B
LeTourneau University, TX	B
Malone College, OH	B
Messiah College, PA	B
MidAmerica Nazarene College, KS	B
Milligan College, TN	B
Mississippi College, MS	B
Mount Vernon Nazarene College, OH	B
North Park College, IL	B
Northwestern College, IA	B
Northwestern College, MN	B
Northwest Nazarene College, ID	B
Nyack College, NY	B
Olivet Nazarene University, IL	B
Palm Beach Atlantic College, FL	B
Point Loma Nazarene College, CA	B

Redeemer College, ON	B
Roberts Wesleyan College, NY	B
Seattle Pacific University, WA	B
Simpson College, CA	A,B
Sioux Falls College, SD	B
Southern California College, CA	B
Southern Nazarene University, OK	B
Spring Arbor College, MI	B
Sterling College, KS	B
Tabor College, KS	B
Taylor University, IN	B
Trevecca Nazarene College, TN	B
Trinity Christian College, IL	B
Trinity College, IL	B
Trinity Western University, BC	B
Warner Pacific College, OR	B
Warner Southern College, FL	B
Western Baptist College, OR	B
Westmont College, CA	B
Wheaton College, IL	B
Whitworth College, WA	B
William Jennings Bryan College, TN	B

Public Administration

California Baptist College, CA	B
Campbell University, NC	B
Cedarville College, OH	B
Dallas Baptist University, TX	B
Evangel College, MO	B
LeTourneau University, TX	B
Mississippi College, MS	B

Public Affairs and Policy Studies

Anderson University, IN	B
Northwest Nazarene College, ID	B

Public Relations

Anderson University, IN	B
Biola University, CA	B
Campbell University, NC	B
John Brown University, AR	A,B
MidAmerica Nazarene College, KS	B
Sioux Falls College, SD	B
Southern Nazarene University, OK	B
Taylor University, IN	B

Radio and Television Studies

Biola University, CA	B
Campbell University, NC	B
Cedarville College, OH	B
Evangel College, MO	B
Geneva College, PA	B
John Brown University, AR	B
Malone College, OH	B
Master's College, CA	B
Messiah College, PA	B
Olivet Nazarene University, IL	B
Sioux Falls College, SD	B
Southern California College, CA	B
Trevecca Nazarene College, TN	A,B

Radiological Sciences

Malone College, OH	B

Radiological Technology
Sioux Falls College, SD — B

Reading Education
Seattle Pacific University, WA — B
Southern Nazarene University, OK — B

Recreational Facilities Management
Indiana Wesleyan University, IN — B
John Brown University, AR — B

Recreation and Leisure Services
Anderson University, IN — B
Asbury College, KY — B
Bethel College, IN — A,B
Bluffton College, OH — B
California Baptist College, CA — B
Calvin College, MI — B
Campbellsville College, KY — B
Central Wesleyan College, SC — B
Eastern Mennonite College, VA — B
Evangel College, MO — B
Gordon College, MA — B
Greenville College, IL — B
Houghton College, NY — B
Huntington College, IN — B
Indiana Wesleyan University, IN — A
Montreat-Anderson College, NC — A,B
Northwestern College, IA — B
Northwest Nazarene College, ID — B
Seattle Pacific University, WA — B
Southern Nazarene University, OK — B
Taylor University, IN — B
Western Baptist College, OR — B

Religious Education
Biola University, CA — B
Calvin College, MI — B
Campbellsville College, KY — B
Campbell University, NC — B
Cedarville College, OH — B
Dallas Baptist University, TX — B
Eastern Nazarene College, MA — A,B
Erskine College, SC — B
Grand Rapids Baptist College and Seminary, MI — A,B
Houghton College, NY — A,B
Indiana Wesleyan University, IN — A,B
John Brown University, AR — B
King's College, NY — B
Lee College, TN — B
Malone College, OH — B
Messiah College, PA — B
MidAmerica Nazarene College, KS — A,B
Milligan College, TN — B
Mississippi College, MS — B
Mount Vernon Nazarene College, OH — B
Northwest College of the Assemblies of God, WA — B
Northwestern College, MN — B
Nyack College, NY — B
Olivet Nazarene University, IL — B
Point Loma Nazarene College, CA — B
Seattle Pacific University, WA — B
Simpson College, CA — B

Southern California College, CA — B
Southern Nazarene University, OK — B
Sterling College, KS — B
Trevecca Nazarene College, TN — B
Trinity Christian College, IL — B
Warner Pacific College, OR — A,B
Warner Southern College, FL — A,B
Western Baptist College, OR — B
Wheaton College, IL — B
William Jennings Bryan College, TN — B

Religious Studies
Anderson University, IN — B
Azusa Pacific University, CA — B
Bethel College, IN — B
Bethel College, KS — B
Biola University, CA — B
Bluffton College, OH — B
California Baptist College, CA — B
Calvin College, MI — B
Central Wesleyan College, SC — B
Eastern College, PA — B
Eastern Mennonite College, VA — B
Eastern Nazarene College, MA — B
Fresno Pacific College, CA — B
George Fox College, OR — B
Goshen College, IN — B
Grand Canyon University, AZ — B
Grand Rapids Baptist College and Seminary, MI — B
Greenville College, IL — B
Houghton College, NY — B
Huntington College, IN — B
Indiana Wesleyan University, IN — B
John Brown University, AR — B
Judson College, IL — B
King College, TN — B
King's College, NY — B
Messiah College, PA — B
MidAmerica Nazarene College, KS — A,B
Mississippi College, MS — B
Montreat-Anderson College, NC — B
Mount Vernon Nazarene College, OH — B
Northwest Christian College, OR — A,B
Northwest College of the Assemblies of God, WA — B
Northwestern College, IA — B
Northwest Nazarene College, ID — B
Nyack College, NY — B
Olivet Nazarene University, IL — B
Palm Beach Atlantic College, FL — B
Point Loma Nazarene College, CA — B
Redeemer College, ON — B
Roberts Wesleyan College, NY — B
Seattle Pacific University, WA — B
Sioux Falls College, SD — A,B
Southern California College, CA — B
Southern Nazarene University, OK — B
Spring Arbor College, MI — B
Sterling College, KS — B
Tabor College, KS — A,B
Taylor University, IN — B
Trevecca Nazarene College, TN — A,B
Trinity Christian College, IL — B
Trinity Western University, BC — B
Warner Pacific College, OR — B
Warner Southern College, FL — A,B
Western Baptist College, OR — B

Westmont College, CA — B
Wheaton College, IL — B
Whitworth College, WA — B

Retail Management
Mississippi College, MS — B

Robotics
Taylor University, IN — B

Romance Languages
Olivet Nazarene University, IL — B
Redeemer College, ON — B

Sacred Music
Anderson University, IN — B
Belhaven College, MS — B
Bethel College, IN — A,B
Bethel College, MN — B
Calvin College, MI — B
Campbellsville College, KY — B
Campbell University, NC — B
Cedarville College, OH — B
Central Wesleyan College, SC — B
Colorado Christian University, CO — B
Dallas Baptist University, TX — B
Evangel College, MO — B
Grace College, IN — B
Grand Canyon University, AZ — B
Greenville College, IL — B
Houghton College, NY — B
Indiana Wesleyan University, IN — B
Malone College, OH — B
MidAmerica Nazarene College, KS — A,B
Milligan College, TN — B
Mississippi College, MS — B
Mount Vernon Nazarene College, OH — A,B
Northwest Christian College, OR — B
Northwest College of the Assemblies of God, WA — B
Nyack College, NY — B
Olivet Nazarene University, IL — B
Point Loma Nazarene College, CA — B
Simpson College, CA — B
Southern Nazarene University, OK — B
Taylor University, IN — B
Trevecca Nazarene College, TN — B
Western Baptist College, OR — B

Science
Bartlesville Wesleyan College, OK — A,B
Belhaven College, MS — B
Bethel College, IN — A,B
Calvin College, MI — B
Cedarville College, OH — B
Eastern Nazarene College, MA — B
Geneva College, PA — B
George Fox College, OR — B
Houghton College, NY — B
Huntington College, IN — B
Indiana Wesleyan University, IN — A,B
Judson College, IL — B
King College, TN — B
Malone College, OH — B
Montreat-Anderson College, NC — A
Mount Vernon Nazarene College, OH — B
North Park College, IL — B

Northwestern College, MN	A
Olivet Nazarene University, IL	B
Palm Beach Atlantic College, FL	B
Redeemer College, ON	B
Roberts Wesleyan College, NY	B
Seattle Pacific University, WA	B
Southern California College, CA	B
Southern Nazarene University, OK	B
Tabor College, KS	B
Trinity Western University, BC	B
Warner Pacific College, OR	B

Science Education

Asbury College, KY	B
Bartlesville Wesleyan College, OK	B
Bethel College, IN	A,B
Bethel College, MN	B
Calvin College, MI	B
Campbellsville College, KY	B
Campbell University, NC	B
Cedarville College, OH	B
Eastern Mennonite College, VA	B
Evangel College, MO	B
George Fox College, OR	B
Goshen College, IN	B
Grace College, IN	B
Grand Canyon University, AZ	B
Grand Rapids Baptist College and Seminary, MI	B
Houghton College, NY	B
Huntington College, IN	B
Indiana Wesleyan University, IN	B
Malone College, OH	B
Mississippi College, MS	B
Mount Vernon Nazarene College, OH	B
Olivet Nazarene University, IL	B
Sioux Falls College, SD	B
Southern Nazarene University, OK	B
Tabor College, KS	B
Taylor University, IN	B
Trevecca Nazarene College, TN	B
Trinity Christian College, IL	B
Warner Pacific College, OR	B
Warner Southern College, FL	B
Wheaton College, IL	B
William Jennings Bryan College, TN	B

Secondary Education

Anderson University, IN	B
Azusa Pacific University, CA	B
Bethel College, IN	B
Bethel College, KS	B
Bethel College, MN	B
Bluffton College, OH	B
California Baptist College, CA	B
Calvin College, MI	B
Campbellsville College, KY	B
Campbell University, NC	B
Cedarville College, OH	B
Colorado Christian University, CO	B
Dordt College, IA	B
Eastern College, PA	B
Eastern Mennonite College, VA	B
Evangel College, MO	B
Fresno Pacific College, CA	B
Geneva College, PA	B
George Fox College, OR	B
Goshen College, IN	B

Grand Canyon University, AZ	B
Grand Rapids Baptist College and Seminary, MI	B
Greenville College, IL	B
Houghton College, NY	B
Huntington College, IN	B
Indiana Wesleyan University, IN	B
John Brown University, AR	B
King's College, NY	B
Lee College, TN	B
Malone College, OH	B
Master's College, CA	B
Messiah College, PA	B
MidAmerica Nazarene College, KS	B
Montreat-Anderson College, NC	B
Mount Vernon Nazarene College, OH	B
North Park College, IL	B
Northwestern College, IA	B
Northwestern College, MN	B
Nyack College, NY	B
Olivet Nazarene University, IL	B
Palm Beach Atlantic College, FL	B
Redeemer College, ON	B
Roberts Wesleyan College, NY	B
Seattle Pacific University, WA	B
Simpson College, CA	B
Sioux Falls College, SD	B
Southern California College, CA	B
Southern Nazarene University, OK	B
Spring Arbor College, MI	B
Sterling College, KS	B
Tabor College, KS	B
Taylor University, IN	B
Trevecca Nazarene College, TN	B
Trinity Christian College, IL	B
Trinity Western University, BC	B
Warner Pacific College, OR	B
Warner Southern College, FL	B
Western Baptist College, OR	B
Westmont College, CA	B
Wheaton College, IL	B
Whitworth College, WA	B
William Jennings Bryan College, TN	B

Secretarial Studies/Office Management

Anderson University, IN	A
Bartlesville Wesleyan College, OK	A
Bethel College, IN	A
Campbellsville College, KY	A,B
Cedarville College, OH	A,B
Dordt College, IA	A
Evangel College, MO	A,B
Grace College, IN	A
Grand Rapids Baptist College and Seminary, MI	A
Huntington College, IN	A
John Brown University, AR	A,B
Lee College, TN	B
Milligan College, TN	A,B
Mississippi College, MS	B
Mount Vernon Nazarene College, OH	A,B
Northwestern College, IA	A
Northwestern College, MN	A,B
Northwest Nazarene College, ID	B
Point Loma Nazarene College, CA	B

Sioux Falls College, SD	A,B
Southern Nazarene University, OK	A,B
Tabor College, KS	A,B

Social Science

Azusa Pacific University, CA	B
Bethel College, IN	A,B
Bethel College, KS	B
Bethel College, MN	B
Biola University, CA	B
Bluffton College, OH	B
California Baptist College, CA	B
Calvin College, MI	B
Campbell University, NC	B
Cedarville College, OH	B
Eastern Nazarene College, MA	B
Evangel College, MO	A,B
Fresno Pacific College, CA	B
Grand Canyon University, AZ	B
Houghton College, NY	B
Indiana Wesleyan University, IN	A,B
John Brown University, AR	B
Judson College, IL	B
The King's College, AB	B
Lee College, TN	B
Malone College, OH	B
Messiah College, PA	B
Mississippi College, MS	B
Montreat-Anderson College, NC	B
Mount Vernon Nazarene College, OH	B
North Park College, IL	B
Northwestern College, MN	B
Nyack College, NY	B
Olivet Nazarene University, IL	B
Roberts Wesleyan College, NY	B
Simpson College, CA	B
Sioux Falls College, SD	A,B
Southern California College, CA	B
Southern Nazarene University, OK	B
Spring Arbor College, MI	B
Tabor College, KS	B
Taylor University, IN	B
Trevecca Nazarene College, TN	B
Trinity College, IL	B
Trinity Western University, BC	B
Warner Pacific College, OR	A,B
Warner Southern College, FL	B
Western Baptist College, OR	B
Westmont College, CA	B

Social Work

Anderson University, IN	B
Asbury College, KY	B
Azusa Pacific University, CA	B
Bethel College, KS	B
Bethel College, MN	B
Bluffton College, OH	B
Calvin College, MI	B
Campbell University, NC	B
Cedarville College, OH	B
Dallas Baptist University, TX	B
Dordt College, IA	B
Eastern College, PA	B
Eastern Mennonite College, VA	B
Eastern Nazarene College, MA	B
Evangel College, MO	B
George Fox College, OR	B
Gordon College, MA	B

Social Work *(continued)*

Goshen College, IN	B
Grand Rapids Baptist College and Seminary, MI	B
Greenville College, IL	B
Indiana Wesleyan University, IN	B
Malone College, OH	B
Messiah College, PA	B
Milligan College, TN	B
Mississippi College, MS	B
Mount Vernon Nazarene College, OH	B
Northwestern College, IA	B
Olivet Nazarene University, IL	A,B
Roberts Wesleyan College, NY	B
Sioux Falls College, SD	B
Spring Arbor College, MI	B
Tabor College, KS	B
Taylor University, IN	B
Trevecca Nazarene College, TN	B
Warner Pacific College, OR	B

Sociology

Anderson University, IN	B
Asbury College, KY	B
Azusa Pacific University, CA	B
Bethel College, IN	A,B
Bethel College, KS	B
Bethel College, MN	B
Biola University, CA	B
Bluffton College, OH	B
California Baptist College, CA	B
Calvin College, MI	B
Campbellsville College, KY	B
Cedarville College, OH	B
Covenant College, GA	B
Dallas Baptist University, TX	B
Dordt College, IA	B
Eastern College, PA	B
Eastern Mennonite College, VA	B
Eastern Nazarene College, MA	B
Erskine College, SC	B
Evangel College, MO	B
Fresno Pacific College, CA	A,B
Geneva College, PA	B
George Fox College, OR	B
Gordon College, MA	B
Goshen College, IN	B
Grace College, IN	B
Grand Canyon University, AZ	B
Grand Rapids Baptist College and Seminary, MI	B
Greenville College, IL	B
Houghton College, NY	B
Huntington College, IN	B
Indiana Wesleyan University, IN	B
Judson College, IL	B
King's College, NY	B
Lee College, TN	B
Messiah College, PA	B
Milligan College, TN	B
Mississippi College, MS	B
Mount Vernon Nazarene College, OH	B
North Park College, IL	B
Northwestern College, IA	B
Olivet Nazarene University, IL	A,B
Point Loma Nazarene College, CA	B
Redeemer College, ON	B

Roberts Wesleyan College, NY	B
Seattle Pacific University, WA	B
Sioux Falls College, SD	B
Southern California College, CA	B
Southern Nazarene University, OK	B
Spring Arbor College, MI	B
Sterling College, KS	B
Tabor College, KS	B
Taylor University, IN	B
Trinity Christian College, IL	B
Trinity College, IL	B
Warner Pacific College, OR	B
Warner Southern College, FL	B
Westmont College, CA	B
Wheaton College, IL	B
Whitworth College, WA	B

Spanish

Anderson University, IN	B
Asbury College, KY	B
Bethel College, IN	A
Bethel College, MN	B
Biola University, CA	B
Bluffton College, OH	B
California Baptist College, CA	B
Calvin College, MI	B
Campbell University, NC	B
Cedarville College, OH	B
Dordt College, IA	B
Eastern College, PA	B
Eastern Mennonite College, VA	B
Eastern Nazarene College, MA	B
Erskine College, SC	B
Evangel College, MO	B
Fresno Pacific College, CA	B
Geneva College, PA	B
Gordon College, MA	B
Goshen College, IN	B
Grace College, IN	B
Grand Canyon University, AZ	B
Greenville College, IL	B
Houghton College, NY	B
Indiana Wesleyan University, IN	B
King's College, NY	B
Malone College, OH	B
Messiah College, PA	B
MidAmerica Nazarene College, KS	B
Mississippi College, MS	B
Mount Vernon Nazarene College, OH	B
North Park College, IL	B
Northwestern College, IA	B
Point Loma Nazarene College, CA	B
Southern Nazarene University, OK	B
Spring Arbor College, MI	B
Taylor University, IN	B
Westmont College, CA	B
Wheaton College, IL	B
Whitworth College, WA	B

Special Education

Bethel College, KS	B
Bluffton College, OH	B
Calvin College, MI	B
Cedarville College, OH	B
Central Wesleyan College, SC	B
Eastern Mennonite College, VA	B
Erskine College, SC	B
Evangel College, MO	B

Gordon College, MA	B
Grand Canyon University, AZ	B
Greenville College, IL	B
Huntington College, IN	B
John Brown University, AR	B
Malone College, OH	B
Milligan College, TN	B
Mississippi College, MS	B
Mount Vernon Nazarene College, OH	B
Northwestern College, IA	B
Seattle Pacific University, WA	B
Sterling College, KS	B
Tabor College, KS	B
Trevecca Nazarene College, TN	B
Whitworth College, WA	B

Speech Pathology and Audiology

Biola University, CA	B
Calvin College, MI	B
Geneva College, PA	B
Mississippi College, MS	B

Speech/Rhetoric/Public Address/Debate

Anderson University, IN	B
Asbury College, KY	B
Bethel College, MN	B
Bluffton College, OH	B
Calvin College, MI	B
Cedarville College, OH	B
Evangel College, MO	B
Geneva College, PA	B
Grace College, IN	B
Grand Canyon University, AZ	B
Grand Rapids Baptist College and Seminary, MI	B
Greenville College, IL	B
Judson College, IL	B
North Park College, IL	B
Olivet Nazarene University, IL	B
Palm Beach Atlantic College, FL	B
Sioux Falls College, SD	B
Southern California College, CA	B
Southern Nazarene University, OK	B
Spring Arbor College, MI	B
Sterling College, KS	B
Taylor University, IN	B
Trevecca Nazarene College, TN	B
Wheaton College, IL	B
Whitworth College, WA	B

Speech Therapy

Biola University, CA	B
Point Loma Nazarene College, CA	B

Sports Administration

Bluffton, OH	B
Campbell University, NC	B
Cedarville College, OH	B
Erskine College, SC	B
LeTourneau University, TX	B
Mount Vernon Nazarene College, OH	B

Sports Medicine

Anderson University, IN	B

George Fox College, OR | B
John Brown University, AR | B
Malone College, OH | B
Messiah College, PA | B
Mount Vernon Nazarene College,
OH | B
North Park College, IL | B
Whitworth College, WA | B

Stringed Instruments

Belhaven College, MS | B
Covenant College, GA | B
Houghton College, NY | B
Olivet Nazarene University, IL | B
Point Loma Nazarene College, CA | B
Wheaton College, IL | B

Studio Art

Bethel College, MN | B
Biola University, CA | B
Campbell University, NC | B
Eastern College, PA | B
Grand Canyon University, AZ | B
Indiana Wesleyan University, IN | B
Point Loma Nazarene College, CA | B
Roberts Wesleyan College, NY | B
Wheaton College, IL | B
Whitworth College, WA | B

Systems Engineering

Eastern Nazarene College, MA | B

Teacher Aide Studies

Eastern Mennonite College, VA | A
Olivet Nazarene University, IL | A

Teaching English as a Second Language

Eastern Mennonite College, VA | B
Goshen College, IN | B

Technical Writing

Cedarville College, OH | B

Telecommunications

Calvin College, MI | B
George Fox College, OR | B

Textiles and Clothing

Bluffton College, OH | B
Olivet Nazarene University, IL | B
Seattle Pacific University, WA | B

Theater Arts/Drama

Anderson University, IN | B
Bethel College, IN | A
Bethel College, KS | B
Bethel College, MN | B
Biola University, CA | B
California Baptist College, CA | B
Campbell University, NC | B
Cedarville College, OH | B
Colorado Christian University, CO | B
Dordt College, IA | B
Goshen College, IN | B
Grand Canyon University, AZ | B
Greenville College, IL | B
Huntington College, IN | B
Judson College, IL | B

King College, TN | B
Lee College, TN | B
Malone College, OH | B
Mount Vernon Nazarene College,
OH | B
Northwestern College, IA | B
Northwestern College, MN | B
Northwest Nazarene College, ID | B
Point Loma Nazarene College, CA | B
Redeemer College, ON | B
Seattle Pacific University, WA | B
Sioux Falls College, SD | A,B
Southern California College, CA | B
Southern Nazarene University, OK | B
Sterling College, KS | B
Taylor University, IN | B
Trevecca Nazarene College, TN | B
Trinity Western University, BC | B
Westmont College, CA | B
Wheaton College, IL | B
Whitworth College, WA | B

Theology

Azusa Pacific University, CA | B
Bethel College, MN | B
Biola University, CA | B
Calvin College, MI | B
Campbell University, NC | B
Cedarville College, OH | B
Colorado Christian University, CO | B
Dordt College, IA | B
Eastern Mennonite College, VA | B
Grand Canyon University, AZ | B
Greenville College, IL | B
Huntington College, IN | B
Indiana Wesleyan University, IN | B
John Brown University, AR | B
Lee College, TN | B
Malone College, OH | B
Master's College, CA | B
Messiah College, PA | B
Mount Vernon Nazarene College,
OH | B
North Park College, IL | B
Northwest Christian College, OR | B
Northwestern College, IA | B
Northwestern College, MN | B
Olivet Nazarene University, IL | B
Point Loma Nazarene College, CA | B
Redeemer College, ON | B
Seattle Pacific University, WA | B
Southern Nazarene University, OK | B
Taylor University, IN | B
Trevecca Nazarene College, TN | B
Trinity Christian College, IL | B
Warner Pacific College, OR | B
Warner Southern College, FL | B
Western Baptist College, OR | B

Urban Studies

North Park College, IL | B

(Pre)Veterinary Medicine Sequence

Anderson University, IN | B
Azusa Pacific University, CA | B
Belhaven College, MS | B
Bethel College, MN | B
Campbellsville College, KY | B

Campbell University, NC | B
Cedarville College, OH | B
Dordt College, IA | B
Eastern Mennonite College, VA |
Eastern Nazarene College, MA | B
Evangel College, MO | B
George Fox College, OR | B
Goshen College, IN | B
Grand Canyon University, AZ | B
Greenville College, IL | B
Houghton College, NY | B
Huntington College, IN | B
Indiana Wesleyan University, IN | B
King College, TN | B
LeTourneau University, TX | B
Malone College, OH | B
Messiah College, PA | B
Milligan College, TN | B
Mount Vernon Nazarene College,
OH | B
North Park College, IL | B
Northwestern College, IA |
Olivet Nazarene University, IL | B
Point Loma Nazarene College, CA | B
Redeemer College, ON | B
Sioux Falls College, SD | B
Southern California College, CA | B
Southern Nazarene University, OK | B
Sterling College, KS | B
Taylor University, IN | B
Trinity Christian College, IL | B
Trinity Western University, BC | B
Westmont College, CA | B
Whitworth College, WA | B

Voice

Anderson University, IN | B
Belhaven College, MS | B
Bethel College, IN | A,B
Biola University, CA | B
Calvin College, MI | B
Campbellsville College, KY | B
Campbell University, NC | B
Cedarville College, OH | B
Colorado Christian University, CO | B
Covenant College, GA | B
Dallas Baptist University, TX | B
Erskine College, SC | B
Grand Canyon University, AZ | B
Houghton College, NY | B
Huntington College, IN | B
Indiana Wesleyan University, IN | B
John Brown University, AR | B
Judson College, IL | B
Lee College, TN | B
Messiah College, PA | B
Mount Vernon Nazarene College,
OH | B
Nyack College, NY | B
Olivet Nazarene University, IL | B
Point Loma Nazarene College, CA | B
Roberts Wesleyan College, NY | A,B
Sioux Falls College, SD | B
Southern Nazarene University, OK | B
Sterling College, KS | B
Tabor College, KS | B
Taylor University, IN | B
Wheaton College, IL | B
Whitworth College, WA | B

Welding Engineering

LeTourneau University, TX   B

Welding Technology

LeTourneau University, TX   B

Western Civilization and Culture

Trinity Christian College, IL   B

Wind and Percussion Instruments

Covenant College, GA   B
Grand Canyon University, AZ   B
Houghton College, NY   B
Indiana Wesleyan University, IN   B
Mount Vernon Nazarene College, OH   B
Olivet Nazarene University, IL   B

Point Loma Nazarene College, CA   B
Sioux Falls College, SD   B
Southern Nazarene University, OK   B
Wheaton College, IL   B

Zoology

Southern Nazarene University, OK   B

Athletics Index

M—for men; W—for women;
(s) scholarship offered

Badminton

Redeemer College, ON	M,W

Baseball

Anderson University, IN	M
Asbury College, KY	M
Azusa Pacific University, CA	M(s)
Belhaven College, MS	M(s)
Bethel College, IN	M(s)
Bethel College, MN	M
Biola University, CA	M(s)
Bluffton College, OH	M
California Baptist College, CA	M(s)
Calvin College, MI	M
Campbellsville College, KY	M(s)
Campbell University, NC	M(s)
Cedarville College, OH	M(s)
Central Wesleyan College, SC	M
Dallas Baptist University, TX	M(s)
Eastern College, PA	M(s)
Eastern Mennonite College, VA	M
Eastern Nazarene College, MA	M
Erskine College, SC	M(s)
Evangel College, MO	M
Geneva College, PA	M(s)
George Fox College, OR	M
Gordon College, MA	M
Grace College, IN	M(s)
Grand Canyon University, AZ	M
Grand Rapids Baptist College and Seminary, MI	M(s)
Huntington College, IN	M
Indiana Wesleyan University, IN	M(s)
King's College, NY	M
LeTourneau University, TX	M
Malone College, OH	M(s)
Master's College, CA	M(s)
Messiah College, PA	M
MidAmerica Nazarene College, KS	M(s)
Montreat-Anderson College, NC	M(s)
Mount Vernon Nazarene College, OH	M(s)
North Park College, IL	M
Northwestern College, IA	M(s)
Northwestern College, MN	M(s)
Northwest Nazarene College, ID	M
Nyack College, NY	M(s)
Olivet Nazarene University, IL	M(s)
Palm Beach Atlantic College, FL	M(s)
Point Loma Nazarene College, CA	M(s)
Sioux Falls College, SD	M

Southern California College, CA	M(s)
Spring Arbor College, MI	M(s)
Sterling College, KS	M
Taylor University, IN	M
Trevecca Nazarene College, TN	M(s)
Trinity Christian College, IL	M
Warner Southern College, FL	M(s)
Whitworth College, WA	M

Basketball

Anderson University, IN	M,W
Asbury College, KY	M,W
Azusa Pacific University, CA	M(s),W(s)
Bartlesville Wesleyan College, OK	M(s),W(s)
Belhaven College, MS	M(s),W(s)
Bethel College, IN	M(s),W(s)
Bethel College, KS	M(s),W(s)
Bethel College, MN	M,W
Biola University, CA	M(s),W(s)
Bluffton College, OH	M,W
California Baptist College, CA	M(s),W(s)
Calvin College, MI	M,W
Campbellsville College, KY	M(s),W(s)
Campbell University, NC	M(s),W(s)
Cedarville College, OH	M(s),W(s)
Central Wesleyan College, SC	M(s),W(s)
Colorado Christian University, CO	M(s),W(s)
Covenant College, GA	M(s),W(s)
Dordt College, IA	M,W
Eastern College, PA	M(s),W(s)
Eastern Mennonite College, VA	M,W
Eastern Nazarene College, MA	M,W
Erskine College, SC	M(s),W(s)
Evangel College, MO	M(s),W(s)
Fresno Pacific College, CA	M(s),W(s)
Geneva College, PA	M(s),W(s)
George Fox College, OR	M(s),W(s)
Gordon College, MA	M,W
Goshen College, IN	M,W
Grace College, IN	M(s),W(s)
Grand Canyon University, AZ	M(s),W(s)
Grand Rapids Baptist College and Seminary, MI	M(s),W(s)
Greenville College, IL	M,W
Houghton College, NY	M(s),W(s)
Huntington College, IN	M(s),W(s)
Indiana Wesleyan University, IN	M(s),W(s)
John Brown University, AR	M(s),W(s)
Judson College, IL	M(s),W(s)
King College, TN	M(s),W(s)
King's College, NY	M(s),W(s)

The King's College, AB	M,W
Lee College, TN	M(s),W(s)
LeTourneau University, TX	M
Malone College, OH	M(s),W(s)
Master's College, CA	M(s),W(s)
Messiah College, PA	M,W
MidAmerica Nazarene College, KS	M(s),W(s)
Milligan College, TN	M(s),W(s)
Mississippi College, MS	M(s),W(s)
Montreat-Anderson College, NC	M(s),W(s)
Mount Vernon Nazarene College, OH	M(s),W(s)
North Park College, IL	M,W
Northwest Christian College, OR	M
Northwest College of the Assemblies of God, WA	M,W
Northwestern College, IA	M(s),W(s)
Northwestern College, MN	M(s),W(s)
Northwest Nazarene College, ID	M,W
Nyack College, NY	M(s),W(s)
Olivet Nazarene University, IL	M(s),W(s)
Palm Beach Atlantic College, FL	M(s)
Point Loma Nazarene College, CA	M(s),W(s)
Redeemer College, ON	M,W
Roberts Wesleyan College, NY	M(s),W(s)
Seattle Pacific University, WA	M(s),W(s)
Simpson College, CA	M,W
Sioux Falls College, SD	M(s),W(s)
Southern California College, CA	M(s),W(s)
Southern Nazarene University, OK	M(s),W(s)
Spring Arbor College, MI	M(s),W(s)
Sterling College, KS	M(s),W(s)
Tabor College, KS	M(s),W(s)
Taylor University, IN	M,W
Trevecca Nazarene College, TN	M(s)
Trinity Christian College, IL	M,W
Trinity College, IL	M(s),W(s)
Trinity Western University, BC	M,W
Warner Southern College, FL	M(s),W(s)
Western Baptist College, OR	M(s),W(s)
Westmont College, CA	M(s)
Wheaton College, IL	M,W
Whitworth College, WA	M(s),W(s)

Basketball (continued)

William Jennings Bryan College,
TN   M(s),W(s)

Crew

Seattle Pacific University, WA   M,W

Cross-Country Running

Anderson University, IN	M,W
Asbury College, KY	M,W
Azusa Pacific University, CA	M(s),W(s)
Bartlesville Wesleyan College, OK	M(s),W(s)
Belhaven College, MS	M(s),W(s)
Bethel College, IN	M(s),W(s)
Bethel College, MN	M,W
Biola University, CA	M(s),W(s)
Bluffton College, OH	M,W
Calvin College, MI	M,W
Campbellsville College, KY	M(s),W(s)
Campbell University, NC	M(s),W(s)
Cedarville College, OH	M(s),W(s)
Covenant College, GA	M,W
Eastern College, PA	M(s),W(s)
Eastern Mennonite College, VA	M,W
Eastern Nazarene College, MA	M,W
Erskine College, SC	M(s)
Evangel College, MO	M(s),W(s)
Fresno Pacific College, CA	M(s),W(s)
Geneva College, PA	M(s),W(s)
George Fox College, OR	M(s),W(s)
Gordon College, MA	M,W
Goshen College, IN	M,W
Grand Canyon University, AZ	M(s),W(s)
Grand Rapids Baptist College and Seminary, MI	M,W
Greenville College, IL	M,W
Houghton College, NY	M(s),W(s)
Huntington College, IN	M(s),W(s)
Indiana Wesleyan University, IN	M(s),W(s)
King College, TN	M,W
King's College, NY	M(s),W(s)
LeTourneau University, TX	M,W
Malone College, OH	M(s),W(s)
Master's College, CA	M(s),W(s)
Messiah College, PA	M,W
MidAmerica Nazarene College, KS	M(s),W(s)
Mississippi College, MS	M(s)
North Park College, IL	M,W
Northwestern College, IA	M(s),W(s)
Northwestern College, MN	M(s),W(s)
Olivet Nazarene University, IL	M(s),W(s)
Point Loma Nazarene College, CA	M(s),W(s)
Redeemer College, ON	M,W
Roberts Wesleyan College, NY	M(s),W(s)
Seattle Pacific University, WA	M(s),W(s)
Sioux Falls College, SD	M(s),W(s)
Southern California College, CA	M(s),W(s)
Spring Arbor College, MI	M(s),W(s)
Sterling College, KS	M(s),W(s)
Tabor College, KS	M,W
Taylor University, IN	M,W
Trinity College, IL	M,W
Westmont College, CA	M(s),W(s)
Wheaton College, IL	M,W

Whitworth College, WA	M(s),W(s)
William Jennings Bryan College, TN	M(s),W(s)

Field Hockey

Eastern College, PA	W(s)
Eastern Mennonite College, VA	W
Gordon College, MA	W
Houghton College, NY	W(s)
Messiah College, PA	W

Football

Anderson University, IN	M
Azusa Pacific University, CA	M(s)
Bethel College, KS	M(s)
Bethel College, MN	M
Bluffton College, OH	M
Campbellsville College, KY	M
Evangel College, MO	M(s)
Geneva College, PA	M(s)
Greenville College, IL	M
Malone College, OH	M(s)
MidAmerica Nazarene College, KS	M(s)
Mississippi College, MS	M(s)
North Park College, IL	M
Northwestern College, IA	M(s)
Northwestern College, MN	M(s)
Olivet Nazarene University, IL	M(s)
Sioux Falls College, SD	M(s)
Sterling College, KS	M(s)
Tabor College, KS	M(s)
Taylor University, IN	M
Trinity College, IL	M(s)
Wheaton College, IL	M
Whitworth College, WA	M(s)

Golf

Anderson University, IN	M
Bartlesville Wesleyan College, OK	M(s)
Belhaven College, MS	M(s)
Bethel College, IN	M(s),W(s)
Bethel College, MN	M
Bluffton College, OH	M
Calvin College, MI	M,W
Campbellsville College, KY	M(s)
Campbell University, NC	M(s),W(s)
Cedarville College, OH	M(s)
Central Wesleyan College, SC	M(s)
Colorado Christian University, CO	M(s)
Dordt College, IA	M,W
Eastern Mennonite College, VA	M
Erskine College, SC	M(s)
Goshen College, IN	M
Grace College, IN	M(s)
Grand Canyon University, AZ	M(s)
Grand Rapids Baptist College and Seminary, MI	M(s)
Greenville College, IL	M
Huntington College, IN	M(s)
Indiana Wesleyan University, IN	M(s)
King College, TN	M,W
Lee College, TN	M(s)
Malone College, OH	M(s)
Messiah College, PA	M
Milligan College, TN	M(s)
Mississippi College, MS	M(s)
Mount Vernon Nazarene College, OH	M(s)
Northwestern College, IA	M(s),W(s)

Northwestern College, MN	M(s),W(s)
Olivet Nazarene University, IL	M
Point Loma Nazarene College, CA	M(s)
Spring Arbor College, MI	M(s)
Taylor University, IN	M
Trinity Christian College, IL	M,W
Trinity College, IL	M(s)
Wheaton College, IL	M

Gymnastics

Seattle Pacific University, WA   W(s)

Ice Hockey

Bethel College, MN	M
Calvin College, MI	M
Dordt College, IA	M
Gordon College, MA	M
The King's College, AB	M
Redeemer College, ON	M,W

Lacrosse

Eastern College, PA	W(s)
Gordon College, MA	M

Rugby

Trinity Western University, BC   M

Soccer

Anderson University, IN	M
Asbury College, KY	M
Azusa Pacific University, CA	M(s),W(s)
Bartlesville Wesleyan College, OK	M(s),W(s)
Belhaven College, MS	M(s)
Bethel College, IN	M(s)
Bethel College, KS	M(s)
Bethel College, MN	M
Biola University, CA	M,W
Bluffton College, OH	M,W
California Baptist College, CA	M(s),W(s)
Calvin College, MI	M,W
Campbellsville College, KY	M(s)
Campbell University, NC	M(s),W(s)
Cedarville College, OH	M(s)
Central Wesleyan College, SC	M(s)
Colorado Christian University, CO	M(s),W(s)
Covenant College, GA	M(s)
Dallas Baptist University, TX	M(s)
Dordt College, IA	M
Eastern College, PA	M(s),W(s)
Eastern Mennonite College, VA	M
Eastern Nazarene College, MA	M
Erskine College, SC	M(s),W(s)
Fresno Pacific College, CA	M(s)
Geneva College, PA	M(s),W(s)
George Fox College, OR	M(s),W(s)
Gordon College, MA	M,W
Goshen College, IN	M,W
Grace College, IN	M(s)
Grand Canyon University, AZ	M(s)
Grand Rapids Baptist College and Seminary, MI	M(s)
Greenville College, IL	M,W
Houghton College, NY	M(s),W(s)
Huntington College, IN	M(s)
Indiana Wesleyan University, IN	M(s),W(s)
John Brown University, AR	M(s)

Judson College, IL	M(s)
King College, TN	M(s)
King's College, NY	M(s),W(s)
Lee College, TN	M(s),W(s)
LeTourneau University, TX	M
Malone College, OH	M(s)
Master's College, CA	M(s)
Messiah College, PA	M,W
Milligan College, TN	M(s)
Montreat-Anderson College, NC	M(s)
Mount Vernon Nazarene College, OH	M(s)
North Park College, IL	M
Northwest College of the Assemblies of God, WA	M
Northwestern College, MN	M(s)
Northwest Nazarene College, ID	M
Nyack College, NY	M(s),W(s)
Olivet Nazarene University, IL	M
Palm Beach Atlantic College, FL	M(s)
Point Loma Nazarene College, CA	M(s)
Redeemer College, ON	M,W
Roberts Wesleyan College, NY	M(s),W(s)
Seattle Pacific University, WA	M(s)
Simpson College, CA	M
Southern California College, CA	M(s)
Southern Nazarene University, OK	M(s)
Spring Arbor College, MI	M(s)
Sterling College, KS	M(s),W(s)
Tabor College, KS	M(s)
Taylor University, IN	M
Trevecca Nazarene College, TN	M(s)
Trinity Christian College, IL	M
Trinity College, IL	M(s),W
Trinity Western University, BC	M,W
Warner Southern College, FL	M(s)
Western Baptist College, OR	M(s)
Westmont College, CA	M(s),W(s)
Wheaton College, IL	M,W
Whitworth College, WA	M(s),W(s)
William Jennings Bryan College, TN	M(s)

Softball

Anderson University, IN	W
Asbury College, KY	W
Azusa Pacific University, CA	W
Bethel College, IN	W(s)
Biola University, CA	W
Bluffton College, OH	W
California Baptist College, CA	W(s)
Calvin College, MI	W
Campbellsville College, KY	W(s)
Campbell University, NC	W(s)
Cedarville College, OH	W(s)
Dordt College, IA	W
Eastern College, PA	W(s)
Eastern Mennonite College, VA	W
Eastern Nazarene College, MA	W
Erskine College, SC	W(s)
Evangel College, MO	W
Geneva College, PA	W
George Fox College, OR	W
Gordon College, MA	W
Goshen College, IN	W
Grace College, IN	W(s)

Grand Rapids Baptist College and Seminary, MI	W(s)
Huntington College, IN	W
Indiana Wesleyan University, IN	W(s)
King College, TN	W
King's College, NY	W
Lee College, TN	W(s)
Malone College, OH	W(s)
Messiah College, PA	W
Mount Vernon Nazarene College, OH	W(s)
North Park College, IL	W
Northwestern College, IA	W(s)
Northwestern College, MN	W(s)
Nyack College, NY	W(s)
Olivet Nazarene University, IL	W(s)
Point Loma Nazarene College, CA	W
Simpson College, CA	W
Southern California College, CA	W(s)
Spring Arbor College, MI	W(s)
Sterling College, KS	W
Taylor University, IN	W
Wheaton College, IL	W

Swimming and Diving

Asbury College, KY	M,W
Calvin College, MI	M,W
Campbellsville College, KY	M(s),W(s)
Dordt College, IA	M,W
John Brown University, AR	M(s),W(s)
Wheaton College, IL	M,W
Whitworth College, WA	M(s),W(s)

Tennis

Anderson University, IN	M,W
Asbury College, KY	M,W
Azusa Pacific University, CA	M(s)
Bartlesville Wesleyan College, OK	M(s)
Belhaven College, MS	M(s),W(s)
Bethel College, IN	M(s),W(s)
Bethel College, KS	M(s),W(s)
Bethel College, MN	M,W
Biola University, CA	M(s),W(s)
Bluffton College, OH	M,W
California Baptist College, CA	M(s),W(s)
Calvin College, MI	M,W
Campbellsville College, KY	M(s),W(s)
Campbell University, NC	M(s),W(s)
Cedarville College, OH	M(s),W(s)
Colorado Christian University, CO	M(s),W(s)
Dordt College, IA	M,W
Eastern College, PA	M,W
Eastern Mennonite College, VA	M,W
Eastern Nazarene College, MA	M,W
Erskine College, SC	M(s),W(s)
Geneva College, PA	M(s),W(s)
Gordon College, MA	M,W
Goshen College, IN	M,W
Grace College, IN	M(s)
Grand Canyon University, AZ	W(s)
Grand Rapids Baptist College and Seminary, MI	M(s)
Greenville College, IL	M,W
Huntington College, IN	M(s),W(s)
Indiana Wesleyan University, IN	M(s),W(s)
John Brown University, AR	M(s),W(s)

Judson College, IL	M(s),W
King College, TN	M,W
Lee College, TN	M(s),W(s)
Malone College, OH	M(s),W(s)
Messiah College, PA	M,W
Milligan College, TN	M(s),W(s)
Mississippi College, MS	M(s),W(s)
Montreat-Anderson College, NC	W
North Park College, IL	M,W
Northwestern College, IA	M(s),W(s)
Northwestern College, MN	M(s),W(s)
Northwest Nazarene College, ID	W
Olivet Nazarene University, IL	M,W
Point Loma Nazarene College, CA	M(s),W(s)
Southern California College, CA	M
Spring Arbor College, MI	M(s),W(s)
Sterling College, KS	M(s),W(s)
Tabor College, KS	M(s),W(s)
Taylor University, IN	M,W
Trevecca Nazarene College, TN	M(s),W(s)
Trinity College, IL	M(s),W(s)
Westmont College, CA	M(s),W(s)
Wheaton College, IL	M,W
Whitworth College, WA	M(s),W(s)

Track and Field

Anderson University, IN	M,W
Azusa Pacific University, CA	M(s),W(s)
Bethel College, KS	M(s),W(s)
Bethel College, MN	M,W
Biola University, CA	M(s),W(s)
Bluffton College, OH	M,W
Calvin College, MI	M,W
Campbell University, NC	M(s),W(s)
Cedarville College, OH	M(s),W(s)
Dordt College, IA	M,W
Eastern Mennonite College, VA	M,W
Evangel College, MO	M(s),W(s)
Fresno Pacific College, CA	M(s),W(s)
Geneva College, PA	M(s),W(s)
George Fox College, OR	M(s),W(s)
Goshen College, IN	M,W
Greenville College, IL	M,W
Houghton College, NY	M(s),W(s)
Huntington College, IN	M(s),W(s)
Indiana Wesleyan University, IN	M(s),W(s)
LeTourneau University, TX	M,W
Malone College, OH	M(s),W(s)
Messiah College, PA	M,W
MidAmerica Nazarene College, KS	M(s),W(s)
Mississippi College, MS	M(s)
North Park College, IL	M,W
Northwestern College, IA	M(s),W(s)
Northwestern College, MN	M(s),W(s)
Northwest Nazarene College, ID	M,W
Olivet Nazarene University, IL	M,W
Point Loma Nazarene College, CA	M(s),W(s)
Roberts Wesleyan College, NY	M(s),W(s)
Seattle Pacific University, WA	M,W(s)

Sioux Falls College, SD	M(s),W(s)
Spring Arbor College, MI	M(s),W(s)
Sterling College, KS	M(s),W(s)
Tabor College, KS	M(s),W(s)
Taylor University, IN	M,W
Trinity College, IL	M,W
Westmont College, CA	M(s),W(s)
Wheaton College, IL	M,W
Whitworth College, WA	M(s),W(s)

Volleyball

Anderson University, IN	W
Asbury College, KY	W
Azusa Pacific University, CA	W(s)
Bartlesville Wesleyan College, OK	W(s)
Bethel College, IN	W(s)
Bethel College, KS	W(s)
Bethel College, MN	W
Biola University, CA	W(s)
Bluffton College, OH	W
California Baptist College, CA	W(s)
Calvin College, MI	W
Campbell University, NC	W(s)
Cedarville College, OH	W(s)
Central Wesleyan College, SC	W(s)
Colorado Christian University, CO	W(s)
Covenant College, GA	W
Dallas Baptist University, TX	W(s)
Dordt College, IA	W
Eastern College, PA	W(s)
Eastern Mennonite College, VA	M,W
Eastern Nazarene College, MA	M,W
Erskine College, SC	W(s)
Evangel College, MO	W(s)
Fresno Pacific College, CA	W
Geneva College, PA	M,W(s)
George Fox College, OR	W(s)
Gordon College, MA	W
Goshen College, IN	W
Grace College, IN	W(s)
Grand Canyon University, AZ	W(s)
Grand Rapids Baptist College and Seminary, MI	W(s)
Greenville College, IL	W
Houghton College, NY	W(s)
Huntington College, IN	W(s)
Indiana Wesleyan University, IN	W(s)
John Brown University, AR	W(s)
Judson College, IL	M,W(s)
King College, TN	W(s)
King's College, NY	W(s)
The King's College, AB	M,W
Lee College, TN	W(s)
LeTourneau University, TX	W
Malone College, OH	W(s)
Master's College, CA	W(s)
Messiah College, PA	W
MidAmerica Nazarene College, KS	W(s)
Milligan College, TN	W(s)
Mississippi College, MS	W(s)
Montreat-Anderson College, NC	W(s)
Mount Vernon Nazarene College, OH	W(s)
North Park College, IL	M,W
Northwest College of the Assemblies of God, WA	
Northwestern College, IA	W(s)
Northwestern College, MN	W(s)
Northwest Nazarene College, ID	W
Nyack College, NY	W
Olivet Nazarene University, IL	W
Palm Beach Atlantic College, FL	W(s)
Point Loma Nazarene College, CA	W(s)
Redeemer College, ON	M,W
Seattle Pacific University, WA	W(s)
Simpson College, CA	M,W
Sioux Falls College, SD	W(s)
Southern California College, CA	W(s)
Southern Nazarene University, OK	W(s)
Spring Arbor College, MI	W(s)
Sterling College, KS	W(s)
Tabor College, KS	W(s)
Taylor University, IN	W
Trevecca Nazarene College, TN	W(s)
Trinity Christian College, IL	M,W
Trinity College, IL	M,W(s)
Trinity Western University, BC	M,W
Warner Southern College, FL	W(s)
Western Baptist College, OR	W(s)
Westmont College, CA	W(s)
Wheaton College, IL	W
Whitworth College, WA	W(s)
William Jennings Bryan College, TN	W(s)

Wrestling

Campbell University, NC	M(s)
Messiah College, PA	M
Northwestern College, IA	M(s)
Northwestern College, MN	M(s)
Olivet Nazarene University, IL	M(s)
Trinity College, IL	M
Wheaton College, IL	M

Study Abroad Index

Africa
King College, TN
Malone College, OH
Westmont College, CA

Asia
Wheaton College, IL

Australia
George Fox College, OR
Taylor University, IN

Austria
Calvin College, MI
Gordon College, MA

Belgium
Gordon College, MA

Belize
Eastern Nazarene College, MA

Brazil
Grand Canyon University, AZ

Central America
Bluffton College, OH
Taylor University, IN

China
Bethel College, KS
California Baptist College, CA
Calvin College, MI
Eastern Mennonite College, VA
Fresno Pacific College, CA
George Fox College, OR
Geneva College, PA
Grand Canyon University, AZ
Lee College, TN
Messiah College, PA
Sioux Falls College, SD
Taylor University, IN
Whitworth College, WA

Colombia
Messiah College, PA

Commonwealth of Independent States
Bluffton College, OH
Eastern Mennonite College, VA
Geneva College, PA
George Fox College, OR
Gordon College, MA

Grand Canyon University, AZ
King College, TN
Roberts Wesleyan College, NY
Taylor University, IN
Warner Pacific College, OR

Costa Rica
Azusa Pacific University, CA
Biola University, CA
Calvin College, MI
Dordt College, IA
Eastern Mennonite College, VA
Fresno Pacific College, CA
George Fox College, OR
Goshen College, IN
Huntington College, IN
King College, TN
Malone College, OH
Northwestern College, IA
Southern California College, CA
Southern Nazarene University, OK
Westmont College, CA
Whitworth College, WA

Dominican Republic
Goshen College, IN
King's College, NY
Roberts Wesleyan College, NY

East Asia
Westmont College, CA

Ecuador
Azusa Pacific University, CA

Egypt
Eastern Mennonite College, VA
George Fox College, OR

England
Asbury College, KY
Bethel College, KS
Bethel College, MN
Biola University, CA
Calvin College, MI
Campbellsville College, KY
Central Wesleyan College, SC
Dallas Baptist University, TX
Eastern Mennonite College, VA
Erskine College, SC
Fresno Pacific College, CA
Gordon College, MA
Huntington College, IN
King's College, NY

Lee College, TN
Messiah College, PA
Milligan College, TN
Mississippi College, MS
Nyack College, NY
Roberts Wesleyan College, NY
Southern Nazarene University, OK
Taylor University, IN
Westmont College, CA
Wheaton College, IL
Whitworth College, WA

Europe
Geneva College, PA
Palm Beach Atlantic College, FL
Seattle Pacific University, WA
Westmont College, CA

France
Asbury College, KY
Bethel College, KS
Calvin College, MI
Campbellsville College, KY
Campbell University, NC
Eastern Mennonite College, VA
Eastern Nazarene College, MA
Erskine College, SC
Fresno Pacific College, CA
George Fox College, OR
Gordon College, MA
Grace College, IN
King College, TN
King's College, NY
Messiah College, PA
Northwestern College, IA
Redeemer College, Canada
Roberts Wesleyan College, NY
Taylor University, IN
Wheaton College, IL
Whitworth College, WA

Germany
Bethel College, KS
Bethel College, MN
Biola University, CA
Calvin College, MI
Dordt College, IA
Eastern Mennonite College, VA
Eastern Nazarene College, MA
Fresno Pacific College, CA
George Fox College, OR
Gordon College, MA
Goshen College, IN
Grace College, IN

Germany (continued)
King College, TN
King's College, NY
Lee College, TN
Messiah College, PA
Mississippi College, MS
Wheaton College, IL
Whitworth College, WA

Great Britain
Eastern Nazarene College, MA
George Fox College, OR
King College, TN

Greece
Fresno Pacific College, CA
George Fox College, OR
Gordon College, MA
Messiah College, PA

Guatemala
George Fox College, OR
Malone College, OH
Warner Pacific College, OR
Whitworth College, WA

Honduras
Warner Pacific College, OR
Whitworth College, WA

Hong Kong
Malone College, OH
Whitworth College, WA

Hungary
Grand Canyon University, AZ

Israel
Bethel College, MN
Biola University, CA
Campbellsville College, KY
Eastern Mennonite College, VA
Fresno Pacific College, CA
George Fox College, OR
Gordon College, MA
King College, TN
Messiah College, PA
North Park College, IL
Northwest Christian College, OR
Northwestern College, MN
Simpson College, CA
Southern California College, CA
Taylor University, IN
Westmont College, CA
Wheaton College, IL
Whitworth College, WA

Italy
George Fox College, OR
Gordon College, MA

Ivory Coast
Goshen College, IN

Jamaica
Huntington College, IN

Japan
Azusa Pacific University, CA
Bethel College, KS
Eastern Mennonite College, VA
George Fox College, OR
Gordon College, MA
Messiah College, PA
Seattle Pacific University, WA
Sioux Falls College, SD

Kenya
Gordon College, MA
Messiah College, PA
Taylor University, IN

Korea
King College, TN
Seattle Pacific University, WA
Whitworth College, WA

Latin America
Asbury College, KY
Palm Beach Atlantic College, FL

Mexico
Bluffton College, OH
Calvin College, MI
Campbell University, NC
Dordt College, IA
Eastern Mennonite College, VA
Fresno Pacific College, CA
George Fox College, OR
Grace College, IN
King College, TN
North Park College, IL
Whitworth College, WA

Morocco
King College, TN

The Netherlands
Calvin College, MI
Dordt College, IA
George Fox College, OR
King College, TN
Northwestern College, IA
Redeemer College, Canada
Wheaton College, IL

New Guinea
King College, TN

New Zealand
Taylor University, IN

Nicaragua
Whitworth College, WA

Poland
Bluffton College, OH

Scandinavia
Gordon College, MA

Scotland
Erskine College, SC

Singapore
Taylor University, IN

Spain
Bethel College, KS
Calvin College, MI
Cedarville College, OH
Dordt College, IA
Eastern Mennonite College, VA
Eastern Nazarene College, MA
Fresno Pacific College, CA
George Fox College, OR
Gordon College, MA
Grace College, IN
Grand Canyon University, AZ
King College, TN
King's College, NY
Messiah College, PA
Northwestern College, IA
Taylor University, IN
Trinity Christian College, IL
Wheaton College, IL

Sweden
Bethel College, MN
North Park College, IL

Switzerland
Eastern Nazarene College, MA
George Fox College, OR
Gordon College, MA

Taiwan
Azusa Pacific University, CA

Ukraine
Lee College, TN

Wales
Calvin College, MI
Campbell University, NC

Graduate Programs Index

M—master's degree; D—doctoral degree; P—professional degree; O—other advanced degree

Art Education
Calvin College	M
Mississippi College	M

Art/Fine Arts
Mississippi College	M

Bilingual and Bicultural Education
Eastern College	M
Fresno Pacific College	M
Point Loma Nazarene College	M

Biology and Biomedical Sciences
Mississippi College	M

Business Administration and Management
Azusa Pacific University	M
Campbell University	M
Central Wesleyan College	M
Dallas Baptist University	M
Eastern College	M
Grand Canyon University	M
Indiana Wesleyan University	M
Mississippi College	M
Olivet Nazarene University	M
Seattle Pacific University	M
Southern Nazarene University	M
Trevecca Nazarene College	M

Clinical Psychology
George Fox College	M,D
Wheaton College	M

Communication
Mississippi College	
Southern Nazarene University	
Wheaton College	M

Computer Education
Azusa Pacific University	M
Fresno Pacific College	M

Computer Science
Azusa Pacific University	M

Counseling Psychology
California Baptist College	M

Counseling Psychology
Eastern Nazarene College	M
Southern Nazarene University	M

Counselor Education
Campbell University	M
Dallas Baptist University	M
Fresno Pacific College	M
Mississippi College	M
Point Loma Nazarene College	M
Trevecca Nazarene College	M
Whitworth College	M

Curriculum and Instruction
Campbell University	M
Eastern Nazarene College	M
Fresno Pacific College	M
Seattle Pacific University	M
Simpson College	M
Southern Nazarene University	M
Trevecca Nazarene College	M

Early Childhood Education
Calvin College	M
Dallas Baptist University	M
Eastern Nazarene College	M
Southern Nazarene University	M

Economics
Eastern College	M

Education
Azusa Pacific University	M
Biola University	M
Calvin College	M
Campbell University	M,D,O
Covenant College	M
Dallas Baptist University	M
Eastern College	M
Eastern Nazarene College	M
Fresno Pacific College	M,O
Grand Canyon University	M
Grand Rapids Baptist College and Seminary	M,P
Malone College	M
Milligan College	M
Mississippi College	M
Northwestern College, IA	M
Northwest Nazarene College	M
Olivet Nazarene University	M
Point Loma Nazarene College	M,O
Seattle Pacific University	M
Simpson College	M
Sioux Falls College	M

Counseling Psychology
Southern Nazarene University	M
Trevecca Nazarene College	M
Wheaton College	M
Whitworth College	M

Educational Administration
Azusa Pacific University	M
Calvin College	M
Campbell University	M,D,O
Dallas Baptist University	M
Fresno Pacific College	M
Mississippi College	M
Point Loma Nazarene College	M,O
Seattle Pacific University	M
Trevecca Nazarene College	M
Whitworth College	M

Educational Media/ Instructional Technology
Fresno Pacific College	M

Education of the Gifted
Grand Canyon University	M
Whitworth College	M

Education of the Multiply Handicapped
Fresno Pacific College	M

Elementary Education
Campbell University	M
Dallas Baptist University	M
Eastern Nazarene College	M
Grand Canyon University	M
Mississippi College	M
Northwestern College, IA	M
Olivet Nazarene University	M
Southern Nazarene University	M
Trevecca Nazarene College	M

Engineering and Applied Sciences
Azusa Pacific University	M

English
Mississippi College	M
Southern Nazarene University	M

English Education
Calvin College	M
Campbell University	M
Olivet Nazarene University	M

Finance and Banking
Dallas Baptist University | M
Eastern College | M

Health Education
Eastern College | M

Health Services Management and Hospital Administration
Eastern College | M
Mississippi College | M

Higher Education
Azusa Pacific University | M

History
Mississippi College | M

Human Resources Management and Personnel
Azusa Pacific University | M
Eastern College | M

Interdisciplinary Programs in the Humanities and Social Sciences
Mississippi College | M
Wheaton College | M

International Business
Azusa Pacific University | M
Dallas Baptist University | M

Journalism
Wheaton College | M

Law
Campbell University | P
Mississippi College | P

Liberal Studies
Dallas Baptist University | M

Linguistics
Biola University | M

Management Information Systems
Seattle Pacific University | M

Marketing
Dallas Baptist University | M
Eastern College | M

Marriage and Family Therapy
Azusa Pacific University | M
Eastern Nazarene College | M
Mississippi College | M
Northwest Christian College | M
Seattle Pacific University | M

Mass and Organizational Communication
Mississippi College | M

Mathematics Education
Campbell University | M
Fresno Pacific College | M
Mississippi College | M

Middle School Education
Campbell University | M

Missions and Missiology
Biola University | M,D
Grand Rapids Baptist College and
  Seminary | P,M
Nyack College | M
Simpson College | M
Wheaton College | M

Music
Azusa Pacific University | M
Mississippi College | M
Seattle Pacific University | M

Music Education
Calvin College | M
Mississippi College | M

Nonprofit Management
Eastern College | M

North American Studies
Wheaton College | M

Nursing
Azusa Pacific University | M
Indiana Wesleyan University | M
Seattle Pacific University | M

Nursing Administration
Seattle Pacific University | M

Pastoral Ministry and Counseling
Azusa Pacific University | M
Bethel College, IN | M
Central Wesleyan College | M
Eastern Nazarene College | M
Grand Rapids Baptist College and
  Seminary | P,M
Huntington College | M
Indiana Wesleyan University | M
Olivet Nazarene University | M
Trinity Western University | P,M
Whitworth College | M

Pharmacy
Campbell University | P

Physical Education and Human Movement Studies
Azusa Pacific University | M
Campbell University | M
Seattle Pacific University | M
Whitworth College | M

Psychology
Biola University | D
California Baptist College | M
Eastern Nazarene College | M
Fresno Pacific College | M
Geneva College | M

George Fox College | M
Southern Nazarene University | M
Wheaton College | M

Public and Community Health
Indiana Wesleyan University | M

Public Health Nursing
Indiana Wesleyan University | M

Radio, Television, and Film
Wheaton College | M

Reading
Calvin College | M
Dallas Baptist University | M
Eastern Nazarene College | M
Fresno Pacific College | M
Grand Canyon University | M
Olivet Nazarene University | M
Seattle Pacific University | M
Sioux Falls College | M
Southern Nazarene University | M
Whitworth College | M

Religion
Azusa Pacific University | M
Dallas Baptist University | M
Eastern Nazarene College | M
Grand Rapids Baptist College and
  Seminary | M
Northwest Christian College | M
Northwest Nazarene College | M
Olivet Nazarene University | M
Point Loma Nazarene College | M
Seattle Pacific University | M
Simpson College | M
Trevecca Nazarene College | M
Warner Pacific College | M
Wheaton College | M

Religious Education
Calvin College | M
Grand Rapids Baptist College and
  Seminary | P,M
Wheaton College | M

School Psychology
Fresno Pacific College | M

Science Education
Calvin College | M
Fresno Pacific College | M
Mississippi College | M
Olivet Nazarene University | M

Secondary Education
Campbell University | M
Eastern Nazarene College | M
Grand Canyon University | M
Mississippi College | M
Olivet Nazarene University | M

Social Sciences Education
Calvin College | M
Campbell University | M

Sociology

Mississippi College   M

Special Education

Azusa Pacific University   M
Calvin College   M
Eastern Nazarene College   M
Fresno Pacific College   M
Point Loma Nazarene College   M
Whitworth College   M

Speech and Interpersonal Communication

Southern Nazarene University   M

Sports Administration

Seattle Pacific University   M

Teaching English as a Second Language

Azusa Pacific University   M,O
Biola University   M
Grand Canyon University   M
Whitworth College   M

Theology

Anderson University   P,M
Azusa Pacific University   P,M
Bethel College, IN   M

Biola University   P,M,D
Calvin College   M
Grand Rapids Baptist College and
    Seminary   P,M
Huntington College   M
Master's College   P,M
Nyack College   P,M
Olivet Nazarene University   M
Simpson College   M
Southern California College   M
Southern Nazarene University   M
Wheaton College   M,O

Urban Education

Grand Canyon University   M